FIRES & FURIES

THE LOS ANGELES RIOTS OF 1992

James D. Delk

FIRES & FURIES

THE L. A. RIOTS

What Really Happened

Library of Congress Cataloging-in-Publication Data

Delk, James D., 1932-
    Fires and furies: the Los Angeles riots of 1992 / by
James D. Delk.
        p.   cm.
    Includes bibliographical references (p.   ) and index.
    ISBN 0-88280-123-6
    1. Riots--California--Los Angeles--History--20th
century. 2. Los Angeles (Calif.)--Race relations.
I. Title.
F869.L857D45   1995
979.4'94053-dc20   94-13804
                              CIP

Published by ETC Publications
      700 East Vereda del Sur
      Palm Springs, CA 92262-4816

Published in the United States of America.

Jay Brookner

Dedicated
to the thousands of soldiers
who served so exceptionally well,
usually in the absence of specific orders

Thanks for all you do for all states and nature —

Jim Dew

TABLE OF CONTENTS

Preface *xii*

ix

PREFACE

Memories again flooded back when we were called to duty in Los Angeles. Born there in 1932, for a time our family lived in what is now Watts, in a modest home almost precisely between the two points where the riots of 1965 and 1992 both started. No one then could have guessed that the neighborhood would later be engulfed by riots. Many older California National Guardsmen served in Watts during the riots there in 1965. Younger National Guard men and women knew that the Watts riots were part of the California Guard's history, even if they didn't know that innocent people were killed during those riots. However, details of those innocent deaths were very much on the minds of all senior commanders as we headed towards the more recent riots.

Police officers are carefully trained with a focus on restraint. Armed soldiers, on the other hand, are trained to respond to threats using deadly force. As a consequence, there was considerable concern when thousands of National Guardsmen were sent into the streets to restore order. As might be expected, there were dozens of assaults on the military forces. These assaults are recorded, as well as the extraordinary restraint exercised in responding to those assaults. Unlike the many civilians killed during the Watts riots, only one civilian was killed and one wounded by soldiers during the 1992 riots. Both of those unfortunate incidents involved felons who assaulted military or law enforcement personnel.

The Los Angeles riots of 1992 were influenced by long-standing tensions between civilians and the Los Angeles Police Department, though sparked by the Rodney King incident. While this book is written from the military perspective, the tensions between the citizenry and law enforcement, politicians and law enforcement, and between various law enforcement agencies, played a key role and are briefly explored. Problems also developed between the Governor and his National Guard. I take Governor Pete Wilson to task for his actions during the 1992 riots. In fairness, however, it should be noted that he did a complete turnaround during the devastating 1994 earthquake, and worked particularly well with his National Guard.

In the writing of this narrative, I apologize for overuse of the personal pronoun. Rather than any special credit accruing to what we senior officers did, the author would feel vindicated if the reader ends up sharing our deeply held conviction that the extraordinary performance of our noncommissioned officers at all levels is what really made the difference. Our sergeants were simply superb!

* * *

Perceptions of what actually happened during the early hours of the riots were often distorted, sometimes for political reasons. Fortunately, many people of integrity and conviction helped in digging out the facts and "the rest of the story" in making this narrative factual. I am deeply grateful for the candor and forthrightness shown by soldiers and marines, law enforcement personnel, government officials, and gang members during literally hundreds of interviews.

Many soldiers were especially helpful, including Specialist David P. Andrews, Sergeant Carvel Gay, and Lieutenant Colonel Bill Wenger of 3/160th Infantry. Sergeant First Class Dan Black, and his brother, First Sergeant Pat Black of the 40th Military Police Company, provided insights, tapes, and photographs. Sergeant First Class Toby Bogges of the 2/160th Infantry provided journal entries, photos, and other help. First Sergeant Jim Brown of 4/160th Infantry, and many others of his battalion, provided invaluable details and photographs. I'm indebted to Sergeant First Class Jim Ober of the Headquarters, 40th Infantry Division (and Trackside Photo), who went above and beyond in helping me with photographs. Brigadier General Robert J. Brandt was helpful during all stages of this effort.

Law enforcement officials have consistently been helpful. Chief Paul Myron and Lieutenant Dick Odenthal of the Los Angeles Sheriff's Department provided valuable help during and after the civil disturbances, as did Commander Bayan Lewis and Captain Keith Bushey (both since promoted) of LAPD.

Elected politicians and government officials proved to be the most difficult to work with in obtaining interviews and digging out facts. Surprisingly, it was easier to gain access to various gang members. Nonetheless, details were confirmed, although often only after promising anonymity. Needless to say, nothing was written unless I was confident of the accuracy.

Finally, I gratefully acknowledge the help of those who read, reread, and read again the manuscript in assisting with the editing process. I am particularly indebted to my father, James H. Delk, himself a published author; my youngest son, Jack A. Delk; and an old and trusted mentor and friend, Major General (Retired) Thomas K. Turnage.

CHAPTER ONE

THE PRELUDE

Sirens wail quite often during the day, and even more so at night. The wail of sirens is often accompanied by the beat of helicopter blades as the police wage their ceaseless war against lawlessness, with no victory in sight. The tension as you drive through at night is almost palpable. It seems as though for every pleasant face one sees, there is another that looks at you with suspicion, or downright antagonism. Almost every night one can hear gunshots, though you can't tell from a distance whether those shots are meant to kill, frighten, or just to make a statement. Even some humble homes have bars on the windows, giving the appearance (and perhaps reality) of people being prisoners in their own homes. Much of the business district in the area is literally covered with graffiti, and paint is peeling almost everywhere. Where there is new paint, it quite often is a patchwork of a different shade or color, covering graffiti or peeling paint that was not scraped before new paint was slapped on. There is too little beauty in this area of decay, generally described as South Central Los Angeles.

South Central Los Angeles has been in a state of decline for a very long time, even prior to the Watts riots of 1965. The county unemployment rate in 1965 was less than 6%, but exceeded 15% for blacks and Hispanics. The area was a tinderbox, ready for any spark to ignite the conflagration. Voters had repealed anti-discrimination legislation in 1964.

The mayor of the all but ungovernable City of Los Angeles, Sam Yorty, had been squabbling with federal officials over disbursement of the government's anti-poverty funds. The weather was hot and humid as tension in the area grew, especially between blacks and the police. This was demonstrated in the escalation that resulted from what started as a relatively minor traffic stop the early evening of August 11, 1965 on Avalon Boulevard near 116th Place. The California Highway Patrol stopped 21-year-old Marquette Frye and his older brother Ronald in their mother's 1955 Buick one block from their home. What started as a routine arrest of Marquette for driving under the influence of alcohol rapidly grew out of control. The crowd that gathered swelled rapidly, and increasingly became a concern to the two arresting officers. They made the first of several calls for back-up. The law enforcement contingent grew with the addition of more Highway Patrolmen, and eventually included Los Angeles police from the 77th Street Division, as well as Sheriff's deputies. The sirens drew even more of a crowd as the situation generally escalated. Before the incident ended, both brothers had been arrested, as well as their mother and another woman who had joined the onlookers. As the police disengaged, bottles were thrown, and the riots rapidly spread.

The Watts riots lasted six days, and required a massive response by law enforcement and almost 14,000 National Guardsmen before the riots were quelled six days after they began. There were at least 34 people killed, that figure being the historically accepted number, though some in the Los Angeles Police Department now suspect the figure was more likely close to fifty. Those riots have been described as a "free fire" zone, with far too many shootings by law enforcement officers and National Guardsmen. The National Guard fired all kinds of weapons from handguns up through .50 calibre machine guns. Too many innocent people were killed. In addition, there were over 1,000 injured, 4,000 arrested, and hundreds of buildings burned.

The riots hastened the decline in the area as many burned-out businesses decided not to rebuild. Comparatively few of the large chain stores can be found in South Central Los Angeles even twenty five years later, where the void was filled by small businesses.

Los Angeles has enjoyed a diverse economy for many years. Famous for being the capitol of the entertainment industry, fewer people know that Los Angeles' garment industry is second only to New York. There is a sizeable food industry, and a very large fishing fleet (primarily tuna). All this contributed to a healthy economy, with a very low unemployment rate from the end of the Sixties. Unfortunately, the area is overly dependent on another sector of the economy, the Defense and Aerospace Industry. Such giants as Hughes, Litton, Lockheed, McDonnel Douglas, Northrop, and Rockwell International all have large plants here. When defense cutbacks hit the industry, the unemployment rate in the county doubled.

The unemployment rate was exacerbated by revised recruiting standards in the armed forces. Alternative employment in a uniformed service was effectively precluded starting in the Eighties, when enlistment standards were significantly raised. Thereafter, only the most intelligent, best educated high school graduates were able to pass the entrance tests. In effect, the bottom half lost the option of joining the military simply because they could no longer pass the test. The situation became even worse in the Nineties when the size of the armed forces began to be sharply reduced.

The urban sprawl in the Los Angeles basin has been described as hundreds of suburbs pretending they are cities, with most having no real sense of community. In an area covering hundreds of square miles, one community runs right into the next, and you can cross borders without even knowing it unless you carefully observe the signs on lampposts as you drive through. It is a crazy quilt of communities where if you feel uncomfortable, just drive for five more minutes and you'll feel perfectly safe. Observing the constant change in the communities here is almost like looking through a kaleidoscope.

Yesterday's ugly oil wells are today's beautiful shopping mall or modern glass-enclosed steel office building. In the last thirty years, billions have been invested building in the City Center, West Los Angeles, and Orange County. Unfortunately, other areas have seen very little investment, as yesterday's middle class neighborhoods deteriorate into slum-like areas of marginally profitable or dying businesses and run-down houses. The area where most of the blight is concentrated has come to be called South Central Los Angeles.

South Central is a significant part of the extraordinary megalopolis generally called Los Angeles, and is much larger in size than most cities in the United States. While suffering decay, the appearance is much different than seen in much of the Midwest and East. The orientation, like most of the area, is lateral rather than vertical. Almost all buildings are no more than three or four stories high. Much of this is due to earthquake concerns. As a consequence, there are no dark, crumbling tenements. In fact, there are comparatively few tall buildings anywhere in

4

South Central. In spite of the uncrowded appearance, however, the population density in South Central is over 10,000 per square mile, more than double the county average.

In order to get around this large area, most people rely on the automobile. The automobile ratio per capita is extraordinarily high. Surrounded by the world's largest freeway system, life all but revolves around the automobile. As a result, unlike so many large cities elsewhere, an unusual percentage of real estate is devoted to parking lots. Unfortunately, automobiles are often involved in crimes, from car jacking and drive-by shootings to get-aways from crime scenes.

The huge areas to be traversed led to extensive reliance on the helicopter. Los Angeles had its own scheduled helicopter transport system with Los Angeles Airways providing transportation in 30-passenger Sikorsky S-61 helicopters between ten locations in the Los Angeles basin. Started in 1948, this service continued until 1971, when the construction of freeways made L. A. Airways no longer cost effective.

Helicopters are still widely used to shorten trips in the basin. They are used for VIP transportation, courier service, medical evacuation, and law enforcement. Many of the taller buildings in Los Angeles have helicopter landing pads on the roof. A look skyward at any time, day or night, shows helicopters crisscrossing the sky.

Perhaps the biggest impact has come from the media helicopter. No major station is without at least one helicopter. Originally not used for much more than reporting of traffic conditions, they are now much more sophisticated. They can quickly fly to a crime scene or newsworthy incident, and instantly transmit the scene into everyone's living room.

Unfortunately, this ability may have inflamed the 1992 riots. Many believe this was a *media-created* riot.

Unofficial borders are in a constant state of flux as the population make-up changes. Whites today comprise only about a third of the population. Blacks have been leaving the city, with their declining numbers, primarily in South Central Los Angeles, now counting about 17% of the population. In the city itself, Hispanics (the largest concentration outside of Mexico) now make up the greatest percentage of the population at about 40%, with most concentrated in East Los Angeles. As a consequence, many former ghetto areas are now better described as barrios. There are also a great many undocumented aliens in the area, a fact that became glaringly obvious when arrests were analyzed following the riots. Asians number about 7%, with the balance of the population made up of other minorities.

Many of those Asians are Koreans. They often bought failing businesses, and then made them profitable by investing long hours of hard work, and doing business on a cash-only basis. Unfortunately, the fact that the Koreans use family members and rarely hire outsiders, coupled with the fact they often choose to live in nicer neighborhoods elsewhere, is often resented by those who patronize their businesses.

Already strained relationships between Koreans and blacks were struck a blow by an unfortunate incident that occurred in the Spring of 1991. A Korean grocery owner, Soon Ja Du, shot and killed 15-year-old LaTasha Harlin. The following November she was convicted of manslaughter in the death of the unarmed black teenager. The judge then gave the store owner five years probation rather than imprisoning her, a move that adversely impacted on perceptions of the judicial system by some blacks in the area, thus exacerbating tensions between the Korean and black communities.

Law enforcement in the area is complicated by many factors. There are 88 cities in Los Angeles County. About half the cities have their own police departments, with the others policed by the Los Angeles Sheriff's Department. This polyglot arrangement is an obvious complication for law enforcement agencies, some of which cannot even talk to each other via radio. Each culture in this multi-cultural area requires a different approach by law enforcement. The growth of gangs and their increasing predilection towards violence is particularly troubling.

*   *   *   *   *   *

The well-publicized problems with gangs are not new. The first gangs of significance seem to have been Hispanic gangs which were recognized in the 1930's and 1940's, although there was some gang activity shortly after the turn of the century. Gangs seem to surface, here as well as other parts of the nation, when poverty-stricken neighborhoods began to deteriorate amidst less than effective church, school and recreation programs.

Hispanic gangs start recruiting youngsters by the time they are ten or eleven. Hispanics are very turf conscious, and join for the protection of the neighborhood, or barrio. Some don't go to school simply because they would have to cross the turf of another gang.

Each Hispanic gang tends to dress in a distinctive manner, although that rule is not as rigid as it once was. They often wear clothes that are too large, especially khaki pants and

Pendleton-style shirts. The pants are often highly starched, worn very high above the waist, and are baggy. Trench coats may be worn, both to appear machismo and to conceal weapons. Colors, as in almost all gangs, are significant. For instance, Eastside Torrance wears black pants and brown bandanas. Keystone wears brown pants and red bandanas, while Tortilla Flats wears gray pants and blue bandanas.

Hispanic gang members are often very heavily tattooed, usually with tattoos of animals, birds, frogs, insects, rodents and snakes. They will tattoo their nicknames, and the names of past and present girlfriends. They will also have the names of fallen "homeboys" tattooed, or "R.I.P." (Rest In Peace).

The behavior of Hispanic gangs differs from gangs rooted in other cultures. Hispanic members tend to consider themselves "soldiers," and strive to be considered "Vato Loco" (Crazy Guy). They want to be considered the craziest, and therefore most respected, member of the gang.

Black gangs have not been around as long as Hispanic gangs, and the uninitiated feel they are easier to understand. Perhaps that is because black gangs, unlike Hispanic gangs, are organized into two distinct groups, the Bloods and the Crips. The Bloods are believed to have been organized first, becoming a factor in the 1960's. The origin of the names is obscure, although many claim they have the only correct answer. The name "Bloods" as assumed to come from referring to other blacks as "blood," or from the color red. The title "Crip" is assumed by many to have originated in reference to a cripple in the gang. Some members of the Crip gangs even walked with a limp so others would know they were Crips.

Black gangs in the county originated in the Compton, Watts and Willowbrook areas of South Central Los Angeles. Those who lived in the area of Piru Street, a comparatively insignificant residential street running generally east and west, called themselves the Compton Pirus. They later expanded into different factions, calling themselves "Pirus," and later "Bloods." Some experts feel the two names should be used interchangeably.

The color blue is associated with the Crips, and red is associated with the Bloods. But there are important exceptions. For instance, the Lime Street Piru wear green, the Santana Block Crips wear black, and the Grape Street Watts Crips wear purple. Crips will sometimes wear British Knights tennis shoes because of the "BK" monogram (signifying "Blood Killer") on the side of the shoe. Bloods feel the same way about the initials "CK."

As noted, Hispanic gangs have been a significant factor much longer, and blacks adapted some Hispanic gang culture in the evolution of their own gangs. Nonetheless, the migration of gang cultural styles goes as much from blacks to Hispanics nowadays as vice versa.

Most black gangs are involved in drug dealing to some degree. There have been occasional truces between some of the Crips and Bloods, as during portions of April and May 1992. Crips and Bloods, however, rarely work together unless a mutual deal involving large drug profits makes it advantageous to do so. The explosive growth of drug dealing is acknowledged, with felony drug convictions more than doubling in the last ten years.

There are a great many more Crips than Bloods. For self preservation, Bloods don't usually fight other Bloods. Crips fight Bloods, and will also fight some other Crips.

There are other gangs representing Polynesians, Asians, and White Supremacists. Samoan gangs primarily originated within the large Samoan community in Carson, but have since migrated to surrounding communities, including Compton. The other Pacific Islander gangs may look similar, but come from such diverse places as Tonga or the Hawaiian Islands. These gangs often have historic enmities based on religion, such as Mormon versus Catholic influences.

The behavior of Pacific Islander gangs is heavily influenced by Hispanic and black gangbanging. When the Pacific Islanders first came to the area, they joined the gangs that already existed. This continued until the population and distribution of Pacific Islanders grew to the point that it made sense to form their own gangs. They did so, but brought with them the behavior patterns they had learned from their previous associations with Hispanic and black gangs.

Asian gangs are less territorial than other gangs, but tend to be much more secretive. They also tend to prey on their own kind rather than outsiders. Chinatown has the Cantonese "Wah Ching" gang, which is particularly violent, and found generally in the northern part of Chinatown. The Vietnamese of Chinese ancestry, or "Viet Ching," are found more to the south. The Taiwanese have the United Bamboo or "Chu Lien Bon" gangs.

Filipino gangs have many of the same characteristics as Chinese gangs, and are growing due to recent immigration. Members often have burn scars as a result of rituals to prove their courage.

Dress can range from long trench coats to white shirts and black trousers, but Asians generally dress more fashionably than other gangs. Japanese and Korean gangs exist, but they are highly secretive, and not much is known about them.

Law enforcement is particularly challenged in fighting the problem of Asian gangs. Asians, especially recent immigrants, trust law enforcement less than people from other cultures. For one thing, they consider our law extremely complex. For another, law enforcement in some parts of Asia (and elsewhere in the world, for that matter) is often greatly affected by bribes and other forms of influence. Crimes by Asian gangs in the United States are almost always underreported. Asians also tend to mistrust banks, and often keep large quantities of cash around their homes. Asian gang members know that, and take advantage of the fact.

White youth tend to join Hispanic gangs if they live in neighborhoods that are dominated by those gangs. If they are disposed to gangbanging (members tend to use the term "banging"), and don't live in a neighborhood dominated by a gang, they might join one of the comparatively few white gangs.

White gangs are much less territorial than other gangs. Some are into white supremacy. Skinhead groups are both racist and non-racist. They originally cut their hair so it couldn't be pulled in street fights, although some let their hair grow longer now. Other groups are into Satanism, or Hitlerism. Many wear polo shirts or tank tops, and suspenders. Boots are key to their uniform, and they wear their pants rolled up to expose their boots. Comparatively small in numbers, but many are violent. The police tend to treat them as violent political extremists rather than street gangs.

Other white gangs can best be termed "motorcycle gangs." The notorious Hell's Angels motorcycle gang originated in Fontana, not far from Los Angeles.

Stoner gangs tend to be multiracial, both white and Hispanic, and from multiracial neighborhoods. A common theme tends to be the Heavy Metal culture, complete with names and pictures of Heavy Metal stars, and lots of drugs. Their hair tends to be longer, they seem to care less about their personal appearance, and they tend to wear predominantly red or black clothing. There is a lot of occultism, or Satanism.

Efforts to understand the role of gangs other than Hispanic and black during the riots may be pretty much a waste of time. White gangs played almost no role during the riots, other than some relatively unimportant demonstrations and counter demonstrations. The Asian gangs are so secretive that no one really knows what role, if any, they played in the violence.

As noted before, colors of clothes worn by gangbangers often identify their gang affiliation. Gang markings can be seen in the color of hats and headbands. Colored bandanas are also worn around the head, hat, or neck; hung from a specific pocket, and sometimes tied around the lower thigh. Colors can also be seen in earrings, shoe laces, and belts. The color of automobiles may also be significant, but to a lesser degree. However, a Crip would never be seen in a red car, for instance, any more than he would wear a red shirt. A Blood would never wear blue, except for Levis.

Most of the gangs use hand signs, particularly to identify what gang they belong to. They use one or both hands, and occasionally their arms. Sometimes the positioning of the hands adds a geographical dimension, such as hand above the chest for north, and left of the chest for west, etc. They also use "hand jive" to send simple messages.

The black gangs have, to a considerable degree, adopted their own language. All black gang members consider themselves "gangsters" (unlike the Hispanic "soldier"). Crips curl their thumb and index finger to form a "C." Bloods curl their index finger to the thumb, but then point the other three fingers straight to form what can be considered either a "b" for Blood or "P" for Piru.

Blood gang members will avoid using the letter "C" if at all possible. Students in school have even been known to substitute the letter "B" for the letter "C" on homework. The opposite is true for Crips.

The gangs favor certain vehicles, although that often depends on the particular part of the county where the gang is based. Many of the vehicles have darkly tinted windows, making it all but impossible to see inside. Others have all-terrain vehicles, complete with light bars, even though they rarely leave city streets.

The size of the gangs varies from as small as five or ten up to as many as a thousand. Young members usually make the decision to join a gang by the time they are in the sixth grade, although the decision may be reached at ages as young as eight. Mothers are increasingly dressing their children, as young as two-years-old, in gang colors. In the old days, gang members used to leave the gang by the age of twenty or so. Now some of them remain until their forties (if they live that long).

In many neighborhoods where gangs are dominant, every young man must make a decision. He can be either an active or passive member of the gang. It is rare for someone to be forced to join a gang, but he is not permitted to be anti-gang, or a member of an enemy gang. In that way all gang members in the neighborhood can focus on the police and other enemies, and not worry about people on their "turf." Someone may occasionally be permitted in a friendly gang elsewhere, especially if he has just moved into the neighborhood, but that is dangerous. Gang alliances don't always endure.

Graffiti is seen everywhere, especially in South Central Los Angeles. Gang graffiti marks the gang's turf. The study of graffiti is an art in itself, and an expert can derive a surprising amount of information from the graffiti in an area. Police experts can tell which gang is dominant in an area, or whether there are conflicts with other gangs. Contested areas will often have rival gang "tags" crossed out. Graffiti can also tell others which members of the gang were killed by the police or rival gangs, plus who is marked for death.

The most basic element of gang graffiti is the name of the gang...its name, placa (Spanish for "plaque"), or logo. Gang graffiti has developed a language of its own. For instance, "13" means the gang is loco (crazy), or more recently, can mean the artist/writer is from Southern California. There are many abbreviations in the symbology, such as "ACMD" (All Cops Must Die). One must be very familiar with street slang to interpret much of the Spanish, for Castilian Spanish is all but useless in the barrio Interestingly, some of the black gangs use Hispanic graffiti artists in their territory. Hispanics have been painting graffiti for much longer than black gangs, and their distinctive style is considered much more attractive by most gangbangers. That is not the case with those business owners and highway crews who must constantly paint over the graffiti.

Gangs were a constituent and significant part of the neighborhood during the Watts Riots of 1965. However, they were much less pervasive, and much less dangerous than they have become in recent years. Not too many years ago, a typical gang "rumble" would involve bats, sticks, chains and knives. Guns were often present, but not routinely used. Now there

14

are literally tens of thousands of firearms scattered among the gangs.

An excellent street gang manual called "L. A. Style" was developed by the Los Angeles County Sheriff's Street Gang Detail and distributed just prior to the 1992 riots. The manual notes that poverty often leads to gangbanging. They point out that the location of gang concentrations almost precisely duplicates a map profiling poverty areas. The manual, in describing the insidious effects of gangsterism, says:

"Not only is the citizenry in mortal danger from street gangs, but the influence wielded by the gangs has a trickle-down effect on all aspects of life for the residents of an area afflicted with a street gang. Street gangs prey upon their neighborhood much like a malignant growth which continues to spread through its host until only a wasted shell remains."

There is some behavior relatively common among gang-bangers. There are a lot of hand signals, even directed at people or troops who could not be expected to understand the signals. Weapons are often flashed, with gangbangers simulta-neously, as if on signal, raising their weapons up so they can be seen as their car slowly drives by. Gang members will often walk up to someone to ask a question, with one hand held behind their back as though holding a weapon. Others will have their hands in their pockets as though they had a weapon. It is never safe to assume the gangbanger is just pretending to have a weapon.

There often are "car trains (or caravans)," where gang-bangers form a string of cars and drive slowly through a terri-tory. They sometimes do it with their lights off, and ignore traffic signals as they arrogantly demonstrate their power.

The gangbangers practice "mad-dogging." This is the stare-down or staring contests not unlike those games kids used to play in grammar school. The consequences, however, can be much more serious when gang members are involved. Many people in South Central Los Angeles make a habit of avoiding eye contact so they don't inadvertently get caught in this behavior so widely practiced by gang members. Where a young gangbanger comes from a poor family (and most do), his reputation may be his most prized possession. A "hard look" from a rival gang member is seen as an insult impacting on self-esteem. As L. A. Style puts it, "(hard looks) by a rival gang member must be avenged, for such 'hard looks' threaten not only his own self-esteem, but his standing within the gang, and by extension, his identity. The blood baths seen on Los Angeles streets are often the result of this attitude."

This discussion of gangs, and gang behavior, has been lengthy. However, it should be recognized that by far the most serious challenges faced by both law enforcement officers and the military during the riots came from gang members. The gangs are extremely well armed, to include having a wide variety of sophisticated automatic weapons. They do on occasion have cooperative ventures, and demonstrate enough discipline to be a very serious threat to law and order.

*   *   *   *   *   *

Each year the number of gang-related problems seems to grow, as well as the number of killings involving gang members. In 1991, 771 deaths were directly attributed to the estimated 102,000 gang members in Los Angeles County. This was approximately half the homicides in the county, where death by gunfire per 100,000 inhabitants is more than triple the national average.

It was in this atmosphere of tension that the Rodney King incident occurred.

Rodney G. King, an unemployed 25-year-old construction worker on parole after serving a term for armed robbery, had two passengers with him as he was chased by the California Highway Patrol late at night in the San Fernando Valley. The high speed chase was joined by police from Los Angeles Police Department's Foothill Division, who pulled King over shortly after midnight on March 3, 1991. The chase had ended in Lake View Terrace. There George Holliday, a resident of Lake View Terrace, videotaped police officers beating King about 175 feet from his apartment. The tape was over eighty seconds in length. It showed King lunging at a police officer after being hit with two Taser darts when he refused to be handcuffed, and then being repeatedly beaten with police batons. *In the shortened version repeatedly shown on television*, an officer was seen stepping on King's head or neck, as well as repeated blows by police batons. Tests taken several hours after the event showed King with a blood alcohol content well over California's legal limit.

The tape was sold to Los Angeles television station KTLA (Channel 5) the next day, and was repeatedly shown over several television networks. This was followed by a series of events culminating in the Los Angeles Grand Jury indicting four of the police officers on March 15, 1991.

All four police officers: Sergeant Stacy Koon (41), Officers Laurence Powell (29) and Theodore Briseno (39), and Probationary Officer Timothy Wind (32); were charged with assault with a deadly weapon and assault under color of authority. In addition, both Koon and Powell were charged with filing a false police report, and Koon was charged with being an accessory after the fact.

In November of 1991, it was announced that the trial had been moved to the city of Simi Valley in Ventura County as a consequence of a motion for change of venue based on massive pretrial publicity. Pretrial motions began in February of 1992, and jurors were selected by March.

In the meantime, there were manifestations of mistrust and dislike between Mayor Tom Bradley and Chief of Police Daryl F. Gates. There also were rumors that there was considerable discomfort in the relationship between both Gates and the County Sheriff, Sherman Block. These were all allegations of long standing. These issues were to play a significant role in varying degrees later, when tensions were erupting into violence in an escalating situation that begged for close and continuing cooperation.

As the trial progressed, law enforcement officials began to express concern over the consequences should the four police officers not be found guilty. The public had been inflamed by repeated showings of the videotape in which the police officers beat Rodney King, especially since the portion of the tape almost always aired was a shortened version depicting what appeared to be the most brutal portion. The shortened version didn't show King lunging at the police officers. In addition, many people didn't believe some of the information that had been released about the incident. For instance, the chase had been described as exceeding well over 100 miles per hour. Some felt that the small car King was driving, especially when carrying three comparatively large men, was incapable of such speeds.

18

Some unusual meetings between rival gangs were getting the rapt attention of law enforcement officials in April of 1992 as the King trial approached a verdict. There had been reports of meetings for a couple of years involving attempts to defuse the intense rivalry and feuds between gangs that were costing so many lives. These became much more intensive following three unrelated accidental killings of babies by gang members in drive-by shootings that spring. There were reports of meetings in churches and celebrity's homes, any place that could be considered neutral territory. Representatives of both Bloods and Crips discussed a truce to stop the killing of their babies. While no individuals, or even a group, can claim to represent all of the gangs in the county, it nonetheless was a promising start.

Members of some gangs privately admitted they looked forward to moving around without constantly having to look over their shoulders for fear of getting "capped" (shot) by rival gang members.

More ominous were a series of meetings that occurred during the last week in April. One meeting took place on April 27th in the Imperial Courts Housing Projects between rival gangs from Imperial Courts and the Jordan Downs Housing Projects. The next day a reciprocal and expanded meeting was conducted in the Jordan Downs Housing Projects. The meetings involved gangs with long standing feuds including the "Project Crips," "Grape Street Watts Crips," the "Main Street Crips," and the "Bounty Hunters" (Bloods). The stated objective of the truce was so gang members could direct their efforts towards "killing a police officer."

Stopping the killing of their own babies, and killing a police officer, are very different objectives. Nonetheless, they aren't necessarily mutually exclusive, nor should they be considered incompatible. The various groups are so diverse that almost any motivation could apply somewhere. Regardless, there was active discussion and speculation "on the streets" regarding a truce.

In the month of April, 1992, the pot was simmering. Tensions were raised for a variety of reasons. Unemployment was high, and poverty was growing. There was a lot of frustration among the increasing number of broken families. There had also been the incidents that increased the tensions between the black and Korean communities. Gang violence in the news recently had been particularly brutal. There was considerable street talk and threats surrounding the ongoing trial in Simi Valley involving the Rodney King incident. A huge city with a rather amorphous self-image had been Balkanized, and was ready to explode.

The Headquarters of the California National Guard (also called "The Military Department") in Sacramento received a call from the California Highway Patrol on April 6, 1992. The California Highway Patrol indicated there was some potential for civil disturbances depending on the trial outcome. The Military Department was asked if the Los Alamitos Armed Forces Reserve Center could be made available for staging of Highway Patrolmen if needed. This was quickly approved. On April 13th, the Military Department was asked for body armor and other equipment by the Los Angeles Police Department.

This last request raised some alarm signals. The department was apprehensive about loaning civil disturbance equipment they might need themselves. There had been a series of meetings by Military Department staff planners in the Spring of 1989, that in addition to others, involved the Office of Emergency Services (a state agency), the Los Angeles Sheriff's

Office, and the Los Angeles Police Department. These meetings reviewed the potential role of the California National Guard in future civil disturbance operations, and resulted in an important policy shift. Law enforcement response capabilities and systems had vastly improved over the years, and because of increased confidence in the law enforcement mutual aid system, it was determined that the National Guard would probably not be employed in a civil disturbance "on-street" role in the future. Mutual aid is a system sponsored by the Office of Emergency Services whereby law enforcement agencies from elsewhere can be requested and brought in to assist law enforcement agencies that need help. Reliance on mutual aid was reinforced in August of 1990 by Office of Emergency Services assurances that the National Guard would simply not be needed "on-street" in the future.

Based on the foregoing, and an estimate that law enforcement mutual aid resources would be more than adequate to handle any civil disturbances that might result from the Rodney King trial, the Military Department approved the loan of civil disturbance equipment to civil authorities. The Los Angeles Police Department was provided armor vests, Kevlar (the Army's newer, more protective "German-style") helmets, and filters for gas masks. Loans were also requested on April 29th (and later) and approved for 1,210 armor vests for the Los Angeles County Fire Department, 625 vests for the Los Angeles City Fire Department, and 500 vests for the Orange County Fire Department.

The Los Angeles Police Department continued their precautionary planning in the event riots erupted. They were handicapped for several reasons. An important factor was the fact that the department had been frustrated by a series of increasingly stringent annual budgets. There were only about 7900 police officers for a population of about 3.5 million scattered over an extremely large area. This ratio of officers to population is one of the worst in major metropolitan areas. Another factor, considered important at the time, was the fact that a whole generation of officers had left the department since the Watts riots. There were very few police officers with riot control experience available to do any contingency planning for another possible riot. However, that may not have been as serious as it was considered at the time, because most planning assumptions in the Los Angeles Police Department (and other agencies for that matter) were based on the Watts experience. Law enforcement agencies had fallen into the same trap often experienced by the military. They were preparing to fight the last war. Unfortunately, they didn't realize what they would face would bear little similarity to the Watts riots of 1965.

In late April of 1992 it was business as usual for the California National Guard. Most California National Guard training was oriented toward wartime contingencies in the Pacific, but some support units were earmarked for possible European requirements. Most of those relationships had existed for many years. This was especially true for units focused on NATO requirements in Germany. The California National Guard had exchanged contingents with the German Territorial Army annually since 1984 during "Exercise Lasting Response" in Central California each Spring, and NATO exercises in Germany. As a consequence, some of us from headquarters in Roseville and Sacramento were involved in Exercise *Lasting Response* in San Luis Obispo with a group of German officers led by Major General Berthold Schenk Graf von Stauffenberg (the son of Count von Stauffenberg, who was executed after making the assassination attempt on Hitler in July, 1944). Most other National Guard men and women were involved in normal, everyday civilian occupations while widely scattered around the state.

This all changed following the announcement of the trial verdicts mid-afternoon on Wednesday, April 29th.

CHAPTER TWO

Wednesday, April 29, 1992
THE FIRST DAY AND NIGHT

Cameramen aggressively recorded the scene both inside and outside the courthouse in Simi Valley about 3:15 p.m. Wednesday afternoon as the jury announced the verdicts. The four policemen were found not guilty on all counts except for Officer Powell, where a mistrial was declared on the single charge of using excessive force "under color of authority."

Reaction to the verdicts in the King trial developed rapidly, and showed that much of the public clearly expected a guilty verdict. Chief Gates later reflected the view of other factions during an interview by Ted Koppel on ABC New's Nightline program on May 28, 1992. "Expectations of a guilty verdict were brought on by the electronic media and the print media. The electronic media replayed that thing (the videotape) over and over and over and kept saying how terrible that was." However, public expectations were vindicated in a second, Federal trial almost a year later when two of the four police officers were convicted of violating King's civil rights.

Initial reaction from elected officials also tended to inflame emotions. Mayor Bradley described the defendants as "renegade cops" who should be fired, and said "I do not seek to explain the jury's decision, because frankly, no explanation makes sense." A couple of city councilmen publicly expressed similar sentiments, which did little to cool passions.

Immediately following the verdict, Chief Gates named Deputy Chief Ronald A. Frankle as the Department Commander for the "incident," and the department's Emergency Operations Center (EOC) was opened. The EOC is located in a secure facility deep under ground, the fourth sub-level of City Hall East, across the street from Police Headquarters in Parker Center. Chief Gates later left for a fund raiser in Brentwood which, in retrospect, he admitted was a mistake.

The riots that followed had an initial flash point that is commonly acknowledged to be the intersection of Florence and Normandie Avenues, almost precisely four miles from where the Watts riots started in 1965. The area around Florence and Normandie is not particularly bad. In fact, the area to the southwest of the intersection is especially well kept, with several churches and neat, well maintained homes and lawns. However, the nearby intersection of Florence and Normandie has an unsavory reputation.

The southeast corner of Florence and Normandie had a Union Oil of California (Unocal) Service Station. The southwest corner had a Shell Service Station which was closed some months before the riots. The northwest corner had a mini-mall with a radiator shop, a mom and pop grocery, and a small auto parts store. However, the real problem appeared to be on the northeast, with a liquor and delicatessen at the corner, next to ABC Furniture. That liquor store was described by a local resident as a place frequented by known gang members and other undesirables. A place generally cluttered with trash and a lot of cars, there had been nine or ten shootings over the years, mostly drug-related. Further described as "a place where church-going folk don't go," some of the people who normally hung around the liquor store were described as the catalyst for the violence that erupted.

The problem had started with an initial confrontation between police and others just north of Florence and Normandie. The riotous crowd gathered at that key intersection about 4:00 p.m. and soon became a destructive mob---demonstrating and yelling at pedestrians and motorists. The activity gradually escalated into throwing various missiles at people. The first call to the police was recorded at about 4:30 p.m.

Police from the department's 77th Street Division responded. Rocks, bricks, pieces of concrete and bottles were being thrown at cars, people and through shop windows, as the situation rapidly deteriorated. In a highly controversial decision, the police retreated from the scene rather than being reinforced. Later there were several explanations for pulling out. One was that there were not enough police officers, and they were poorly equipped for a riot. Another was the conviction that police were the targets of the anger, so removing the targets should defuse the crowd's anger. This was the same rationale that was often used to explain actions that led up to the Watts riot, and didn't work any better this time than it did back then. Pulling the police out seemed to merely embolden the rioters.

Individual small-scale attempts were made by police thereafter to rescue individuals and positively impact on the situation at Florence and Normandie. In spite of several heroic attempts, some of which were successful in rescuing people, they were too little and too late to make a significant impact. As the situation deteriorated, abandoned cars, growing crowds, and sniper fire severely hindered law enforcement efforts for several hours.

The police from 77th Street Division were awaiting help from the Metro Squad. The Metro Squad members are specially trained, and had been augmented in anticipation of possible civil disturbances resulting from the verdict. They are considered to be the Los Angeles Police Department's most tactically proficient officers. Knowing when the verdicts were due, police leadership had directed Metro to report for work at 6:00 p.m. This timing decision was based on experiences during the Watts riots (and most other riots for that matter), when very little violence occurred during daylight hours. Unfortunately, Metro ended up being too late to be a factor in what occurred at Florence and Normandie.

Television crews in helicopters overhead recorded scenes of what followed the pullout of the police, with images that will be seared in many people's memories forever. Rioters were seen pulling people from their cars and beating them. The most memorable scene, shown repeatedly that night and many times thereafter, was the beating of 36-year-old truck driver Reginald O. Denny. Denny was driving a large truck that pulled right into the middle of the intersection of Florence and Normandie. He was yanked from the truck, beaten, kicked, hit on the head by what appeared to be a fire extinguisher, and robbed.

A similar incident involved Fidel Lopez, driving his pickup home after a long day on a construction job. He had his windshield smashed with a pipe, and then was also pulled from his truck and severely beaten. He also had his face and genitals sprayed black by one of the mob as he lay almost unconscious in an unforgettable scene shown on television. He was finally rescued by black minister Bennie Newton.

The above two are perhaps the most memorable incidents that day. However, there were many more just as terrifying and memorable to those involved. There was a lady alone in her car who was quickly surrounded by about fifty rioters at Florence and Normandie. Her car was smashed and she was beaten unconscious and severely injured before police rescued her. A young couple with a one-year-old child had a similar incident. Elsewhere firebombs were thrown and people beaten and shot almost indiscriminately as mob rule prevailed. This activity is described as "almost indiscriminately" because it eventually became apparent that some businesses were being particularly targeted. These included gun shops, pawn shops, liquor stores and businesses owned by Koreans.

There were so many television helicopters over the Florence and Normandie area that some were concerned there might be an air disaster to match the ground action that was being transmitted and taped. Before long, every business at the intersection had been trashed and burned with the single exception of the Shell Station which had been boarded up and fenced long before.

Mayor Bradley; Phil Depoian, his liaison to law enforcement; and Deputy Chief Matt Hunt were attending a rally at the First African Methodist Episcopal (AME) Church. While there they received a phone call from their press secretary saying, "There's been a guy getting beat up at Florence and Normandie, and there's been no response...(it has been) on the air now for ten minutes." They then saw on the television that the Reginald Denny incident was what the press secretary was talking about. Phil turned to Matt Hunt and said "Matt, can you get some guys out there?" Matt looked at the television, picked up the phone, and as Phil said, "That's the last time I see Matt Hunt for about a week!" They communicated again over the telephone a little later, and Matt said "Phil, it's very bad out here." When

Phil asked how bad, Matt responded "We're going to need the National Guard!" When Phil asked him how many, Matt estimated that 2000 Guardsmen would be needed.

The Los Angeles Sheriff's Department was mobilizing at the same time as the city police. A tactical alert was declared shortly after 4:00 p.m., followed by a briefing to their Executive Planning Council. Shortly after the briefing, Assistant Sheriff Jerry Harper ordered more deputies to duty and the establishment of two forward command posts. The Northern Command Post was established at the Crescenta Valley Sheriff's Station, with the Southern Command Post at the Carson Sheriff's Station. At 6:30 p.m., Lieutenant Dick Odenthal mobilized two additional platoons. At 6:45 the Sheriff's Emergency Operations Center was activated, and then four additional platoons were mobilized, including the Sheriff's Special Weapons and Tactics (SWAT) team.

Elsewhere in the city, people were taking to the streets. On the corner of Florence Avenue and Hoover Street, Rene Vamorano, a private security officer, videotaped the activity as daylight turned to dusk. The segment lasts less than three minutes, but illustrates what was happening all over South Central Los Angeles. Car horns were blaring, with people hanging out the windows and yelling and laughing at each other. People on the sidewalks were running and dancing, waving at each other, and yelling, "Free at last, free at last!" Cars often ignored the traffic signals and ran red lights.

The carnival-like atmosphere at that corner began to change as time passed and the sun began to set. Some drivers of cars running red lights appeared to be concerned about their safety and in a hurry to get home. Street thugs began to take advantage of the situation. Fires were started in trash dumpsters that were then pushed into the street, followed by fires started in buildings. Perhaps most ominous of all, in that one short tape, was the sound of twenty-nine gun shots. Rene Vamorano, the Security Guard, later that evening made the transition to Sergeant Vamorano the Military Policeman, and reported for duty with his National Guard unit at Los Alamitos Armed Forces Reserve Center.

In the meantime, at about 6:00 p.m., a Forward Command Post was set up by LAPD according to the published plan. It was established at the Rapid Transit District (RTD) Division Number Five, at the corner of 54th and Arlington. This facility, used for maintenance and dispatch of up to 265 city buses, was considered ideally suited for this purpose. Close to the affected area, it is about two city blocks in size, and surrounded by a ten foot cinder block wall, making it easy to secure. In order to empty out the yard to obtain space, the RTD dispatcher sent his buses to other RTD districts, primarily Division 18 in the City of Carson, and Division 2 off of Interstate Highway 10. The main building became the hub of the Forward Command Post. One area in the yard was cordoned off for use as a heliport, and another area was used to control fire engines dispatched from the yard.

The gangbangers quickly found out where the action was being controlled from. An intelligence report came in warning that there would be an attempt by some gangs to disrupt operations at the Forward Command Post. Four police officers with shotguns were then placed at the main entrance, charged with keeping people out. In the meantime, several hundred people, including a large contingent from the media, gathered outside the entrance and across the street at a liquor store.

31

One of the police officers working out of 54th and Arlington was Officer John Dalbey. John normally worked traffic out of the LAPD substation at the Baldwin Hills Crenshaw Shopping Mall. He is also a Military Policeman in the National Guard. His first night in the riots was performed as a police officer, arriving at the Forward Command Post with his partner just before dark.

One of Dalbey's first missions was to rescue two drivers supposedly stranded with their buses at Vermont and 68th. "We headed out, accompanied by one other cruiser with two cops. We went by one corner with about a hundred people who were jeering, hollering, and holding up flags and banners. It was really wild! A kid about twenty years old stepped off the curb with a brick about eighteen inches long raised over his head. When I saw what he was doing, I hit the brakes and the brick crashed off the left front quarter panel. I then floored it and left. We got to 68th and Vermont, but couldn't find any buses."

Police were then being dispatched from the Forward Command Post to accompany fire engines. They would set up a perimeter when the firemen got to a fire to protect them from snipers and drive-by shootings. Dalbey had his left rear tire shot out by a sniper at 58th and Broadway. "Later, while protecting firefighters, we had two Hispanic kids come up to us who had just left the Lakers game at the Forum. They were a 19-year-old and his 15-year-old brother. They didn't know what they were getting into and ended up in the melee with their late model Cadillac. Unfortunately their car was having serious engine problems, and wasn't going to get them home. The older one asked me what to do. I then asked him how important to him his car was. He wisely made it clear they were more interested in their own skins. We turned them over to a news crew who took them home. God knows what happened to the car!"

"Later we pulled up to a Pep Boys Store on Slauson and Western so the firemen could fight fires that were burning everywhere. People were like ants hauling stuff out of there. They took off when we arrived. Unfortunately we were about a hundred yards from a J. J. Newberry's that was being looted. There were people loading up their cars with loot. Some of them had even rented trailers to haul away the stuff. Anything not nailed down was taken. It was extremely frustrating just standing there watching them, but our mission was to protect the firemen, and we had been told not to leave our posts.

"There was lots of gunfire everywhere. We had one looter who was shot in the hand by another looter. He came by for help, so we had the paramedic with us check him out. The number of fires burning around us was unbelievable!" As night became morning, Officer Dalbey changed uniforms, and reported to the armory at Los Alamitos as Platoon Sergeant Dalbey of the 40th Military Police Company, California Army National Guard.

Fires were set all over the city. Unlike the Watts riots, which were limited to the central part of the city, these riots spread at breakneck speed, with incidents occurring all the way from the Hollywood Hills in the North, to Long Beach over thirty miles to the South. Fire departments were quickly overwhelmed by the sheer numbers of fires that arsonists set, and were plagued by snipers as they tried to bring the fires under control. Some of the injuries were serious, as gang members sniped at fire engines racing to fires, and sniped at firefighters while they were fighting fires.

This was particularly frustrating to firefighters, who had been assured they would be escorted by the police. In fact, that was what LAPD's plan called for. The plan didn't work. While many firemen were provided escorts as was described previously, the need was so great that the police were unable to fully meet their commitment to their fire fighting brethren.

There typically are 32 structure fire incidents a day in the City of Los Angeles. They tallied 601 on the first day of the riot. The firemen couldn't begin to keep up with the sheer numbers of fires. Even worse, they had to battle rioters and gangbangers as well as fires. They faced rocks, bottles and bullets, sometimes on the way to fires, and more often after they arrived on the scene. Several firefighters were severely injured. The most seriously injured was fireman Scott Miller, shot in the face as he drove to a fire in South Central on a hook-and-ladder truck. The shot was fired from a car that pulled up beside the truck as it was racing to the fire. His partners applied first aid as he was hauled in the truck, barely conscious, to Cedars-Sinai Medical Center. There he underwent several hours of surgery. Reports of such injuries spread rapidly, and more and more of the firefighters refused to leave their station houses without police escort.

Increasingly, firefighters were facing snipers in their station houses, as well as on the way to and at fires. The police quickly agreed to let fire companies stage out of the Forward Command Post at 54th and Arlington. The word rapidly spread, and more and more fire engines showed up at the Forward Command Post rather than going to their own station houses. Three queues eventually formed, consisting of a line of fire engines, a line of ambulances, and a line of law enforcement vehicles. Initially a combination of LAPD and Highway Patrol vehicles, the protective mission eventually was almost exclusively handled by the California Highway Patrol. Units would be dispatched from the three lines as needed, with returning units placed at the rear of the queue to await new missions.

More and more police units were gathering at the Forward Command Post. The plan for the Forward Command Post was carefully designed, but unfortunately didn't work as well as it should in practice. So many vehicles congregated there that the situation in the yard rapidly approached gridlock, with vehicles having great difficulty using the facility. By the second night, there were not only a great many police and fire vehicles from Los Angeles, but also police from neighboring cities responding to requests for mutual aid.

The police were having other problems. In an unfortunate twist of fate, many senior leaders in the department were away at a training seminar in Oxnard when the riots broke out. The scene at Parker Center, the downtown headquarters of the Police Department near the Civic Center, grew tense as crowds began to gather. Parker Center served as a form of lightning rod for those with pent-up emotions to vent or causes to push. The crowd included people of every color and culture. They ranged from gangbangers flashing their arm and hand signs, to Revolutionary Communist Party members with hand lettered signs.

Under the lights of television crews, they threw rocks and bottles, and broke windows. Eventually they began to batter at the doors, and destroyed what looked like a kiosk or guard shack outside the building. A police car was overturned and burned on Main Street across from Parker Center. Shortly after 9:00 p.m. there were a series of phone calls between the

Los Angeles Police and Sheriff's Departments discussing the possibility of evacuating Parker Center.

At 9:20 a report came in that the Hall of Justice, just two blocks up from Parker Center, was being broken into. Lieutenant Mike Sparkes of the Los Angeles Sheriff's Department immediately responded, followed ten minutes later by Undersheriff Bob Edmonds with reinforcements. By 10:00 the area was secured , though the Criminal Courts Building across from the Hall of Justice sustained damage to windows, doors and metal detectors. The Hall of Records across the street had broken windows.

The police knew that gun shops would be targeted, so the response plan called for police to provide protection to gun shops in the affected area. As the riots spread, they abandoned two gun shops because of the lack of policemen. Both of the gun shops were quickly looted and burned, with the loss of about 3000 handguns and shoulder fired weapons. Many months later, only 200 of those weapons had been recovered.

Television coverage shifted back to South Central Los Angeles, with more scenes of fires and looting. The impression given over television was that there were very few police in the area, and looting was going unpunished. The looting swiftly spread.

The journal (or log) in the various Emergency Operations Centers established that night rapidly began to fill with entries. Following the verdicts, more and more incidents of civil disorder including fires, bomb threats, vandalism and looting were reported. Some examples included workers being chased from construction jobs. One sewer job in the county, on Century Boulevard in South Central Los Angeles, resulted in spillage because workers were chased off. There were reports of police being shot at, and pelted with rocks and bottles. There were reports of demonstrations and marches. Violence began to erupt in the housing projects. Police and fire stations were targeted for thrown rocks and bottles, and later for sniping attacks to include using high powered rifles. People started shooting at ambulances as well as fire engines and police cars, with one ambulance sustaining six hits. There were too many reports of shootings to record. To cap it off, there was a prison riot in the medium security South Facility of the Peter J. Pitchess (formerly named the Wayside Honor Rancho) Honor Rancho near Castaic, with many inmates injured before it was quickly brought under control.

The Adjutant General of the California National Guard, Major General Robert C. Thrasher, was in Coronado (near San Diego) for a speaking engagement. He was contacted by Larry Goldzband of the Governor's Office at about 8:30 p.m. to ensure he was available in the event the National Guard was needed. Mayor Bradley and Chief Gates had not talked for many months, for as described previously, there was little love lost between the two. Nonetheless, both were involved in a conference call with Governor Pete Wilson sometime after 8:30 at which time Mayor Bradley requested 2000 National Guardsmen. Larry Goldzband then called General Thrasher again, saying the Governor had made the decision to call 2000 Guardsmen following a call from Mayor Bradley. The specific missions were to be defined later.

General Thrasher passed the word to his Chief of Staff in Sacramento, Colonel Terry G. Tucker, at about 9:05 p.m. He directed Colonel Tucker to have the 2000 troops, plus support troops as needed, report to the armories. He further directed that Tucker focus on troops in proximity to Los Angeles first.

37

While Colonel Tucker activated the National Guard's EOC to get troops rolling, General Thrasher phoned Dr. Richard Andrews, Director of the Office of Emergency Services. Dick Andrews advised that he would coordinate with the Los Angeles Police and Sheriff's Departments, noting that the Police Department had already been requested to inform State agencies regarding who was in charge. General Thrasher reconfirmed guidance with Colonel Tucker, restating that troops were to stage in armories, and await specific mission guidance. He then made arrangements to fly back in his C-12 aircraft to Sacramento following a conference call with the principals.

It was becoming increasingly clear that normal law enforcement request channels had been circumvented. The Sheriff is the chief law enforcement official in the county, and is the official who would normally request mutual aid and coordinate efforts in his county. This is especially true in Los Angeles County, which as noted before is a huge megalopolis with a mixture of cities and neighborhoods, some with their own police departments, but with many relying on the Sheriff for protection.

Shortly after 10:00 p.m., there was a conference call arranged by Mike Guerin of the Office of Emergency Services. Participants included Governor Wilson, Mayor Bradley, Sheriff Block, Chief Gates, Commissioner Maury Hannigan of the California Highway Patrol, OES Director Andrews, Randi Rossi of the Attorney General's Office, and General Thrasher.

Chief Gates reported there were many fires out of control and looting in the forty to fifty square miles in South Central Los Angeles involved, but there were not as many people in the streets as during the Watts riots. One or two firemen had been shot. The California Highway Patrol would be needed to help shut down the perimeter, and they then intended to sweep the streets to get the looters. The Los Angeles Police Department had been completely mobilized, with approximately a thousand on duty and more coming, and 400 to 500 in the area.

Sheriff Block acknowledged the fires and looting, but felt no areas were out of control. He didn't feel there was a need for State resources immediately, as he had 500 deputies available and more coming in to assist. He described what he called a "Mardi Gras" atmosphere, with young whites, blacks and Hispanics involved. It became clear later that the "Mardi Gras" atmosphere deteriorated and became much more dangerous across the county as time passed.

Both Gates and Block agreed that there was no need for the National Guard at that time. General Thrasher said he would have 1000 mobilized in armories shortly, with the other 1000 within six hours. Commissioner Hannigan said he could provide 1500 Highway Patrolmen very quickly, but needed the Los Alamitos Armed Forces Reserve Center for staging. General Thrasher assured him that Los Alamitos was ready.

The Governor held a press conference at midnight, during which he looked nervous and tired. His staff later explained that the Governor was tired from some other activities that occurred during the week, even before the riots. He was to get much more tired before the week was over.

General Thrasher flew back to Sacramento, arriving at Mather Air Force Base at about 1:00 a.m. He received a series of briefings at the EOC, and then called to inform me that I was to be the Military Field Commander. There is only one television station available at Camp San Luis Obispo, so after a social event on post with the Germans, I had returned to my quarters to read, without a clue about what was going on. General Thrasher gave me a brief overview. I then talked to the Officer in Charge of the EOC, Colonel Guido J. Portante Jr., and was given a situation update. He advised which troops were being mobilized (see Troop List in Appendix 1) and that a Military Police unit from Northern California had been added to the list. Ammunition, flak vests, and lock plates were to arrive by noon on Thursday. A lock plate is a device which can be installed on the M16 rifle to prevent accidentally putting the selector on automatic. It is required by Federal regulation for use in civil disturbances, to ensure the rifle can only be fired semi-automatically.

National Guard soldiers all over the state were making preparations on their own volition based on what they learned over the radio or television. The commander of the 40th Infantry Division, Major General Daniel J. Hernandez, had been at division headquarters most of the day Wednesday. He had discussed with Colonel Peter Gravett, the full time division Chief of Staff, that the verdict was coming. When General Hernandez heard the verdict, he was "absolutely stunned." He told Pete, "I'm sure we're going to get a call. In the meantime, I'm going home and getting some sleep, because we've got a big day coming." Pete also left shortly afterwards, and picked up personal gear from home before returning to division head-quarters.

Colonel Richard W. Metcalf commands the Second Brigade of the division, headquartered in San Diego. He was driving home from work as the Human Resources Manager for Beckman Instruments in Fullerton at about 6:30 p.m. He heard about the trial verdict and its aftermath over the radio, so immediately switched on the television when he got home. By

8:00 p.m. the extent of the problem was becoming obvious, so on his own authority, he placed his entire brigade on alert. He directed the brigade be alerted down to the company level, with all commanders to remain near their phones.

Similar actions were being initiated all over the division, which consists of approximately 12,000 soldiers in that portion of the division which is located in California. Lieutenant Colonel Joseph R. Mathewson, general manager of Foster Wheeler Corporation, an environmental site remediation firm, was watching Canadian Television in Toronto while on a business trip. He jumped on a plane and was back with his battalion by Thursday afternoon. Other California National Guardsmen scattered around the country, seeing the crisis as reported on television, immediately flew back to their units in California from as far away as New York.

Lieutenant Colonel Gregory C. Peck, Vice President for Information Systems at Pioneer Electronics, is a Vietnam veteran and third generation Guardsman. As soon as he got home, he grabbed his "ready-bag" (most Guardsmen, like the Minutemen of old, keep a bag packed with field gear, underwear and other necessities for emergencies), and headed for Division Headquarters at the Los Alamitos Armed Forces Reserve Center. There he found Colonel Lawrence S. (Mac) McAfee, Jr., the division's Senior Army Advisor. Together they watched the situation develop on television. They quickly established a temporary EOC and opened the staff journal in which key events and communications are logged.

California National Guard men and women all over Southern California were getting calls to report for duty. At 9:25 p.m. the 40th Infantry Division was directed to assemble 2000 troops. In the meantime, the EOC in Sacramento received the official word at 10:00 p.m. from OES that the Governor had authorized the mobilization of 2000 "on street" troops plus support as necessary. When Colonel Gravett returned to the division headquarters about 10:00 p.m., he was briefed by Lieutenant Colonel Peck, and the official EOC was opened.

Lieutenant Colonel Carl Lawrence, commander of Los Alamitos Armed Forces Reserve Center, was told to prepare a staging area to receive 500 California Highway Patrolmen that were being flown in. He was authorized to bring twenty people on duty for that mission and others to follow.

Major William V. Wenger is vice president and general manager for the Shuwa Investments Corporation, and commander of the Third Battalion, 160th Infantry in Inglewood. His wife had alerted him regarding the deteriorating situation elsewhere in the city. When he got home, he got a call from Sergeant First Class Raymond D. Grafton, a full time Guardsman at the armory. Sergeant Grafton told him that Guardsmen were reporting in voluntarily, and they were getting organized in the event troops were needed.

Major Wenger got a call from Lieutenant Colonel Peck shortly after 10:00 p.m., telling him to mobilize the battalion. He started the process, using his alert roster. It was a tough time to leave, as his young son was having a severe asthma attack. In addition, his wife, like so many others, was concerned about his safety as the violence in the streets was being vividly portrayed on television.

Major Wenger left home for his armory in Inglewood, not far from the Los Angeles International Airport and the increasingly riot-torn area of South Central Los Angeles. He could see the glow of fires as he headed out the San Diego Freeway (I-405) before exiting on Manchester Boulevard heading east.

He stopped in the turn lane behind a small red sedan waiting at a red light to make a left turn up La Brea Avenue. The car was crowded with six black youths, who were yelling at some other youths at the Unocal gas station at the northwest corner. As the light changed so they could turn left, things suddenly became violent. "The youth in the left rear seat pulled out what appeared to be a .357 magnum, and fired approximately five rounds at the two cars waiting (to our left front coming south on La Brea) at the stop light on La Brea.

"It appeared to me that people in both cars waiting there were hit. They (in the red sedan) then punched the accelerator and screeched around the corner heading north up La Brea." Major Wenger was unarmed, so there wasn't much he could do. "Everything (seemed to) turn into slow motion. I couldn't believe this was actually happening in front of me." He thought "My God, he just shot two people, and I watched him do it! I followed them to see where they were going. Very quickly one, and then two more squad cars joined in the chase. We went the two or three blocks to where Florence Avenue and the railroad tracks head northeast off La Brea. The cop cars surrounded the vehicle and arrested them."

Major Wenger turned around and headed for the armory. He only went a block before seeing another cluster of police cars. He stopped to tell them what he had seen, only to find out they were arresting some other individuals who had just shot at them. They were delighted to hear the National Guard was being mobilized.

The two shooting incidents within eight blocks of his armory reinforced the sense of urgency as he arrived just prior to midnight. He found his battalion headquarters already operational, and guards posted on the roof and at the gates around the armory. He phoned First Brigade Headquarters to talk to his commander, but found that Colonel William E. Weil was up in Sacramento. He then updated Lieutenant Colonel Charles M. Arce, the brigade executive officer. He found another officer more than familiar with tensions on the street, as Charlie had taken his two sons to the Lakers basketball game at the Forum in Inglewood earlier that night.

The 3-160th Infantry Battalion in Inglewood is primarily black. Guardsmen providing security at the armory were quickly being hassled by gangbangers. "Hey, bro', what are you doing on that side of the wire? You should be out here helping us get Whitey, and showing them what the revolution is all about! You are a traitor!" This was reported to commanders by the Guardsmen, but didn't overtly seem to phase the troops. Many of the Guardsmen were gang members, or had relatives and friends that were, so they knew what was going on in the street.

Few commanders knew for sure how many, if any, members of their commands belonged to gangs. Gang membership is not listed on enlistment contracts for any of the services. Some commanders in the Los Angeles area estimate over ten percent of their units are current or former members of gangs. As previously mentioned, law enforcement officials estimate there are 102,000 gang members in Los Angeles County. Gangs and gang members are therefore endemic in many parts of the county. Nonetheless, no commander during the riots found reason to question the loyalty or dedication of his soldiers.

The 40th Division called to duty that first night:

-- 1st Brigade, commanded by Colonel William E. Weil, and headquartered at Fort MacArthur in San Pedro. They assembled in armories located in Apple Valley, Bakersfield, Ban-

44

ning, Burbank, Delano, Fresno, Glendale, Hanford, Indio, Inglewood, Palmdale, Porterville, Reedley, San Bernardino, San Pedro, Tulare and Visalia.

   -- 2nd Brigade, commanded by Colonel Richard W. Metcalf, and headquartered in San Diego. They assembled in armories located in Brawley, Calexico, Corona, El Centro, Escondido, Fullerton, National City, Orange, Redlands, Riverside, San Diego, Santa Ana and Vista.

   -- 1st Squadron, 18th Cavalry, commanded by Lieutenant Colonel Marvin G. Metcalf (no relation to Richard) and headquartered in Ontario. They assembled in armories located in Colton, Los Alamitos, Pomona and Ontario.

   -- Division Support Command, commanded by Colonel Manuel F. (Red) Silva, with headquarters in Long Beach, called to duty to provide support. They assembled in Bell, Compton, El Cajon, Gardena, Long Beach, Lynwood, Montebello, Ontario and San Diego.

Shortly after midnight, Chief Gates was interviewed on nationwide television. He was asked if an additional 2000 troops might be needed, and responded that not only was that not likely, but that it might not be necessary to deploy the first 2000. He felt that law enforcement was well prepared for the emergency.

In spite of those assurances, the 40th Division Commander shortly afterwards directed that the entire division be placed on an alert status so they could be quickly mobilized if necessary.

As late night became early morning, it was becoming rapidly clear to everybody that this was very different from the Watts riots. The Watts riots involved only about sixty square blocks. These riots extended over thirty miles the first night. All races were involved, rather than being race-specific (blacks) as during

45

the Watts riots. Just as important, we were to find that these riots were not restricted to the hours of darkness.

As dawn began to break, the news media reported the first day's toll:

At least ten killed, nine of which were shooting victims.

Dozens of injured, with almost two dozen treated in just one emergency room.

There were 601 structure fires in the city, with 792 calls for emergency medical support

CHAPTER THREE

Thursday, April 30, 1992
THE SECOND DAY

General Hernandez headed for his headquarters at the Los Alamitos Armed Forces Reserve Center very early in the morning. When he was waved through the main gate he had to drive through concrete anti-terrorist barriers that had been placed during the night. California Highway Patrol sedans were beginning to fill the parking lot, with Highway Patrolmen starting to arrive from all over the state.

When he reached his office, he found a message saying the Adjutant General wanted a call at 6:00 a.m. After exchanging pleasantries, General Thrasher told General Hernandez he was pleased that the division had 2000 soldiers in the armories by 4:00 a.m. He advised that I had been appointed the Military Field Commander, and would be down later in the morning to take overall command. General Thrasher then emphasized his concern that there not be another Kent State. General Hernandez assured the Adjutant General that all commanders were very conscious of the necessity for fire discipline and restraint, and would emphasize that in their orientation for the troops prior to their commitment.

General Hernandez had requested an early morning staff briefing to assure himself the division was adequately preparing for action. During the briefing, he became increasingly concerned about having enough transportation for his soldiers.

The 40th Infantry Division is mechanized, with the great majority of the soldiers transported in tracked vehicles. He didn't want to come rolling into the city in tanks, armored personnel carriers and self-propelled artillery, so the logisticians were scrambling to find commercial transportation. The problem was eventually solved by using commercial bus systems from both Los Angeles and Orange Counties.

The garrison command at Los Alamitos was preparing for a huge influx of law enforcement people and soldiers. The California Division of Forestry started rolling in their mass feeding trailers, supported by prison trustees and California Conservation Corps personnel. The National Guard was delighted to see the California Division of Forestry arrive. They have a reputation for preparing great meals with plenty to eat, as their cooks are trained to replenish the extraordinary caloric output generated by firefighters. Having others handle feeding operations also permitted assignment of riot control duties to soldiers who would normally have to cook or pull kitchen police.

In the Pentagon, Pete Williams, the Assistant Secretary of Defense for Public Affairs, wanted input prior to his twice weekly briefing, normally held on Tuesday and Thursday mornings. He asked Dan Donahue of the National Guard Bureau for the latest on Los Angeles, and also wanted to know what the procedures were for federalizing the National Guard. The calls between Washington and California began to warm up on Thursday. They would sizzle on Friday!

The Air National Guard was busy also. Their C-130 aircraft were shuttling Highway Patrolmen from around the state to Los Alamitos. Before the end of the day, C-130's from the 146th Tactical Airlift Wing based at Port Hueneme in Ventura County would fly 49 sorties loaded with Highway Patrolmen and Guardsmen from around the state.

The Air National Guard C-26 that flew in that morning to pick me up in San Luis Obispo already had several passengers from Sacramento. They included Commissioner Hannigan of the Highway Patrol and three of his top staff, plus several Guardsmen including Colonel Edmund C. Zysk who was to serve on my staff, and Colonel Roger L. Goodrich Jr., the Military Department's Public Affairs Officer.

Colonel Ed Zysk, who has extensive experience managing emergency operations, handed me the Rules of Engagement that had been drafted for my approval. We were particularly pleased that they were short (see Appendix 2), as too often they are quite lengthy, and too long for effective application without constant referral and study. These could be and later were printed on a single page. The rules had been drafted by Major William A. Hipsley, an officer with extensive law enforcement experience. He commanded about 500 full time National Guard men and women working on the counterdrug mission in California, who often were faced with making decisions regarding the application of force. Major Hipsley took their Rules of Engagement, and slightly modified them for application during riot control.

While we were airborne, the Guard's EOC in Sacramento received a call at 10:07 a.m. from Fritz Patterson, the Office of Emergency Services' liaison officer to the Los Angeles County Sheriff's Department, advising that LAPD and LASD were considering three specific missions to be assigned to the California National Guard, but not before 4:00 p.m. that day. The three missions were security of specific locations to

49

prevent further looting and fires, guarding of inner perimeter areas, and protection of firefighters.

At about the same time Fritz Patterson was informing the Guard they wouldn't be needed until 4:00 p.m., General Thrasher told the Los Angeles County Sheriff's Department that National Guardsmen were ready to deploy. This mistake was apparently a consequence of misunderstandings during a staff briefing earlier that morning in Sacramento. The ammunition and equipment weren't even promised to arrive in Southern California until noon, although some officers were convinced it would arrive much earlier. Unfortunately, it arrived almost two hours late.

The C-26 landed at Los Alamitos Armed Forces Reserve Center shortly before 11:00 a.m. We were immediately met by Colonel Pete Gravett who was representing the division, Lieutenant Colonel Jim Ghormley (the Airfield Commander); and LAPD's Captain Keith Bushey (a Marine Corps Reserve Lieutenant Colonel), who was assigned by LAPD to be their liaison officer to us. After a quick update, they were asked "who is in charge?" They acknowledged that they did not know the answer to that very key question. Commissioner Hannigan heard that response, and after he had an opportunity to visit with his staff and Highway Patrolmen who had been airlifted into Los Alamitos, said he would work the issue of who was to provide operational guidance.

We then traveled the short block to the headquarters of the 40th Infantry Division (Mechanized), located in what used to be base headquarters on this former Naval Air Station. There I met briefly with General Hernandez, the division commander, and an old friend.

We talked about the command relationships. The Military Field Command system is unique to California, and works extraordinarily well when the California National Guard is inserted into comparatively small, emergency situations in a deliberate way. The system is based on a combination of full time and volunteer traditional (part time) Guardsmen who have been trained in state administrative requirements. In an emergency-prone state like California, we have found this system works very well for forest fires and floods. However, neither General Hernandez nor I were comfortable with *ad hoc* command and staff arrangements in life threatening, high tempo operations like the Los Angeles riots. I had relinquished command of the division less than three years before, when General Hernandez had been one of my two Assistant Division Commanders, so I knew all the key players. Most important of all, General Hernandez and I have a great deal of confidence in each other, and the complete leadership chain. All of this impacted on one of the more important decisions made during the riots.

The key decision we made was to not implement the *ad hoc* Military Field Command system, and rely instead on the traditional military system. That way we would not be inserting another headquarters between the EOC in Sacramento and the division. Instead, I would serve as overall commander at the scene, working strategy and policy issues, with the Office of the Adjutant General in Sacramento providing assistance (primarily administrative and logistical) as necessary. In effect, General Hernandez and his staff would run the tactics, with my support, while I ran interference. As the overall commander, I could not abrogate responsibility for everything the soldiers did or failed to do. I could, however, organize the effort my way. Besides, it was becoming increasingly apparent that there would be problems in overall direction of efforts to combat the riots, and those had to receive priority.

After agreeing generally on how we would approach the mission, we headed for the conference room for an update briefing by the division staff. In the audience for the update briefing were about thirty members of the division staff, Captain Bushey from LAPD, a representative from LASD, plus Paul Flores and Ken Jourdan of OES. Two things were immediately evident. One was that the division headquarters was fully operational and had things well in hand. This was to be expected in a division headquarters that had recently participated in several Army-sponsored "Warfighter" Exercises. Those computer-assisted exercises are run for the division by the I Corps staff at Fort Lewis, Washington, and a special team at the Command and General Staff College at Fort Leavenworth, Kansas. The exercises, which run continuously day and night for several days, fully stress a headquarters while requiring that responsive, fully coordinated guidance be provided to subordinate units.

The other issue obvious to us all was an appropriate sense of urgency. The Intelligence Officer (G-2), Lieutenant Colonel Bill Humphreys (in civil life the Principal Consultant for San Diego Data Processing Corporation), painted the picture of Wednesday night's riot activities, mainly drawn from television. It was too early in the "battle" for intelligence summaries to be generated by law enforcement. He also briefed the locations of police and sheriff's stations, and the locations of school yards that could be used for helicopter landing zones. The full time Operations Officer (G-3), Lieutenant Colonel John Bernatz, advised that no missions had been received yet. Training

52

guidance sent out to the commands required refresher training in riot control formations, use of force, arming orders, and the Rules of Engagement. We were very concerned about fire discipline and the necessity of our soldiers showing restraint. Most of our older soldiers had served in Watts, and they didn't want a repeat of the "free fire" atmosphere that prevailed in those riots. As added insurance, Sacramento had directed that every soldier sign the Rules of Engagement, attesting that he read and understood them.

Shortly after the briefing, Commissioner Maury Hannigan told me that there would be a meeting in the Sheriff's Office at 2:00 p.m. to organize efforts to combat the riots. I passed this information to Colonel Ed Zysk and Paul Flores, and asked the division for a helicopter flight to be scheduled.

Riot activities began to pick up steam in the middle of the morning. This came as a surprise to everyone who had any knowledge of previous riots. In fact, LAPD's Metro Squad had been told to report for duty at 4:00 p.m., earlier than the 6:00 p.m. report time they had been given on Wednesday, but still not early enough for what transpired this Thursday.

Some morning activities that were reported included demonstrations and rallies in scattered parts of the county that grew into disturbances. Riotous activity was reported at the Forum Amphitheater in Inglewood, and at the Court and City Hall in Pasadena. At 10:40 a.m., about fifteen gang members were reported to be breaking into businesses at the corner of Colorado and Rosemead. At 10:45 a.m., additional law enforcement officers were dispatched to the Baldwin Hills Crenshaw Shopping Center where 74 looters were arrested. Some of those officers were then moved to a mini-mall at Vernon and Figueroa where 43 looters were taken into custody. At 11:28 a.m. looting was reported on Willowbrook Avenue. A few minutes later a Compton Police Officer requested assistance at the corner of Long Beach and Compton Boulevard. It was rapidly becoming apparent that this was to be a very different kind of civil disturbance, and looters were not going to wait until it got dark.

At about noon, we got a phone call from Undersheriff Bob Edmonds of the Los Angeles Sheriffs Department. The number two man in that department, subordinate only to Sheriff Sherman Block, he is well known to and respected by the California National Guard. This is because of his reputation and popularity among law enforcement officers in Southern California, in addition to his dedication over the last several years in helping get counterdrug efforts organized among local, state and federal agencies.

Bob told me that he would like a National Guard presence on the streets quickly for the psychological value. It wasn't until three months after the riots that we found out the Sheriff's Department, as already stated, had been told at about 10:00 a.m. that the National Guard was ready to deploy. At this time, none of us in Southern California knew the ammunition had been delayed. Bob said he would like to get television coverage in helicopters over our troops, so the word would quickly get out that the National Guard had arrived. I told him we probably ought to use our 40th Military Police Company for the mission. He told me he wanted to initially send them to Lakewood Sheriff's Station, where he would have escorts meet our troops and guide them into the area of operations. We were familiar with that location, as the 40th Division's former Command Sergeant Major, John W. Jackson, had worked out of there in his full time capacity as a sergeant in the Sheriff's Department. We went to work on it.

It was then announced that the supply flight due at noon hadn't arrived yet. We put out a call for ammunition from Task Force Grizzly, our counterdrug force at Los Alamitos A.F.R.C. While it was being sent over, Lieutenant Colonel Bernatz, the Division G3, put together an operations order to get the troops dispatched.

There were several calls back and forth between the Sacramento EOC, Los Alamitos, and General Thrasher. It was clear that there was an increasing sense of urgency. General Thrasher was told about the ammunition and supply problem, and the challenges involved in getting the Rules of Engagement reproduced and out to the troops scattered in forty-three armories around Southern and Central California. The call after noon was the first time some of the staff in Sacramento knew the ammunition and equipment were delayed. The progress (or lack of it) was evidently not even being monitored by senior staff officers there.

There were a series of phone calls from various senior officials in state government to General Thrasher about the delay in getting troops into the street. Though the accepted standard for National Guard commitment in civil disturbances is twenty-four hours, phone calls started getting rather strident about sixteen hours after we were first notified.

Paul Flores of the Office of Emergency Services had seen all the activity in preparing to send troops on the street, and he called me over to one side. There he told me that law enforcement mutual aid had not been fully invoked, and we shouldn't be sending out troops yet. I told him "O.K.," but did nothing to actually stop any troops from getting prepared. I did tell Sacramento about the conversation during the next call.

It didn't take long for that message to reverberate around the state. Within a very few minutes we received a call from an understandably upset Undersheriff Edmonds. He clearly was feeling operational pressure as the civil disturbances picked up steam even though it was still very early in the afternoon. I explained the logistical problems, and promised him that as soon as we had two platoons of Military Police ready, we would dispatch them.

That decision to initially send only two platoons is not as risky as it might seem for several reasons. Our Military Police are doctrinely expected to perform their duties in widely dispersed units as small as three-person teams, and are routinely trained for riot control. In addition, the 40th Military Police Company has an extraordinarily high percentage of police officers among its ranks. But perhaps most importantly, it is a unit in which we had a great deal of confidence. The risk was in sending troops out before the overall management structure had been agreed to, and that decision hadn't been made yet.

The division had the second and fifth platoons of the Military Police company ready to roll by 1:30 p.m. There were a series of phone calls changing the destination of the Military Police from Lakewood Station to Vernon and Vermont, and then to Martin Luther King Boulevard. Finally it was decided to hold them at Los Alamitos A.F.R.C. where law enforcement would pick them up and guide them to where they were most needed. When law enforcement escorts arrived to guide them at 2:35 p.m., the full company was ready to roll. However, I didn't find this out until at least an hour later, because Colonel Zysk and I had already headed for a UH-60 Blackhawk helicopter which departed at 1:31 p.m. for the meeting with law enforcement officials to establish the management guidelines.

We landed on top of City Hall East, which has a helipad just large enough to handle two military helicopters. It is always a thrill landing in a helicopter on top of a skyscraper downtown, but we were too engrossed in the problems at hand to enjoy the excitement. We were met by a Sheriff's Deputy, who drove us to the Sheriff's Office in the Hall of Justice two blocks away.

Commissioner Hannigan and a couple of his deputies were already in the Sheriff's Conference Room. We were shortly joined by Chief Gates, Sheriff Block and Undersheriff Edmonds. It was just after 2:00 p.m., as we were getting ready to start the meeting, when we were informed that Governor Wilson was on the phone with a conference call.

We all moved to the Sheriff's office suite where the Sheriff, Chief of Police, Commissioner of the Highway Patrol, and some others got on the phone. There weren't enough phones so I didn't hear the first part of the conversation. I went into another room where the Sheriff's secretary set me up with a phone.

Governor Wilson was on the phone, as well as General Thrasher, and Dick Andrews of OES. The Governor asked me why Guardsmen were not out in the street. I did not know what General Thrasher had shared with the Governor, but I did know that lock plates had not been installed in our weapons. So I told him that we had not had enough time to install the lock plates required by federal regulation to keep our weapons from firing on automatic and endangering innocent people. Someone (Chief Gates during an interview on television later said he was the one) suggested that each soldier be given one bullet with additional ammunition held by squad leaders.

Governor Wilson asked Sheriff Block if that was acceptable to him, and he responded affirmatively. He then asked Chief Gates the same question and got the same response. He then directed us to handle it that way.

There clearly was a sense of urgency during that conference call, but I heard none of the profanity or vituperation that was later reported in Time Magazine. More on that later.

Many units were committed before the lock plates were installed. The chain of command in the units handled the issue their own way. Almost all issued somewhere between twenty and forty rounds of ammunition to each individual, and counted on the fire discipline of their soldiers. No one wanted to subject their soldiers to the "Barney Fife" rule (only one bullet per soldier), nor did any leader want to report to surviving relatives that their loved one had been killed because he had only one bullet for his weapon.

As we broke up around 2:20 p.m., I was told by one of my staff that the ammunition, lock plates and other supplies had landed at Los Alamitos at 1:55 p.m. The distribution of ammunition and equipment was quickly started, a tough challenge for logisticians because the soldiers were so widely scattered.

We reconvened the meeting in the Sheriff's Conference Room to get organized. Sheriff Block sat at the head of the conference table. To his right sat Undersheriff Edmonds and then Chief Gates. I sat to his immediate left, followed by Commissioner Hannigan and two of Hannigan's deputies.

There were a few brief comments about mutual aid, and the fact that 2000 Guardsmen had been requested. I interpreted Chief Gates' comments as his wanting soldiers rather than more law enforcement mutual aid because of the historical enmity between the police and the residents in the affected area. Chief

Gates looked directly across the table at Commissioner Hannigan, who in response to a question, advised that he would soon have more than a thousand Highway Patrolmen on hand, with more on the way.

Chief Gates then said "Maury, firefighters are refusing to leave their stations because they are being shot at. Would you handle the mission of escorting fire units?"

Commissioner Hannigan quickly agreed to do that, and sometime later also accepted the mission of escorting ambulances. I was then asked if the National Guard would handle all other missions, and we agreed to that division of responsibility.

There was a short general discussion of how to best use the National Guard. The police had been frustrated by rioters and looters who would disperse when police arrived on the scene, only to return as soon as the police left to handle a situation elsewhere. It was agreed that one of the primary roles of the National Guard would be to secure areas behind the police.

The final important order of business was determining how mission tasks were to flow. When this issue was raised, there was a brief but pregnant pause as we looked from Sheriff Block to Chief Gates. Undersheriff Edmonds quickly stepped into the breach. He said that operations should be run from the Sheriff's Emergency Operations Center, with representatives there from the Sheriff's Department, Police Department, the National Guard, and the Office of Emergency Services. Requests were to flow into the EOC, where they would be prioritized by the police and sheriff's representatives, and then converted into military orders by our representatives. We all agreed to that arrangement, and the meeting broke up just before 3:00 p.m. I briefed Colonel Zysk on the results of the meeting before he headed for the Sheriff's EOC, and I flew back to Los Alamitos.

Colonel Zysk earlier had dispatched Major David K. Appel with Sergeant First Class Mark Carrasco to establish liaison with the Sheriff's EOC. We were quite pleased with ourselves for having the foresight to immediately dispatch a liaison team to the Sheriff's EOC. However, our team faced their own set of challenges when they got there.

During major emergencies, there are representatives in the EOC from the County Administrative Officer (the county's chief executive officer), the County Fire Department, the County Road Department, the Department of Public Social Services (welfare department), the Department of Health Services (controls hospitals and ambulance services in the county), and many other non-law enforcement agencies. During emergencies of significant magnitude, there routinely are representatives from the Los Angeles Police and Fire Departments, the California Highway Patrol, and the Office of Emergency Services.

Major Appel and Sergeant Carrasco were more than a little surprised to find eighty people in an EOC designed for about forty-five people. There were even representatives from the Department of Animal Regulation as, well as U.S. Postal Inspectors. The phone system, somewhat obsolescent and scheduled for upgrading in a new EOC planned for construction in a few years, was already overburdened.

The military liaison team was met by Chief Paul Myron of the Los Angeles Sheriff's Department, a highly regarded artillery battalion commander when he was in the National Guard, and later a colonel in the Army Reserve. They discussed the availability of troops, and were told that while the situation was very serious, it was not out of control. The strategy described by Chief Myron called for law enforcement to move to an area, quell whatever disturbance was involved, arrest lawbreakers, and have the National Guard occupy the area. The Guard would secure the area, conduct patrols, and prevent the return of riotous conditions.

Chief Myron introduced Major Appel to Chief William A. Baker, who was the daytime or "Shift A" Incident Commander for the EOC. Later he met Chief Larry Anderson, who handled the night shift for the Sheriff's Department. Chief Baker asked Major Appel to advise when troops would be ready for dispatch, as they wanted them in place, especially in larger shopping malls, before dark. They were expecting more trouble when it got dark, and they wanted to prevent roaming groups from considering the shopping malls easy prey, thus requiring law enforcement intervention to remove looters.

Various agencies began to make direct requests without having them screened and prioritized by the Sheriff's representative. There were about a hundred the first hour, which included:

-- Fire Departments wanted flak jackets.

-- The County Health Department wanted flak jackets for ambulance drivers and emergency medical technicians.

-- The County Fire Department wanted fire stations guarded while they were out fighting fires, and wanted Guardsmen to accompany the trucks when they were on runs.

-- The County Department of Cultural Affairs wanted all museums and art galleries guarded.

-- The County Department of Public Social Services wanted all welfare offices guarded.

-- Public telephone companies wanted all central offices and remote switching stations guarded.

-- Public utilities wanted all substations and control centers guarded.

When we landed at Los Alamitos, we were quickly updated by my deputy, Colonel Richard E. Beardsley, and then met with General Hernandez. We were getting a better "sense of the street," and decided it would be prudent to immediately ask for authority to mobilize another 2000 troops. It seemed to us that if over 10,000 police, sheriff's deputies and highway patrolmen were having trouble keeping the peace, the first 2000 National Guardsmen would not make enough of a difference. Law enforcement officials had similarly recognized the need for more Guardsmen, and passed a requirement up through their channels. Our request for an additional 2000 troops was passed to Sacramento, and quickly approved.

While we were conducting the meetings to determine how the Highway Patrol and the National Guard were to be used, the looting had been gaining momentum. There was some commentary that even people who were normally law-abiding took to the streets to get their share of loot before it was all gone. More fires were set.

Between noon and 2:00 p.m. there were a series of disturbing incidents. It was reported there were at least two shootings involving police officers in Compton and the City of Commerce. Looters were reported ransacking businesses all over the affected area, especially hitting markets, liquor stores, pawn shops and gun stores. A cameraman and reporter were attacked in Compton. There were reports of more shopping centers being targeted by dissidents and hoodlums. An LAPD Community Resources Against Street Hoodlums (called "CRASH") anti-gang unit followed some vehicles loaded with Crips gang members that were headed for Simi Valley where the Rodney King trial took place. The Crips changed direction when they spotted the CRASH unit.

Elsewhere, people were stocking up on food, topping off their gas tanks, and in some cases, trying to buy weapons and ammunition to defend their homes or businesses. In the meantime, National Guard units were arriving on the streets of Los Angeles.

The 40th Military Police Company, commanded by First Lieutenant Dieter Trippel, Vice President of a San Bernardino corporation involved in vocational training, had received its mobilization notification at 11:10 p.m. on Wednesday night. Before noon on Thursday the company was conducting platoon level refresher civil disturbance training, after which they signed the Rules of Engagement and Arming Orders. Everyone was concerned about fire discipline and ammunition accountability, so ammunition was carefully counted out for issue to each soldier, before Sheriff's cruisers arrived at 2:35 p.m. to guide the company into the riots.

The convoy consisted of about thirty Military Police "Hummers," escorted by the Sheriff's cruisers. Hummers are more formally called High-Mobility, Multipurpose Wheeled Vehicles (HMMWV) pronounced "Hum-vee" or "Humvees" (or simply "Hummers") by soldiers. They took the place of the ubiquitous jeep, but are much larger and more powerful. They can normally transport four soldiers (Military Police teams consist of three soldiers in a Hummer), but some Hummers are configured like pickups, and can transport more troops, though not as comfortably. The Hummer became the primary *tactical* mode of transportation for all soldiers during the riots, while buses were used to transport larger numbers of troops.

Military Policemen were understandably tense as they headed into the unknown. The tension was increased by instructions to keep their windows rolled up and be prepared for rocks, Molotov cocktails, and snipers. Their mission was changed twice en route as the situation in the streets changed, and they ended up going north on the Harbor Freeway. There were very few cars on that freeway, and they were surprised at how dark it got from all the smoke that obscured the sky and blew across the freeway. There was graffiti everywhere in black, red and blue. Fresh gang graffiti welcomed them with such messages as "F--- the Police," "F--- the National Guard," and "Kill Whitey." They took the Vernon off ramp and pulled into the Ralph's Supermarket and Thrifty Drug complex at the corner of Vernon and Figueroa.

There they found a couple of LAPD sedans plus a platoon of Sheriff's deputies. Cars were overturned and torched in the street, with litter everywhere. Produce thrown in the streets and parking lots made it slippery, and there were all kinds of trash and dropped loot. There were people scattered all over the place, with a few flashing guns, and some looting going on across the street. There were a lot of taunts and threats from the crowd, with some not convinced the soldiers were serious. One of the gangbangers came up to a Guardsman and tried to yank his M16 rifle away from him. As they struggled, another soldier used his own M16 to butt stroke the individual in the head. He immediately collapsed on the pavement. Some of his friends tentatively approached, then quickly grabbed him and took him away. The pressure from the crowd then eased off, and most of the crowd faded away.

There were too many Hummers to fit the parking lot, and help was needed elsewhere. The assistant Provost Marshal of the division, Major Gary Adams, had accompanied the unit. The Administrative Assistant to the Chief of Police in Santa Ana in his civilian job, Adams discussed the situation with the LASD commander at the scene.

Military Policemen just after arriving in supermarket parking lot. First military deployed during the riots, note smoke in the background. (Photo by SFC Jim Ober)

After the situation stabilized, the company left the Fourth Platoon, and dispatched the four remaining platoons to three other trouble spots. The Sheriff's platoon took off, and one

LAPD cruiser was left to work with the Military Police platoon that remained.

The company headquarters was moved to the south side of the Coliseum where they found a staging area being established, with LAPD police officers and Highway Patrolmen, and phones being installed. The company First Sergeant, Pat Black, normally a Watch Commander with the Buena Park Police Department, was asked by the phone company where he wanted his phone set up. He pointed, and the 40th Military Police Company quickly had a temporary command post.

The First and Third Platoons were sent to a mini-mall on the corner of Martin Luther King Boulevard and Vermont. There had been a killing there, described as a drug deal gone bad, just before they arrived.

They set up in the mall's parking lot next to the Wonderland Laundry, 99 Cent Store, Golden Bird Fried Chicken and Food Town Mart, all of which had been looted and burned. Across the street a Goodyear Tire and some Thrift Stores had been completely gutted, with the Winchell's Donut Shop across the way fully engulfed in flames when they arrived.

The Second Platoon went to the Baldwin Hills Crenshaw Mall at the confluence of Martin Luther King, Stocker Street, and Crenshaw Boulevard. This beautiful mall had seen more than its share of violence. The platoon relieved the California Highway Patrol there, who immediately left for missions elsewhere. This mall is perhaps the last ostentatious symbol of affluence in that area before immediately making the transition to older, much less affluent neighborhoods to the south. The mall is anchored by three large department stores, a Broadway, a May Company, and a Sears; plus a Lucky Supermarket. The problems had started with the Liquor Barn, a large liquor store just south of the mall. They then expanded to the Imperial Plaza Mini-mall across the street, where several Korean-owned businesses had been looted, before the violence migrated to the big shopping center. Most of the windows in the Broadway had been shot out.

Military Policemen arriving at the corner of Martin Luther King Boulevard and Vermont Avenue. (Photo by MSG Cliff Ellison)

When the troops initially took their posts around the Crenshaw Mall, a man from the Liquor Barn called over, offering the soldiers snacks and drinks. When the troops hollered back that they couldn't leave their posts, he came across the street to them. The troops got a kick out of it, as he came complete with a World War II style helmet on, hauling shopping bags with goodies that were distributed among the troops. It was a gesture much appreciated by all of the Second Platoon.

Barricades had been set up between Martin Luther King and Stocker on Crenshaw Boulevard. Gangbangers cruised very slowly up to the barricades, and did a U-turn while hanging out the window with their fingers fashioned like a gun and telling the Guardsmen they were going to come back when it was dark and kill them. A small light colored Nissan mini-truck with a bullhorn came by at least three times telling the crowd to get off the street or the soldiers would kill them. No one seemed to know who he was or where he came from. The gangbangers that were there did a lot of taunting. Too many people came by, slowed their vehicles, and then rolled their tinted windows down to take a photo. Unfortunately, this was the same technique the unit had been briefed as used for drive-by shootings. Needless to say, it greatly increased the tension, and it was fortunate no one was shot, as it got very difficult to tell the difference between a camera and a weapon as darkness began to descend.

The Fifth Platoon went to Vermont Square at Vernon and Vermont. It was a mess. The fire department had been to this shopping center several times, but had been driven off at least twice by the hostile crowd and gunfire. When the Military Policemen arrived, there were half a dozen police officers with their backs against the wall, being taunted by somewhere between 350-500 people. The ABC Market (now a Boy's Market) was completely gutted and was being looted. There was nothing left of the Swap Meet next door. Other stores in the mall, including Pioneer Chicken, Tong's Tropical Fish and Pets, Tina's Wigs, and the Shoe Repair Store were all burned and looted. Across the street, Golden Jewelry had looters running in and out. They all faded away when the Military Police arrived.

Several Guardsmen checked out the ABC Market to ensure no one was hiding inside. They found it extremely eerie as they went through. The background music was still playing in the market, one of the few places in the affected area that still had electricity. The time clock was still clicking, but cash registers had been ripped out and thrown across the parking lot. Groceries and produce were scattered everywhere. There was lots of gunfire in the neighborhood, some of it automatic fire.

In the meantime, the first troops from Northern California had arrived in Los Angeles. The commander, Captain Edward (Ned) Lee, a Municipal Court Judge in civilian life, received the call at 3:15 a.m. on April 30th to mobilize his 670th Military Police Company. The unit is the only company in the 49th Military Police Brigade that was not mobilized for Desert Shield/Desert Storm in Southwest Asia, so they saw this as their opportunity to demonstrate their readiness. The unit was split between Sunnyvale and Eureka, so aircraft were dispatched by the Air National Guard to fly his soldiers from Moffett Field near Sunnyvale, and the commercial airport at Eureka.

His soldiers landed at Van Nuys Airport, where they were picked up in buses and taken to the Los Angeles Police Academy, arriving by 4:00 p.m. A company command post was established, and ammunition was issued by the police. Some of the soldiers stayed and provided security at the Police Academy, which is located on a rather vulnerable hill in Elysian Park near Dodger Stadium. The balance of 108 Guardsmen loaded up on RTD buses (their Hummers were being convoyed down from Northern California) and were dispatched to the LAPD Forward Command Post at 54th and Arlington. The 670th was then split in half, with two platoons heading for the Martin Luther King Shopping Center and the balance going to 3rd and Vermont in Koreatown.

At 3rd and Vermont, the soldiers of the 670th MP Company found a situation very similar to that experienced by many soldiers of the 40th MP Company. They were in a supermarket parking lot with fires burning everywhere and bullets striking the ground, walls and windows nearby. The air was heavy with smoke. Law enforcement officers were trying to push back a crowd of about 500 who wanted to loot the Ralph's Supermarket. The crowd quickly dispersed upon arrival of the Military Police, who were credited by the police with saving the three markets at 3rd and Vermont from burning.

The troops then went out in teams of three to secure the several blocks in the area. Shortly after their arrival in the area, a sedan pulled up with two men in it. The driver asked for help for his friend who had been shot. The unit called for their medic, Private Scott Shuey, who found that the man was dead. The dead man sat in that car in the parking lot for some hours because the coroner was running several hours behind.

The other detachment from the 670th also had their hands full. Some of them witnessed a drive-by shooting a block away. The officer in command, Second Lieutenant Gary Elliott (a deputy sheriff in Solano County) set up his command post in a second floor security office in the Martin Luther King Shopping Center. They then established a perimeter of defense completely around the center, which had been looted but not burned. Right across the street were the housing projects, with a very high wall. That wall, but only in retrospect, provided one of the funnier memories for the troops. Gangbangers would stick their heads up from behind the wall and yell things at the troops. The troops couldn't tell what they were standing on, but it was funny to see the heads keep popping up and down over an eight foot wall. They would bait the troops, telling them how they would get them after it got dark, calling them names and other epithets, before quickly ducking their heads.

While there was gunfire around the Martin Luther King Center, there was considerably less than in Koreatown. They also usually couldn't tell where the gunfire was directed, not hearing the distinctive sound of high-powered bullets flying by, or the sounds of rounds striking anything close. Just when they thought it was getting quiet, a school one block away exploded into flame.

Gangbangers would occasionally test the Guardsmen at all locations, with taunting and teasing to see what reaction they would get. They sometimes would threaten to come back after dark and shoot the soldiers. Such taunts often would be punctuated by gangbangers flashing their weapons before driving off.

Tensions increased as darkness approached, and the few law-abiding citizens still on the streets hurried to get home.

CHAPTER FOUR

Thursday, April 30, 1992
THE SECOND NIGHT

Tension increased as it grew dark. Gangbangers occasionally had told Guardsmen that they didn't believe the troops had ammunition, a consequence of the unfortunate press reports that put our soldiers at risk. Soldiers faced a dilemma when gangbangers started talking with them. General guidance was to ignore gangbangers, to avoid talking with them for fear of inadvertently revealing sensitive information, and act professional. Nonetheless, recognizing the very real dangers of having gangbangers think they had no ammunition, some soldiers showed them ammunition in one of their loaded magazines. Stress remained high as the evening wore on, harassment and gunfire continued, and crashing sounds came from roofs collapsing into burning stores.

Units were being committed into the riots with little or no guidance regarding what to expect other than what was seen on television. Trained to deploy based on reasonably detailed operations plans, and not having had time for detailed briefings or rehearsals, there was considerable apprehension as Guardsmen headed into the riot-torn areas with a minimum of guidance following receipt of mission orders. Fortunately, with the single exception of the 670th MP Company from Northern California, all units committed initially were from the affected area. They had a sense of what they were getting into.

All senior military officers are taught Karl von Clausewitz's precepts for the systematic study of war, including his famous principles of war. Clausewitz's "fog of war" (state of confusion) not only applies to combat, but to these riots as well. This a time of *great* confusion, but perhaps no different than should be expected in any similar complex crisis involving many widely disparate jurisdictions. Regardless, all activities were greatly impacted by a sense of urgency as lines of responsibility and authority began to emerge based on personal and professional relationships from the past, without waiting for the formal arrangements to solidify.

That sense of urgency certainly permeated the senior leadership in the division. This is not surprising considering divisional leadership was or is from the Greater Los Angeles area. In effect, the division was protecting its home turf. General Hernandez has lived almost all his life in Altadena, in the northeast of the affected area. Born into a very poor family that relied on welfare, he had to sleep on the floor when he was a youngster. He obviously has come a long way since those days and his first work as a mail carrier. His background and heritage, as well as his training and experience, served him well during the riots.

Brigadier General William F. Stewart, one of the Assistant Division Commanders, lives in La Canada to the northwest. His civilian job is Los Angeles County Internal Services Director, with 3800 employees and a budget of over $370 million.

The other Assistant Division Commander, Colonel Robert J. Brandt (who was promoted to Brigadier General immediately following the riots) had just been transferred north from the City of Fountain Valley to the southeast. A veteran of two tours in Vietnam and a former pilot with the now defunct Los Angeles Airways, he had just retired from federal service as the director of Army Aviation in the California National Guard.

The Chief of Staff, Colonel Pete Gravett, is from San Pedro to the southwest. Pete is a retired Watch Commander (Internal Affairs) and holder of the Medal of Valor, LAPD's highest decoration for heroism. Those four senior leaders came from areas that in effect bracketed the riot-torn area from the four corners of the compass.

The other senior officer in the division headquarters was Brigadier General Pat Nappi. Pat had just been transferred in from New York's 42nd (Rainbow) Infantry Division on a temporary assignment. He ended up running the night shift in the division's EOC.

I had organized my personal staff. Colonel Zysk and Major Appel were handling duties at the senior (Sheriff's) EOC. Colonel Dick Beardsley had been sent to Los Alamitos a couple of days earlier from the Military Department in Sacramento to conduct a study. As mentioned earlier, I drafted him as my deputy. Our small staff was rounded out by local soldiers: two Lieutenant Colonels, a Command Sergeant Major, and a Staff Sergeant. The Lieutenant Colonels were Timothy M. Murphy, a logistical expert and experienced commander, and Lieutenant Colonel Ross Moen, an operations officer and Lieutenant of Detectives in LAPD. Command Sergeant Major Jimmie F. Maxey, a highly regarded sergeant major assigned to the post, was asked to serve as my Command Sergeant Major. He was a pillar of strength as we visited the troops each night. Finally, Staff Sergeant Saundra (Sandy) Peralta agreed to serve as executive assistant in keeping us all organized and administratively straight.

Tensions in the Sheriff's EOC began to increase as darkness approached. Some agency representatives went from being merely concerned to a state more akin to panic. The civil agencies were talking to their people on the streets just like the law enforcement agencies were, and pressures in the room were dramatically increasing. As time passed, the tension increased to a level that Major Appel described as "second level arm waving." Efforts to bring order out of chaos were complicated by many factors. One was the fact that these riots were more widespread than anyone had envisioned. In addition, there was too much "*ad hocism*" as senior officials ignored established protocols that had been published and practiced during exercises.

As explained earlier, the senior law enforcement official in the county is the Sheriff. Nonetheless, the Mayor bypassed the Sheriff (and his own Chief of Police) and communicated directly and comparatively often with Governor Wilson. Another example was the routine bypassing of normal mutual aid request channels, which are supposed to flow through the Sheriff and the Office of Emergency Services. For instance, some police officers phoned buddies from other police departments (in one case as far away as Bakersfield) and requested aid which was then dispatched in what obviously became an uncoordinated effort. There were many consequences. One was that no one initially knew what law enforcement resources had been requested nor where they were reporting. Another important consequence to us, as we finally learned later that afternoon, was an *ad hoc* arrangement wherein it was agreed that National Guard support was to be split fifty-fifty between the City and County of Los Angeles. We were told this was based on a political decision that the city and county were to be treated as equals, which was interpreted to mean an equal share of the National Guard.

Biscailuz Center, with Prison Facility in foreground. The Emergency Operations Center (EOC) is underground, beneath the antennas in the background.
(Photo: Author's Collection)

Colonel Zysk's team in the Sheriff's EOC was augmented as Major M. Jan Small, a former Marine, was sent by the 40th Division to assist, along with Major John D. Gordon. Requests for assistance continued to flow into the EOC. These requests ran the gamut from the Red Cross wanting the Guard to secure locations where the homeless were housed, to increasing concern about certain public utilities. This latter issue resulted in a recommendation to the Incident Commander to request additional assets through OES. The Air National Guard was given the mission by our EOC in Sacramento, and deployed Air Security Police by the next day. That mission involved over twenty sensitive sites spread throughout the Los Angeles basin, with the Air Guardsmen later augmented by soldiers from the 40th Division's 140th Chemical Company.

Mission tasks continued to flow through the Sheriff's EOC to the division. Following the dispatch of the two military police units during the afternoon, the division began to dispatch larger units. There was considerable frustration as some of these units waited for hours between the time they were equipped and ready, and the time mission requests were received. This was especially true in Inglewood, where soldiers could see their city burning, and city officials were pleading for help. Nonetheless, the mission directives eventually began to rapidly flow, and troops headed out of their staging areas.

The 499 soldiers of 3rd Battalion, 160th Infantry headquartered in Inglewood were the first to roll. Major Bill Wenger ended up with units scattered from Castaic in the north to Lynwood and Whittier, over forty three air miles to the south. This geographical spread gave him some extraordinary command, control, and logistical challenges over the next several days.

Companies A and E, Wenger's Burbank units, were escorted by police to the Peter J. Pitchess Honor Rancho. This is the large prison complex near Castaic northeast of Los Angeles where the riots occurred Wednesday night. The troops were briefed on the security requirements around the four detention facilities, to include a videotape of the previous night's uprising. The videotape showed the need for tear gas, "sting ball" grenades with rubber pellets, and the Arwen Gun using plastic projectiles, to regain control over about a hundred inmates who were directly involved. Thirty-three inmates received minor to moderate injuries, with one requiring hospitalization. Three deputies also received minor injuries while quelling the disturbance. After receiving their mission briefing, the troops were organized into shifts and positioned to provide security around the prison.

The two companies detailed as prison guards had less excitement than their sister companies. They nonetheless provided a reassuring measure of insurance for a very large detention facility where many additional bus loads of prisoners were sent every day during and immediately after the riots. In addition, they watched the excitement, to include the considerable media attention, as the men accused of beating Reginald Denny the first night were arrested and incarcerated some days later.

Company B of Glendale headed into the East Los Angeles area, to include the eastern portions of Wilshire Boulevard and the area around Whittier and Atlantic Boulevards. There was an entirely different atmosphere here than experienced by troops in South Central Los Angeles. The gangs here were primarily Hispanic, and unlike gangs elsewhere (including Hispanic gangs), told Guardsmen they weren't going to "trash" their own neighborhoods. There was no looting or burning to speak of, and very little violence. Gun shots were heard, but they seemed to come from a considerable distance away. Soldiers of Company B, which has many Hispanic soldiers, soon found themselves adopted by the community. Several soldiers even received marriage proposals before they were pulled out of the area some days later.

Company C of Inglewood, augmented by the battalion Scout and Mortar Platoons, deployed to Lynwood in the heart of the affected area. Escorted by Sheriff's sedans with sirens screaming, the convoy of trucks and Hummers sped through the streets. Captain James A. Keating, the Company Commander, has vivid memories of that night. He perhaps went into action with more trepidation than some others, having heard many stories of the Watts riots from his father. Keating is the son of retired First Sergeant Patrick Keating, a former Guardsman who served during the Watts riots in what was then Company B, 3-160th Infantry in Gardena. Captain Keating remembers the trip that night as "almost surrealistic, as the route they took had very few people on the streets and some random looters hiding as the convoy tore by." The military convoy was held up when it reached the Harbor Freeway, as a convoy of fifty or sixty police cars from the San Diego area came down an off ramp with sirens screaming heading for the LAPD Forward Command Post at 54th and Arlington.

Company C was escorted to the Lynwood Area Sheriff's Youth Athletic League (more commonly called "CPIC," for Crime Prevention Information Center) on Imperial Highway in Lynwood. The local law enforcement officials wanted to quickly get the company into the streets. As they briefed company leadership, others set up a command post at the CPIC. Captain Keating quickly started dispatching troops.

One of the first requirements was for protection of the Lynwood Plaza Shopping Center on Martin Luther King Boulevard. Deputies left the shopping center to guide the Guardsmen there from the CPIC. By the time they returned with the troops a few minutes later, gangbangers had struck and several stores had already been looted.

A security detail was sent to protect the Saint Francis Medical Center at the corner of Imperial Highway and Century Boulevard. Roving patrols were sent up and down Long Beach Boulevard from Compton in the south to the city of Southgate in the north. This thoroughfare had seen considerable violence the first night. In addition, security was provided for firemen, especially along Long Beach Boulevard.

A platoon was sent to the intersection of Atlantic Boulevard and Rosecrans in an unincorporated part of the county. Intelligence had been received that the CV70 (Appendix 3 has a listing of gangs in Los Angeles County) gang was going to assault and loot the 7-11 Store on the northwest corner of that intersection. When the platoon got there, they found gang graffiti everywhere. They didn't have to be told that gangs were a particular nuisance in that area. Guardsmen posted at that intersection said "we had little gang punks in low-riders come by quite often telling us they were coming back that night to kill us."

The El Unico across the street from the 7-11 is an extremely popular Mexican restaurant that was always open, including during the curfew hours. El Unico had an armed guard with an automatic rifle posted all the time, sometimes in front, and sometimes on the roof. This made the Guardsmen uncomfortable at first, but they eventually realized the guard helped keep things comparatively quiet on that corner. The Mexican restaurant later provided outstanding food for the troops, and they discovered for themselves why the place was so popular.

Another platoon from Company C was sent to the Kenneth Hahn Plaza shopping center on Wilmington Avenue and 118th

81

Street. This new shopping center is the pride of the community, and had been repeatedly threatened with looting.

The Chief of Security at Hahn Plaza was Police Captain Barry Ogalue. Captain Ogalue is a Nigerian who came to this country ten years ago. He and his augmented force of security guards had their hands full on Thursday. Customers had been asked to leave based on gang threats. The gates to the shopping center were locked, and the security force braced themselves for the assaults they felt sure were coming. They didn't have to wait long.

A raucous crowd gathered at the center starting at about 4:00 p.m. Help was requested from law enforcement authorities, but they were occupied elsewhere. In fact, it was recommended that the security force abandon the center for their own safety. The mob grew to approximately 250-300 vandals and rioters, who were throwing rocks and bottles. The center is protected by a strong fence system of steel grating supported by large brick columns. The gates held until about 6:00 p.m., when gangbangers crashed a blue Toyota pickup truck into the 119th Street gate on the south.

About fifteen or twenty gangbangers were in by the time security forces reacted. The security force at the Hahn Plaza does not overtly carry firearms. A shot was fired by gangbangers, who assumed the security forces were unarmed. To their great surprise, a security guard fired a shot in return, and they all scrambled back out of the shopping center. In the meantime, other gangbangers in the area crashed a 1991 white Ford Taurus Station Wagon into the Wilmington Avenue main gate of the shopping center. The security force again stopped them in a scene captured by television helicopters overhead.

The station wagon was abandoned in front of the center, and later turned out to be stolen. The only damages to the center, other than to the gates, were broken windows in a Taco Bell and a Nail Traps store. The platoon from Company C showed up to relieve the harassed security guards. Captain Ogalue was later honored by the City of Los Angeles for "outstanding heroism in an unselfish act of bravery and courage," and by the County of Los Angeles with a similar citation. The Guardsmen found him every bit as impressive as the gangbangers did. Interestingly, but perhaps not surprisingly, Captain Ogalue has since been routinely called "g--damned African" by the black gangbangers in the area.

Company D of Glendale went to the Civic Center, and was deployed around Parker Center, the Hall of Justice, the Hall of Records, the Courts Building and other key governmental buildings. They quickly were posted in and around the several block area that was particularly targeted by several groups as well as criminal elements who wanted to set fire to buildings in the hope of having their records burned up.

Company D no sooner took their posts than a fire flared up in a dumpster at a service station across from the federal buildings. Firemen arrived without an escort, so four Guardsmen and two federal police ran across the street to protect the firemen as they quickly put the blaze out. As was too often the case for the first few days, no one caught the arsonist. The large show of force around the Civic Center did, however, help keep further incidents to a minimum. While this was a comparatively quiet area for the next few days, sporadic gunfire could often be heard off in the distance.

The curfew was observed in some areas patrolled by the 3rd Battalion, but not in others. Those other areas were generally the most dangerous, and quite often scofflaws would go tearing by in their automobiles at high speed. There were the taunts and threats that all soldiers got used to the first few nights. Captain Keating, his executive officer and driver were driving south on Long Beach Boulevard shortly after midnight checking on their Guardsmen in the area. As they passed under the new Century Freeway under construction near Imperial Highway, they were forced to dodge a short burst of automatic fire from a sniper on the overpass. By the time police responded, the sniper was gone. Soldiers were routinely fired on, and in several instances they caught the shooters, disarmed them and turned them over to law enforcement personnel.

Lieutenant Colonel Joe Mathewson's 4th Battalion, 160th Infantry, headquartered in Santa Ana, was also deploying their 565 Guardsmen. This went rapidly because the battalion had consolidated their outlying units into the closer Santa Ana and Orange Armories. All units except San Diego's Company A were in place and ready for missions by shortly after 2:00 p.m. Company A arrived a few minutes before 6:00 p.m., and just as the first mission requests arrived for the battalion.

Company A was dispatched to support the Compton Police Department. They secured the large K-Mart Shopping and Circuit City Shopping Centers at Alameda and Compton Boulevard, the Gateway Plaza Mall at Central and Rosecrans, and the Compton Fashion Mall on Long Beach Boulevard. The latter two malls had been hit particularly hard. The Gateway Plaza Mall had about half its businesses burned, and all were looted. The Compton Fashion Mall was completely stripped of everything that had any value.

Company B from Orange was sent to support the Firestone Sheriff's substation and the cities of Florence and Huntington

Park. The sheriff's substation is in a very rough neighborhood surrounded by known gang hangouts, including one right across the street. The company established a Quick Reaction Force for use as needed, and manned guard posts around the sheriff's station. They then cleared, secured and protected businesses along Firestone Boulevard and Florence Avenue, many of which had been hard hit by looting and arson.

Company C from Riverside deployed to the Sheriff's Forward Command Post at Washington High School. There they worked with the Lennox Sheriff's substation and the County Fire Department in the Lennox and Inglewood areas. Traffic control points and barricades were set up to enforce the curfew. They also established vehicle and foot patrols, especially in the area of 108th Street and Normandie, to regain and maintain control.

Company D from Redlands and Banning set up in the Inglewood Armory. They established a Quick Reaction Force, and waited for missions. Unfortunately, they received almost none until noon the following day. After the battalion commander complained about the lack of missions to division headquarters, they were redeployed, working out of the Sheriff Department's Lennox Substation between Hawthorne and Inglewood.

Company E from Fullerton, augmented by the Scout and Mortar Platoons from Santa Ana, reported to the Carson Sheriff's substation. There they established area security and accompanied fire engines. They were quickly dispersed over twenty-eight different trouble spots and areas of concern in the South Compton and Carson areas.

While most gangbangers didn't hassle the troops there, many others did. As units moved into the area to regain control of the streets, there were many confrontations with gang members. Just one unit, Company B, commanded by Captain Ricardo Nicol, an attorney in Santa Ana, detained over 140 curfew violators and other lawbreakers for arrest by the Sheriff's Department that first night.

Law enforcement officers handcuffed a couple of gang members to a telephone pole for several hours until they could get back and haul them in for booking. While that took much longer than on a normal night, it did serve as an example to other curfew violators. Law enforcement officers also decided to barricade some streets where gangbangers were racing up and down in their cars in violation of the curfew, so they used some curfew violators' cars to block the roads. Guardsmen who observed this noted the preponderance of luxury cars, such as Mercedes and Cadillacs, that were then used as roadblocks. They assumed that those cars were being used to block the street because they had been driven by gangbangers who probably purchased them with illicit profits from drug dealing.

General Hernandez decided in the meantime to also have a National Guard liaison officer at the Police EOC which was located under City Hall East. Major Jeffrey J. Kramer, normally the senior full time officer in the Division Artillery in West Los Angeles, arrived about 6:30 p.m. When he first walked in, there was brief pause before the EOC occupants broke into applause. While it embarrassed Jeff, he later admitted it felt good to be appreciated. He quickly got to work. The EOC was jammed, and included representatives from Parks and Recreation, Animal Control, and other departments as well as law enforcement. He met the Watch Commander, Deputy Chief Ron Frankle, who handled the 6:00 p.m. to 6:00 a.m. shift. The next morning he met Frankle's daytime counterpart,

Bill Booth, but in the meantime, the EOC team was notified that the Governor, the Mayor and others would be arriving that night to discuss the situation.

The Governor and his party boarded an Air National Guard C-130 aircraft at Mather AFB near Sacramento, and departed at 6:30 p.m. for Los Alamitos. It was a tense group aboard the aircraft, and the Governor was visibly upset with General Thrasher. It was becoming clear as time passed that the Governor and others did not know the Guardsmen were setting records getting on the street in spite of the ammunition delays. There were several conferences during the flight, which is difficult because the C-130 is extremely noisy. Most involved the Governor, members of his personal staff, and Dick Andrews of OES.

When they landed at Los Alamitos, they were briefed on the current situation before boarding an Army National Guard UH-60 Blackhawk helicopter to meet with law enforcement and political officials. They flew over the affected area, and then landed on top of Piper Technical Center, very near the Civic Center and the LAPD Emergency Operations Center.

The group that eventually gathered at the LAPD Emergency Operations Center included the Governor, the Mayor, Maury Hannigan of the Highway Patrol, Dick Andrews of OES, General Thrasher, Sheriff Block, and Chief Gates. As it approached midnight, the discussion centered on requirements for more mutual aid, especially California Highway Patrolmen. They also felt more National Guardsmen were needed, agreeing that a total of 6,000 "on street" forces plus support were required. In the discussion that followed, Mayor Bradley first raised the possibility of requesting federal troops. It later developed that he was already being urged by Warren Christopher to call in federal troops.

General Hernandez earlier in the evening had decided to give himself some insurance, and called more of the division to duty on his own authority. He already had well over 4,000 soldiers on station or on the way. He provided his insurance by placing several thousand additional soldiers in "Inactive Duty Training" status, the normal status for monthly training assemblies. He considered it merely insurance, because he was convinced he would soon have more than enough troops.

Civil disturbances were erupting all over the nation and in Canada, and General Hernandez was concerned about problems elsewhere in California. He was particularly concerned about the San Francisco Bay area. The military police from the 49th Military Police Brigade were already in Los Angeles or on the way, so the division's Third Brigade was the only large force of combat soldiers left in Northern California. General Hernandez had dispatched one of his Assistant Division Commanders, Colonel Bob Brandt, to the headquarters of Third Brigade in San Jose. Bob was told to be prepared to take charge of division forces in Northern California in case they had to deploy into the bay area.

A series of calls followed, as various people pushed to get more troops to Southern California. General Hernandez pointed out that he had more than enough troops in Southern California, and already had troops sitting in armories awaiting orders. He was overruled by the Adjutant General's Office in Sacramento. Third Brigade was directed about midnight to convoy their three battalions to the Peter J. Pitchess Honor Rancho (prison) just inside the northern boundary of Los Angeles County.

Colonel John D. Zaver, the commander of Third Brigade and a media and advertising consultant, prepared to move his brigade south. He did so reluctantly, as his soldiers needed sleep. They had been at work all day Thursday. They then spent Thursday night mobilizing, loading their equipment, and preparing for action. They were now being asked to begin a grueling convoy of several hundred miles without any sleep.

They borrowed trucks from a National Guard truck company in nearby San Bruno. The 1-184th Infantry Battalion in Modesto and 1-149th Armor Battalion in Salinas were given their movement orders. The former battalion made its movement with the assistance of buses borrowed from Beale Air Force Base. The brigade headquarters then coordinated with Camp Roberts in Central California for refueling, and for the pick up of needed rations, equipment and ammunition. After lining up the brigade headquarters company and the 2-159th Infantry Battalion in the streets of San Jose, they moved out of the city at 2:00 a.m. under police escort.

In the meantime, other National Guardsmen from all over the state were rapidly assembling in Los Angeles. Lieutenant Colonel Gerald P. Minetti was in acting command of the Division Artillery as it mobilized because Colonel Eugene W. Schmidt, the assigned commander, was more than busy in his normal job as a Highway Patrolman. The balance of the First Brigade was beginning to arrive to join the 3rd Battalion, 160th Infantry. The 1st Battalion, 185th Armor was assembled in the San Bernardino area with 376 of their soldiers. In addition, the 2nd Battalion, 160th Infantry was convoying down from Central California to arrive at the West Los Angeles Armory with 569 troops about midnight.

All the troops suddenly crowding the West Los Angeles Armory posed a logistical challenge for the Division Artillery's logistics officer, Major Dennis F. Sullivan. Stores and restaurants weren't open in the area because of the riots, and the late hour. Major Sullivan and his driver decided to give it a try outside of the riot area, and headed for Malibu. The McDonald's on Pacific Coast Highway in Malibu was open. They asked for everything that had already been prepared and was sitting on the warming rack. McDonald's gave all of that to them free, which was much appreciated by the troops that were working late and hadn't had a chance to eat.

Major Sullivan then ordered 1200 Egg McMuffins for early the next morning. This was clearly a challenge, even for McDonald's, but they were all ready when Sullivan returned with two vehicles to pick them up. They obviously had worked through the night. More than law enforcement and military were doing their bit to combat the riots.

The crowded armories presented other problems. There were way too many troops for the limited toilet facilities. One officer phoned the 40th Division G-4 (logistics) Section, and put on his best British accent. "I say, old chap. We can't have troops defecating on the parade field!" Portable latrines ("porta-potties") were delivered very quickly.

The Second Brigade had already committed their 4th Battalion, 160th Infantry. The brigade's two tank battalions, the 2nd and 3rd Battalions, 185th Armor, had moved out of the San Diego area and were staging their 407 and 387 soldiers in armories around the Los Angeles basin.

The 1st Squadron, 18th Cavalry of Ontario, is commanded by Lieutenant Colonel Marvin G. Metcalf, a general contractor and developer in Los Angeles County. Most of his helicopter

90

units were not activated, so his two ground troops (each equivalent to a company in size) were augmented by the 160th Long Range Surveillance Detachment. The Long Range Surveillance Detachment consists of 56 highly qualified (airborne and ranger) soldiers. Combined with the cavalry troopers to total over 400 soldiers, they were a highly potent, versatile force. That night they were sent to the Los Angeles Coliseum in support of LAPD.

Commanders of units got very little sleep the first night they were deployed. Battalion Commanders traveled around with their Command Sergeant Major, or Company Commanders with First Sergeants, making sure their troops were properly deployed and supported, and not taking unnecessary risks.

Captain Ned Lee's 670th Military Police Company had been committed to Koreatown and the mall at 3rd and Vermont earlier in the day. He traveled around with a cellular phone he'd bought to ensure he could communicate with headquarters and his troops. Like all commanders, he found his tactical radios all but useless in the city when he tried to communicate over extended distances. He was struck by several anomalies as he traveled around visiting his Guardsmen that night. One was the striking image of seeing so many fires burning without emergency vehicles responding. He also vividly remembers one incongruous sight. Residents just a block or two away from the fires and looting were putting their trash cans out in front of their homes (vainly, as it turned out) for Friday morning pickup.

The 40th Military Police Company had been working for LAPD Commander Bayan Lewis, a former Tank Battalion Commander in the 40th Division. However, their mission was changed about 11:00 p.m., and they ended up being sent to

91

Captain Bernie Parks' Central Division, and then on to Newton Station.

Sergeant Art Stone is with 5th Platoon of the 40th Military Police, and is normally a police officer working out of Newton Station. Art was accompanying the unit as it headed for his own stomping grounds. He vividly remembers the convoy as they redeployed to Newton Station. "I was shocked on the way to Newton that first night. We went through the intersection of Vernon and Central, which is very heavily traveled, a very popular area. All four corners were fully engulfed in flames. The four corners had a Jack-in-the-Box Restaurant, a little walk-in medical clinic for women, a shoe store, and a gas station. It was just incredible. It was also rather eerie as you tended to lose the sense of where you were. There were almost no vehicles, but there were people, thousands of people, running in every direction. There was a lot of screaming and yelling, with most of it directed at the police and National Guard. It was all negative at that intersection, a lot of racial expletives.

"I had one guy run up (to the Hummer) and yell directly in my face 'Go home you f---ing white mother f---er.' Something else that was very memorable were the little kids being taught the same thing. I doubt they knew what they were saying. One little girl about three years old at the corner of Vernon and Central yelled 'Go home, mother f---ers.' It was really sad."

The utter chaos was particularly memorable to Sergeant Stone, who works in the area daily. "To me it is bad enough that the community should have so many problems on a normal basis. But when it went just completely upside down, and you saw the otherwise good people, that you're out there working for, out there doing things like looting and burning, and ah...I

92

guess the sickening, most heartbreaking thing about this is that they were showing their kids that it was O.K."

This police station on Newton Avenue is in a tough neighborhood. The police had lost control of their area except for the four to five blocks immediately around the station. The police and military leadership got together and discussed how to regain control of the situation. The company set up across the street, in a vacant lot, and half the troops settled down to get some rest. Most of the unit had gone over forty hours with little or no sleep. There were some nerves, involving both veterans and young Guardsmen, as they underwent what one platoon sergeant described as adrenalin "crashes." A couple of soldiers sat on a wall, so giddy they giggled at anything and everything. Nonetheless, most of them finally relaxed and got some sleep. The soldiers that remained on duty at Newton were starting what turned out to be, by all accounts, several days of a mutually rewarding, very special relationship between policemen and soldiers with a common mission.

Lieutenant Colonel Richard L. Throckmorton, a helicopter pilot in civilian life, was handling operations at the Division Artillery on Federal Avenue in West Los Angeles when the Culver City Chief of Police called. The Fox Hills Mall, a beautiful shopping center in Culver City, was being threatened. The Culver City police were understrength because they had sent officers to assist LAPD as part of the mutual aid program. The National Guard unit based in Culver City is Battery B, 3rd Battalion, 144th Field Artillery, commanded by Captain Phillip Butch. A Deputy Sheriff in civilian life, his unit was given the mission and deployed at 1:30 a.m.

When they arrived at the mall, they found much of it boarded up, with barricades in strategic locations. They were

93

briefed by the police, with some of the Guardsmen finding out for the first time that many gangbangers consider the shopping malls their "playground." They established their command post, organized a Quick Reaction Force, and placed sentry posts around the mall.

That artillery battery, equivalent to a company in size, retained the Fox Hills Mall mission for the duration of the emergency. They had gangbangers threaten them, several drive-by shootings, and at least one sniper attack. Some buildings in the mall were struck by bullets, but damage to the mall was very limited.

About 3:00 a.m., the Governor held a staff meeting in the Marriott Hotel. They talked about calling in federal troops as added insurance for the National Guard, "as we can't take chances on not having sufficient forces for law enforcement." If it hadn't been apparent before, his lack of confidence in his National Guard was very evident by this time. Three hours later, the Governor called General Thrasher to advise him he had talked with President Bush and General Colin Powell, and that 3500 federal troops were being sent to El Toro Marine Air Station to stage for possible deployment to Los Angeles. In addition, the National Guard was going to be federalized.

National Guardsmen continued to battle the rioters, as more and more Guardsmen flowed through staging areas and were deployed by the division. Before dawn, two more battalions received mission orders to support the Los Angeles Police Department. When General Thrasher phoned Deputy Chief Bill Booth at 6:30 a.m. to find out how many Guardsmen Booth thought he had, Booth responded that there were 1122 Guardsmen supporting the LAPD. Five minutes later the

Sheriff's Department told him they had approximately 1600 Guardsmen, with "many more being assigned as we speak."

Commanders with Guardsmen committed to the streets were taking a deep breath and reflecting on their first day and night in Los Angeles. Typical of this county and its extremely varied neighborhoods, soldiers were finding situations very different depending on what part of the city they were in. In some areas soldiers had faced massed crowds, while others were facing shadows, hidden snipers and occasional taunts. Regardless of where troops were located, they faced an enemy that differed greatly from what they had been taught to face in basic training. They faced gang members. Violent gang members. Clearly more information on gang members was going to have to be quickly organized and disseminated to the troops.

The worst was over, but by the time dawn broke, Los Angeles had paid a heavy price. The totals estimated that morning:

31 Deaths

1000+ Injuries

3,845 Structure fires in the city (3,244 for the one day)

CHAPTER FIVE

Friday, May 1, 1992
THE THIRD DAY

Intelligence Officers are trained to produce summaries that help commanders visualize the battlefield, anticipate weather and other conditions, and most important of all...to understand the enemy. They are not normally expected, or trained, to describe domestic enemies, but that is precisely what they found themselves doing by this time.

The Intelligence Summary for early Friday morning first described the general situation. It was noted that all roads were open except that off ramps on the Harbor Freeway (I-110) were closed between Century Boulevard and I-10 so motorists couldn't inadvertently drive into the affected area. All utilities were operational except there still wasn't any electrical power in a large portion of South Central Los Angeles. No mail delivery would be made into the affected area, so welfare checks were going to have to be picked up at post offices. The demonstrations in Sacramento, Santa Cruz and other cities in California were described, as well as the more extensive problems in the San Francisco Bay area.

The more significant events during the previous 24 hours were recounted. These included the fact that Korean shop owners were defending their businesses and shooting at looters, especially in the area of Wilshire Boulevard and Western Avenue. There continued to be a great number of fires, looting, and random gunfire. It was confirmed that some criminals were using weapons capable of full automatic fire. About 200 uniforms belonging to both the Los Angeles and Inglewood Police Departments were stolen from a dry cleaners. While this last piece of information was ominous, everyone involved in law enforcement was encouraged by the fact there were only a couple of new fires after midnight. Law enforcement was clearly gaining the upper hand.

The Intelligence Summary recognized that criminal elements had stolen a great number of weapons from gun stores, and remained a serious and continuing threat. The weather forecast another warm day, expected to reach about 80 degrees.

Warren Christopher was a former deputy Attorney General of the United States, a former deputy Secretary of State, and attorney in Los Angeles. After the riots he became Secretary of State in the Clinton administration. He had chaired the citizen's commission that investigated the Los Angeles Police Department following the Rodney King beating, and was closely following the day's events. He called Mayor Bradley late on Thursday to urge federal troops be brought in, asserting the National Guard is less effective than federal troops for riots. He obtained the mayor's permission to call federal officials in Washington, and made a series of calls that night.

Governor Wilson and Mayor Bradley in Los Angeles eventually got involved in the series of phone calls, including discussions with President Bush and General Colin Powell in Washington. While most people on the west coast were still asleep, news was breaking in Washington that federal troops were to be sent to Los Angeles.

Dan Donahue is Special Assistant to the Chief, National Guard Bureau. He quickly found himself working with the public affairs staff at National Guard Bureau in reacting to what he described as a "media crescendo" of 150-200 media inquiries in a very short period of time Friday morning. He also received a call from Terry O'Connell. Terry is a highly decorated, disabled Vietnam veteran and Executive Vice President of Keefe Company, a government affairs firm in Washington. When Terry heard that federal troops were being sent to Los Angeles, he immediately got on the phone to Dan Donahue to find out why.

Unlike Warren Christopher, Terry felt National Guardsmen are much better suited for civil disturbance missions, and involving federal troops was a mistake. Terry asked Dan why the federal troops were needed. Dan assured him he was convinced they weren't needed, and had good reasons for feeling that way. He had sent his own staff officer, Major Bob Dunlap, to Los Alamitos as a direct pipeline to activities there. Dan told Terry that there were a great many National Guardsmen at Los Alamitos and other staging areas just waiting for missions. The discussion also raised the specter of possible negligence, as it appeared someone was failing to give troops mission orders. This failure to give Guardsmen missions was occurring at the same time as everyone was watching the fires and looting on television.

Terry O'Connell knew many politicos in California, having worked on the Carter campaign in California many years ago. Terry phoned Phil DePoian, Mayor Bradley's liaison to law enforcement, and asked him why the mayor felt it necessary to request federal troops. Phil asked Terry if he was representing the National Guard, and was told Terry was not. Phil then responded that the mayor was extremely unhappy with the lack of responsiveness by the National Guard. Phil told Terry that the National Guard had been repeatedly requested, but was not responding. In addition, he did not feel they were out in the numbers claimed.

While Terry was talking to Phil DePoian in Los Angeles, Dan was reconfirming facts with his staff officer in Los Alamitos. Sure enough, there were a great number (over 1000 at Los Alamitos alone) of Guardsmen staged and awaiting missions in various staging areas and armories scattered around the Los Angeles basin. After talking to others, Dan was convinced that either law enforcement officials didn't know that troops were available, or they didn't choose to use them.

Terry and Dan talked again about noon (Eastern Standard Time). Dan told Terry that he felt the issue was serious enough to go public. In his view, if officials continued to claim the National Guard was not responsive, there was a simple solution. He would invite the four major broadcast networks and the ten major print organizations to look for themselves. They would see the Guardsmen waiting for missions, and then be invited to ask the Mayor's Office why the troops were not receiving missions.

Terry again talked to Phil DePoian and explained that National Guardsmen were awaiting missions, and how the tasking channels were supposed to flow through the city's police department to the Sheriff's EOC. He pointed out that National Guardsmen are in support of law enforcement and must be employed. Guardsmen don't employ themselves.

Although the mission tasking system may have suffered from constipation before, it started flowing by mid-afternoon. The LAPD liaison officer, Captain Keith Bushey, was suddenly asking for National Guard troops by the thousands. This came as a surprise to the senior liaison officer in the EOC, Colonel Ed Zysk, because the streets were comparatively quiet. Ed was

100

also concerned that too many troops would be going to LAPD, to the possible detriment of the Sheriff's Department. Captain Bushey wanted all the forces not currently committed. He gave some specific missions, and asked that units without missions be stationed in the Coliseum to constitute a reserve force. There soon were literally thousands of Guardsmen in the Sports Arena/Coliseum complex as the committed forces on the street and in reserve approached 6000 troops.

When the mission orders started flowing, Major Bob Dunlap phoned Dan Donahue to let him know. Dan then informed Terry O'Connell that his phone calls to Los Angeles had the desired effect.

There was some confusion on Thursday night and Friday about how many troops were actually in the street. Both Chief Gates and Sheriff Block felt there were fewer Guardsmen on the street than situation charts in the EOC showed. Sheriff Block had been informed by the Governor that federal troops might be coming. Late Friday morning, Colonel Zysk pointed out to the Sheriff that the National Guard had uncommitted troops, and all LAPD and LASD mission requests had been met. Colonel Zysk showed him the statistics posted on the wall of the EOC. Sheriff Block asked if they were accurate. When Colonel Zysk assured him they were accurate, the sheriff found that hard to believe.

The figures were reverified by police and sheriff watch commanders before Colonel Zysk again showed them to the Sheriff. It was then apparent to Sheriff Block that federal troops were not needed. When it was announced that evening that National Guard troops were being federalized, Sheriff Block called Colonel Zysk over. He said, "Ed, I want you to know I didn't call for federal troops."

101

Chief Gates, during a morning news conference, said he had only about 500 troops actually on the streets of Los Angeles, with another 350 due shortly. That could very well have been accurate. His assistant, Bill Booth, had reported he had 1122 troops "supporting him" just hours earlier. The difference is semantics. The Division's daily personnel report for 6:00 a.m. showed 2743 soldiers in staging areas awaiting missions in addition to the soldiers actually deployed to the streets of the city and county. There were many Guardsmen in staging areas such as the Sports Arena and Coliseum, placed there by the police to be immediately responsive to mission requests from LAPD when requested. Some were sent out, but a great many remained in those forward staging areas without any missions.

Soldiers are used to "hurry up and wait" situations. They did a great deal of waiting in Los Angeles.

To complicate matters, in a City Council Meeting held the previous (Thursday) night, city fathers were told the county was getting most of the National Guardsmen. This is true to some extent. The two initial companies of Guardsmen were sent to the city. Two of the next three battalions went to the county, so most of the troops ended up supporting the county during the first (second night of the riots) night. This was probably happenstance, or the consequence of confusion and the "fog of war" previously described. When mission request sheets are analyzed, it appears as though the preponderance of requests were from the unincorporated parts of the county and cities other than Los Angeles, rather than part of an insidious plot. Regardless, Phil DePoian later said the city viewed it as the Sheriff's Department "siphoning off 1500 troops" that were needed in the city. The truth may have been no more than the

102

fact that the Sheriff's emergency response system seemed to be operating more efficiently early in the crisis.

If there was an imbalance, it was corrected during the early hours of the morning. The next four battalions, one infantry and three armor, were committed in support of the city.

The Second Battalion, 160th Infantry was moved to the Sports Arena early in the morning. They traveled up Vermont Street on the way, and could see some of the businesses still smouldering. They waited until 2:00 p.m. for their first mission, which was to provide security for the Piper Technical Center just northwest of the city's Civic Center. They dispatched 200 troops, but found that the police only needed fifteen or twenty soldiers to protect helicopters on the roof from sniper attacks. The mission was given to the battalion's mortar platoon, and the rest of the soldiers returned to the Sports Arena, where they waited for several hours before receiving additional mission assignments.

Many units took advantage of waiting periods to receive additional training before being committed to the streets. Intelligence summaries and television had already made it clear this was not an ordinary riot. Riot control formations and other typical civil disturbance training was of little value. The most valuable training came from police officers in each unit, most units having at least one present or former officer. One example of many was First Sergeant Dennis Bannon of 3-185th Armor. A veteran of seventeen years with the Santa Ana Police Department, First Sergeant Bannon dedicated himself to preparing his Guardsmen to face gangbangers. As he put it, a "crash course in how to be a street-wise cop."

The First, Second and Third Battalions, 185th Armor were dispatched to various parts of the city. The use of tank battalions during the riots was complicated by the fact that tank crewmen are normally armed with pistols or submachine guns. Those weapons were not optimal for riot control, so 40th Division logisticians had to scramble for M-16 rifles to equip the four tank battalions that were eventually employed.

The 1-185th Armor picked up their ammunition, flak vests, face shields, and other equipment needed prior to deployment into the riots. They called all this their "L. A. Gear," in an obvious play on words. The battalion, commanded by Major John S. Harrel (an attorney in civilian life), split into several units, with the first mission being support of the post office on Vernon Avenue. The convoy headed south on the Harbor Freeway, and had just passed the Santa Monica Freeway when the troops saw two people on a rooftop west of the freeway. Several shots rang out with one Hummer's occupants actually hearing the "crack-thump" of near misses over their heads.

When the troops arrived at the post office, they found about fifty police standing between the post office and about three or four hundred people. There also were quite a few news reporters and cameramen. The post office had stopped handing out welfare and social security checks because of the size of the crowd. The troops were asked to help get things organized. Their biggest immediate problem was keeping the media out of their ranks. Reporters tried to stop the Guardsmen and interview them as they were deploying. However, this was quickly overcome, and the situation was defused when people formed an orderly line and the mail started being distributed again.

The troops then went to the ABC Market at Vernon and Vermont, the same intersection where the 40th Military Police Company had taken control the previous afternoon before being sent to Newton Station. The 1-185th Armor found several dozen police officers backed up against the wall, with considerable tension in the air. The parking lot had been converted to a field headquarters for the police officers.

The intersection of Vernon and Vermont is just a couple of blocks from what the police described as "gang central," with much gang activity and shooting in the area. One of the first people killed during the riots was shot at this intersection. People across the street were on their roofs with weapons, adding to the edgy atmosphere. Most of them were no more than business owners trying to protect what remained of their businesses. The Guardsmen set up a command post in the market and deployed troops around the perimeter of the area.

This intersection had already seen a great deal of action the first two nights, but was to see even more. There was a lot of yelling and heckling from cars and pedestrians. The troops had no sooner arrived and set up when a drunk came reeling into their area with a two by four and a brick. They were taken away from him and he weaved off. The troops settled in for an extended stay, with bunk areas in the market and on the roof. The shooting, yelling, taunts, and flashing of signs continued intermittently all the time they were in this tough part of town.

The 2-185th Armor was sent to the Baldwin Hills Crenshaw Shopping Center. They were picked up at their staging area in the Manhattan Beach armory, and escorted with lights and sirens screaming all the way to the shopping center. When they got there, they set up the Battalion Tactical Operations Center and sent patrols off into the surrounding area.

This battalion from the San Diego area was accompanied by Jim Michaels, a Marine Corps Reserve lieutenant colonel, who was a reporter for the San Diego Tribune. He had parked his small Ford Escort next to the Guardsmen in the parking area early Friday morning. Sergeant Robert A. Matey was leaning against the left side of the sedan in front of the driver's window. Sergeant Duane Neynes was leaning against the left rear talking to Master Sergeant Jim Sexton. Suddenly a shot whacked into the vehicle between Matey and Neynes, shattering the driver's window.

The shot came from the roof of the shopping center. The troops gave chase, but the sniper got away before they got up on the roof.

The commander of 2-185th Armor, Lieutenant Colonel Tarold (Terry) Scott had been told to set up and wait for missions. He set up a perimeter around the shopping center, and placed Traffic Control Points out where the traffic lights were not operating. He had an entire battalion at this shopping center, so he made a point of being very visible, to include having units march around drilling and practicing their manual of arms. Not much happened until LAPD's Commander Lewis came by around noon. He had a grasp of the big picture, listened to Scott's recommendations, and made some decisions. From that point on, the 2-185th Armor was more fully employed.

The 3-185th Armor, also from San Diego, was sent to the Los Angeles High School on Olympic Boulevard. They reported to the Police Station between Pico and Venice Boulevard, just east of La Brea. They were then dispatched to several places that had been hard hit by rioters. One was Koreatown, along Western Avenue. Another was the Midtown Mall right next to the police station, which had been badly burned and looted.

They also provided security for the police department itself, which is just north of an area heavily infested with gang

106

members. In fact, one house directly southeast of the station is commonly acknowledged to be a gang headquarters. There was a lot of what Sergeant First Class David Ardilla of Company C, 3-185th Armor called "mad dogging." A law enforcement officer for San Diego County, he recognized the "stare-down" or "looking daggers" behavior from gangbangers across the street that is so much a part of gang culture.

One of the recurring problems faced by soldiers (and marines later) as they patrolled the streets was the presence of paramilitary organizations and individuals, as well as the presence of reservists who informally called themselves to duty. By some coincidence, this seemed to be especially prevalent in the City of Compton.

One example was encountered by Colonel Richard Metcalf, commander of the 40th Division's Second Brigade, as he traveled around visiting his Guardsmen. He was heading down a main street in Compton when he saw a single soldier standing beside the road with full battle gear to include what looked like an M16 rifle. Next to him was a civilian in blue Bermuda shorts, with a light blue tank top over his "beer belly." When Richard stopped, he saw that the rifle was an AR-15. It turned out this soldier was from another reserve component, and with his buddy, was protecting their law offices. They wanted Guardsmen to protect their business. Richard pointed out to them that the emergency was all but over, their offices had survived, and tried to put the memory behind as he drove off.

The Division Artillery received a mission from the Culver City Police Department just before noon. They loaded a platoon-size element into six trucks and Hummers and were escorted by Culver City Police "Code 3" (lights and sirens) to the Target Shopping Center on Jefferson Boulevard. A typical

107

deployment, it always seemed that when a decision was once made, the police not only wanted them some place in a hurry, but they wanted to make plenty of noise and let everyone know a lot of troops were on the way.

The shopping center was closed, with the entrances blocked with trash dumpsters and barricades. The police showed the troops around the center, with vulnerable spots pointed out. The low-rent housing projects on the eastern edge were a particular concern. As the troops scouted the area, they noted a trail of new shoes and shoe boxes between the shoe store in the mall and the wall separating the mall from the housing projects.

The shopping center had been hard hit by looting. One store at the extreme northern end, Audio Visual City, had suffered losses estimated at $300,000. The artillerymen placed three people with a portable radio on the roof of Audio Visual City, and teams of troops around the perimeter. Finally, they organized a combination roving patrol/quick reaction force, and settled in to protect their new "home."

On Friday afternoon, the 270th Military Police Company from Sacramento was sent to assist the Long Beach Police Department. The company was commanded by Captain Donald J. Currier, a deputy district attorney for Sacramento County with ten years of experience as a police officer in Sacramento plus service as an Army Military Policeman before joining the National Guard. Currier took his unit of Desert Storm veterans up the San Diego Freeway and then south on Long Beach Boulevard.

The police in Long Beach more than had their hands full. There was scattered and sporadic shooting. Fires were burning everywhere, and worst of all, people in the area were ignoring the police. People set up barricades in the street to keep the police and fire engines out. They looted almost at will, and were clearly more than the over-extended police department could handle. This quickly changed with the arrival of the veteran 270th MP Company.

In the lead Hummer Currier placed Platoon Sergeant Paul George. Sergeant George is in property management for a real estate development company in Sacramento. More important during the riots, Sergeant George is a former California Highway Patrolman. He spent six of his twelve years as a highway patrolman working in that part of California, and knew the area well. He led the 270th MP company south down Long Beach Boulevard with the Hummers staggered on each side of the street. Each had two military policemen in front plus one standing in the turret.

Currier's Operations Officer, First Lieutenant Steven J. Pelton, a Butte County deputy sheriff in civilian life, described what happened as they came down the street. "They sure didn't ignore us! They suddenly stopped their activity, dropped their loot, and started dispersing while trying to look innocent." Everyone involved was surprised at how quickly the streets changed for miles around. It was almost as though a jungle telegraph was working, because it seemed that all of the gangbangers knew almost simultaneously that the Guard had arrived. Lieutenant Pelton said "very quickly there was almost no one on the streets but homeless and derelicts wandering around under the influence of alcohol, drugs, or whatever."

They pulled into a large shopping mall while the leaders coordinated with the Long Beach Police Department. They then went on a leader's reconnaissance of the large area the police wanted covered. This included Long Beach Boulevard,

Atlantic Avenue, and the famous Pacific Coast Highway. They saw a lot of people on roofs with weapons. As discovered elsewhere, the great majority of them were merchants trying to protect their businesses. Many of them were displaying American flags. Later they told the Guardsmen they knew troops were on the way, and figured if they showed the American flag, the troops would assume they were "good guys." They guessed right.

While making the reconnaissance, three sergeants in a Hummer following the Police Chief's sedan spotted someone with an automatic weapon duck up an alley that paralleled Atlantic. They took off after him, maneuvering to cover each other as he ducked into what appeared to be a former commercial garage converted into a flophouse. There they found about a dozen of what appeared to be street people, including two women, who had made little tents for privacy inside the garage. Of more interest, there were stacks of loot scattered around the room. The merchandise had obviously come from a sporting goods store, and included bicycles, bike helmets, baseball gloves, sports clothing and baseball hats. Most of the loot was in original cartons or had price tags.

By the time police arrived, the military policemen had six guys spread-eagled on the pavement. They were unable to find the weapon during a cursory search, and turned the incident over to the police. The unit then put three-man Traffic Control Points on each intersection over a sizeable portion of the business district in Long Beach.

In South Central Los Angeles, the 40th Military Police Company was working new missions with LAPD out of Newton Station. They were scattering all over the district in mounted patrols consisting of two or three Hummers and one police car. The police radios worked much better in the city than military radios, so each team had the police cruiser to facilitate communications and maintain liaison. Some teams patrolled in specified areas to maintain a presence and keep the rather tenuous peace. Others responded to calls as needed.

One team headed for a warehouse full of valuable stereo equipment that was being looted. When they arrived they saw four trucks crashed into warehouse doors so looters could get in. The police told the military policemen "You guys got the point, you've got the big sticks (rifles)." Staff Sergeant Gary Ayala, a fork lift operator for Avon Cosmetics, said "That pleased us, giving us the chance for some real action. This was just like the Camp Pendleton (Marine Corps) 'combat town' we had trained in. We caught three looters coming out with the goods, and flex-cuffed them. (However) we immediately got a higher priority call. The cops had no choice except to chew the guys out, cut their flex cuffs, and let them go before we raced off."

Federal troops were moving by this time. President Bush had first signed a proclamation directing all persons engaging in acts of violence and disorder to "cease and desist therefrom and to disperse and retire peaceably forthwith." This was followed by an Executive Order authorizing the use of Armed Forces and Federal law enforcement officers to "suppress the violence described in the proclamation and to restore law and order." The phrase "restore law and order" is key to some of the contention that followed, because law and order had been restored before Federal troops hit the streets.

The Pentagon decided to form a Joint Task Force of soldiers and marines, with Major General Marvin L. Covault as the Joint Task Force commander. General Covault, a career field artilleryman and veteran of four campaigns in Vietnam, was commander of the 7th Infantry Division (Light) at Fort Ord in California.

The 7th Infantry Division was alerted at 4:15 a.m. Friday morning. The first C-141 aircraft left Monterey Airport with troops from the Second Brigade, 7th Infantry Division at 4:30 p.m., arriving at El Toro Marine Corps Air Station in Southern California about an hour later. The air flow continued to this staging area, about forty miles southeast of Los Angeles, until the last aircraft landed just before 5:00 a.m. on Saturday morning.

The Marines at Camp Pendleton first received their call at about 6:00 a.m. from General Edwin H. Burba Jr., Commander in Chief of Forces Command at Fort McPherson, Georgia. This was passed to Colonel Nathaniel R. (Nick) Hoskot, Jr. about twenty minutes later. Nick, in addition to other duties, is the Defense Coordinating Officer for Camp Pendleton. He started the Marine wheels rolling.

The primary Marine elements were the Third Battalion, First Marines (3-1), and the First Light Armored Infantry (1st LAI) Battalion, both of whom served in Desert Storm. The 1st LAI was equipped with Light Armored Vehicles, which are large armored cars. The troops were loaded on their armored vehicles, trucks and Hummers, and sent north with Military Police and California Highway Patrol escorts at about 2:30 p.m. They moved to their staging area at Tustin Marine Air Station, which is slightly closer to Los Angeles than El Toro. It had been recommended they stage at Los Alamitos, but it was obvious that Los Alamitos was already bulging at the seams. They took ammunition for their individual weapons, but had to wait for riot batons and face shields.

112

General Covault sent his Assistant Division Commander for Maneuver, Brigadier General Buck Kernan, ahead to Los Alamitos early in the afternoon. We met Buck, who landed at our airfield with an advance party of about twenty soldiers to set up the Joint Task Force Tactical (or Emergency) Operations Center. After giving him a quick tour of the base, showing him what was available, he selected a building with classrooms where they would have adequate space. His staff officers immediately began to establish their operations center and get communications established.

Colonel Nick Hoskot and his advance party of marines landed shortly thereafter with operations, intelligence, communications and public affairs officers. He joined up with General Kernan and went to work.

Major General Covault landed at about 4:30 p.m. We met my former Army War College classmate when he landed, and after a quick exchange of pleasantries, took him to Major General Hernandez' operations center where he was given a full briefing. General Covault spotted the senior marine present, Colonel Hoskot. He told the Marine Corps colonel that the marines would handle the personnel and logistics actions, while his staff handled operations and intelligence. Each component would then put deputies under the other's staff principal, ending up with a joint staff. For example, the J-3 for Operations was an Army Colonel, with a Marine Corps Deputy (Colonel Chip Gregson). Major General Covault made it clear several times that Joint Task Force Los Angeles (JTF-LA) was to be a truly joint, equally shared task force.

General Covault then met with General Kernan and I in his office. General Covault graciously offered me the job as his deputy. I declined, primarily because his own deputy (Buck

Kernan) was already performing that role. Buck is not only an outstanding soldier who had commanded the Army's only Ranger Regiment, but someone he was used to working with. As explained previously, I greatly prefer established relationships over *ad hoc* arrangements, especially under fast moving conditions. He then asked me to serve as his advisor.

General Covault asked if it would be all right to assign Major General Hernandez as the Army Forces (ARFOR) commander. I quickly agreed for a couple of reasons, explaining that morale among National Guardsmen had plummeted when they heard that the active Federal forces were being called in to "save the situation" after they had brought order to the streets. We were convinced that morale would be immediately restored if General Covault named the Guardsmen's own general as ARFOR commander. He did, and went a step further. He put his own Second Brigade, commanded by Colonel Ed Buckley, under the operational control of General Hernandez. As expected, the morale of National Guardsmen was quickly restored.

It was becoming obvious to Colonel Hoskot that tactical marines, rather than what he called "base guys," should be running the Marine portion of the show. He discussed it with his commander back at Camp Pendleton, and it was agreed Brigadier General Marvin T. (Ted) Hopgood of the First Marine Expeditionary Force (MEF) should handle the show. General Hopgood and his staff arrived later that night, and Colonel Hoskot returned to other duties. General Covault named General Hopgood the Marine Force (MARFOR) commander, giving Covault two subordinate tactical headquarters, one Army and one Marine.

In what was to become an overabundance of forces, the Third Brigade had been rolling since 2:00 a.m. from Northern California. The convoys stretched for many miles. The brigade, except for the 1-184th Infantry, stopped at Camp Roberts just before dawn for fuel and ammunition. It took a couple of hours to refuel all the vehicles, load equipment, and to integrate fuel tankers borrowed from Camp Roberts. The most significant problem during the movement was fuel and fuel tankers. The California National Guard's fifty heavy fuel tankers had been loaned to the Army for Desert Storm, and had still not been returned over a year later. As a consequence, they had to rely on tank and pump units mounted on five ton trucks.

The fuel trucks held the convoys down to as slow as five miles per hour on some uphill stretches. In other places the trucks exceeded 55 miles per hour, with the speed probably averaging somewhere around 30 miles per hour. When the convoys had to cross intersections, the people passing the convoy would wave or give the soldiers a "thumbs up." The people in cars stopped at intersections to let long convoys go by unfortunately were much less happy with the situation.

The brigade met up with the 1-184th Infantry at the junction of State Route 46 and Interstate 5. There the 1-184th Infantry was refueled and all were sent down the freeway as each unit was fueled or topped off. By the middle of the afternoon, they were beginning to arrive at the Pitchess Honor Ranch in Los Angeles County, but it took literally hours for the hundreds of vehicles to pull into the prison grounds and coil up in the staging area.

Those unfamiliar with the size of California may have little appreciation for the logistical challenges in moving large numbers of troops so far. The previous day military police from the 49th Military Police Brigade had been moved from Eureka to Los Angeles. If a map of California were superimposed over a map of Europe, this would parallel a move from Brussels, Belgium to a point below Bologna in Italy. The shorter move of the Third Brigade would be the same as convoying from New York City to Raleigh, North Carolina.

The Governor phoned General Covault in the late afternoon while Marv and I were talking in Marv's office. I only heard one side of the conversation, but it was clear the Governor wanted to know when the Federal troops were going to be deployed. General Covault told him that he had been fully briefed by General Hernandez. He told him he was pleased with General Hernandez' grasp of the situation, and that the National Guardsmen had things well in hand. He also made it clear he was not prepared to deploy his Federal troops that night. If the Governor wasn't aware before that his National Guardsmen had responded quickly, it should have been obvious to him after this phone call.

General Covault would not have all his Federal forces in place until the last aircraft landed after 4:00 a.m. Saturday. There was no need for him to take any precipitous action, as the 40th Infantry Division still had troops without missions. The number of troops without any real mission was only to grow over the next few days. General Covault did what any professional would do under the same circumstances. He made sure his troops were properly equipped and trained. His leaders would also take time to scout out mission areas and rehearse their troops before making any deployments.

CHAPTER SIX

Friday, May 1, 1992
THE THIRD NIGHT

As darkness approached, senior commanders were evaluating the situation. Everyone felt that the previous night had been the turning point, and we were clearly gaining control. At the same time, we were being sent decidedly mixed signals. The federal troops had been requested without any discussion with either General Hernandez or me. We knew we had a lot of soldiers who were not fully committed, and that a full brigade of Guardsmen from Northern California was on the way. To add further confusion, we had suddenly received the flurry of mission requests in the afternoon that would use all of the battalions we had earmarked for street missions, but had not yet committed.

In accordance with requests from LAPD through the Sheriff's EOC, we had deployed all of our battalions by the time it was dark. It was obvious LAPD knew about the 132nd Engineer Battalion we were holding in reserve, as they had requested them also. The troops were either sent to street missions, back-up of forces already deployed, or to the Sports Arena/Coliseum complex. Before the 132nd Engineers departed on their buses, I talked to General Hernandez and Colonel Manuel F. (Red) Silva of the Division Support Command, ensuring that we reconstituted a reserve. Colonel Silva formed two provisional battalions with volunteers from his support battalions, many of whom were women.

117

Major General Dan Hernandez, 40th Infantry Division
Commander, in his Crisis Action Center.
(Photo: Author's Collection)

The Third Brigade had all pulled into the Pitchess Honor Ranch before it got dark. Colonel Brandt again called both the division and state Emergency Operations Centers to keep them informed on progress. Division headquarters told them that the Los Angeles Police Department would send guides for the first battalion of troops.

Colonel Zaver, the Brigade Commander, for the second time asked if he could give his troops at least six hours sleep before they were committed. Most of them had been jammed into the vehicles for the convoy lasting anywhere from twelve to sixteen hours, getting little or no sleep since Wednesday night. He was told the brigade had missions coming from LAPD, and to prepare the soldiers for deployment into the streets.

The brigade had been given a picnic area as a forward assembly area, but it was much too small for all of the vehicles. The one telephone in the area was overworked until the phone company installed a portable bank of eight telephones which helped alleviate the problem. Nevertheless, they made it work, and were delighted when the Sheriff's Department sent over a huge portable kitchen manned by prison trustees to serve them hot chow. It was the first hot meal many of them had seen since the previous day.

The Guardsmen had just started through the chow line at about 6:30 p.m. when police cars from several different police divisions pulled in. Colonel Brandt asked them if there was time to finish feeding the troops. The police agreed there would be no problem, and got in the chow line themselves. The prison's portable kitchen fed about 1400 soldiers and policemen in just one hour. As battalions finished feeding, they were deployed with police escorts.

The 2-159th Infantry was split three ways to augment efforts in Compton, Culver City, and Hawthorne. The 1-149th Armor was deployed to Dodger Stadium in support of LAPD's Central Division. The 1-184th Infantry was sent to Hollywood Bowl, and naturally found themselves quickly dubbed "Team Hollywood." Lots of troops were deployed into quiet areas, such as the San Fernando Valley, where they saw little or no action. Others ended up at the Sports Arena and Coliseum, which was already crowded with military and police vehicles.

Buses were needed to move the 132nd Engineers from Los Alamitos to the Sports Arena. Jack Stites, from the Orange County Transportation District, and a retired marine who had survived the Chosen River ordeal during the Korean War, came to the rescue. He quickly led a column of his buses to Los Alamitos. The troops were loaded up and transported to the Sports Arena, only to sit there for 24 hours before being assigned a mission.

One of the Division Support Command's two provisional battalions had been formed from elements of six different commands totalling about seven hundred soldiers. It was placed under the command of Lieutenant Colonel John S. Gong. They called themselves Joint Task Force Six (JTF-6) for obvious reasons, and were sent downtown.

Lieutenant Colonel Gong went to Parker Center for mission guidance, and was given a couple of missions. The first involved about seventy five of his troops along Pico Boulevard in the LAPD Rampart area. A little later they were moved to Little Tokyo. For this first night they were grossly under-utilized, although the situation would improve somewhat over time.

Gong's task force set up housekeeping in the parking lot next to the California Department of Transportation (CALTRANS). Living on a parking lot normally doesn't have much to recommend it, but the troops didn't complain. The employees of CALTRANS were exceptionally considerate and helpful. Just as important, this lot is located between the New Otani Hotel and the St. Vibiana Cathedral. The New Otani, a world-class hotel, fed the troops in luxurious style. The cathedral offered their facilities for showers, so some of the troops took showers in the same facility that had been used by the Pope during one of his visits.

Emergency responses were very well organized by Friday night. Every emergency vehicle would be escorted by two or three police or highway patrol cars as they screamed up and down the streets. In addition, soldiers found that when they requested help from law enforcement, police or sheriff's deputies would respond very quickly in great numbers. Needless to say, they found this very reassuring.

Also by Friday night, law enforcement authorities had Guardsmen posted in all parts of the city and county where they wanted a presence established. They had troops staged and ready to deploy in a back-up role all over the city. They were not only at the Sports Arena and Coliseum, but had large concentrations in Dodger Stadium, Hollywood Bowl, several high schools, and some armories. There the troops that were not deployed slept, cleaned their weapons, and tried to keep occupied as they awaited missions.

Others weren't having any trouble keeping occupied.

The 1-185th Armor was scattered all up and down the "Alvarado Corridor," on Alvarado Street north and south of MacArthur Park. As it started to get dark, the troops could see a lot of drug trafficking, especially out of crack houses. There were a great many buildings with windows broken and doors kicked in. The glass on the sidewalks crunched and snapped as the soldiers patrolled the area. There also was still a lot of smoke in the air, although comparatively few fires that were actively burning.

The curfew was not well enforced, but the great majority of people were the homeless and street people pushing shopping carts with their possessions. There were drunk or drugged-out

121

derelicts all over. The battalion had placed one tank crew per intersection. Each crew had one marksman with an M16 rifle in addition to other weapons.

The strip of Alvarado between MacArthur Park (7th Street) and 11th Street was a particular challenge for Captain Dwayne P. Eckman and his Company B from this tank battalion. They found themselves helping individuals ranging from the sick to various street victims. One man had been assaulted and was almost incoherent. He had cuts and bruises around his head and face, with his pants pocket torn when muggers ripped off his wallet. The troops treated his injuries, gave him water, and tried to calm him down.

One big crack house near the southern end of their sector was doing a great deal of business. People were coming and going, and hanging out of the windows on the second and third floors. There was a lot of yelling between people hanging out of the windows and people in the streets. Suddenly, at about 9:30 p.m., gunfire broke out. First there was automatic fire from the big crack house directed towards a smaller crack house about half a block to the west. Those in the smaller crack house responded with what appeared to be pistol fire. For about three minutes, Guardsmen were exposed to a crossfire over their heads.

At about the same time, three shots were fired at the intersection of Alvarado and Maryland Streets, just above MacArthur Park. The commander then directed that anyone who came through (it was after curfew) should be patted down for weapons. This unit only found two weapons, but confiscated over a dozen crack pipes and detained one man who was carrying cocaine.

One transvestite dressed like a woman walked up to the Guardsmen and said "Tell your commander to stay out of Koreatown, 'cause that place is going to burn!" This was a message that the troops heard several times, but only remembered it being delivered once by a man wearing a dress. These soldiers from the desert community of Palmdale were getting a quick education about life on the more seedy streets of the big city.

As midnight approached, the troops from Palmdale heard a commotion near MacArthur Park. A platoon leader at the southwest corner of MacArthur Park called for assistance from the commander using his PRC-77 (portable) radio.

When Captain Eckman got there, he found a woman being separated from a comparatively small man she had been chasing. The woman was a very dirty, seedy street person, black, in her mid-twenties. The man was white, about the same age, and well dressed. He was wearing gold necklaces and rings, and was very effeminate. She had been chasing him for literally blocks, evidently after his jewelry, as he yelled for help.

Three soldiers formed a wall between the woman and the hapless man as the officers tried to piece together what had occurred. She kept fighting to get at him, saying "I won't hurt you!" He kept crying "She's crazy! She's crazy!" Troops related how they had seen her chasing him all over the place. Finally, the officers told him to run while they blocked the woman. However, he said he was too tired to run any more.

The woman finally got around the soldiers and took after him again as he yelped and ran (he obviously had some energy left!). The soldiers were forced to manhandle her, grabbing her and holding her against some galvanized fencing used to protect a subway construction project. They became irritated when a television crew then turned on their lights to film them having to be forceful with the street person. The same film crew had shown no interest at all any of the times they had played good Samaritan while assisting people, applying first aid, or summoning needed help for various citizens.

Company D of the same battalion was strung out along Pico Boulevard. Any of the troops assigned to this area remember it vividly. The area around Pico and Vermont Avenue is almost exclusively Hispanic. Hispanic gangs had staked out their territory along Pico many years ago, and "tagged" it with their graffiti. Troops assigned to the area quickly became familiar with gang tags in the area, especially those affiliated with the large Hispanic gang in the area called The Playboys.

Unlike some neighborhoods, the area still had electricity. In spite of that, the street lights had been shot out, making it dangerously dark. As Guardsmen patrolled the spooky streets, gangbangers would whistle their locations to each other, signalling across the street from upper windows and rooftops.

Automatic fire was heard from an alleyway a couple of blocks east of Pico and Vermont. When the troops investigated, gangbangers tried to entice them into the dark alley. They said things like "you f---in' National Guards, come in and get us!" The troops knew that would have been stupid and waited for the police to arrive. The police advised the Guardsmen to just ignore their taunts. They did, although it wasn't always easy.

Drug dealing occurs all through the area. We were on the corner of Pico and New Hampshire, just one block off of Vermont, and watched very conspicuous drug dealing. They watched us watching them, almost with a "what are you going

124

to do about it?" attitude. We have all read about it, but the arrogant blatancy has to be seen to be believed.

Other elements of the battalion had received a request to assist police in securing a surplus store close to the Coliseum. They got there just as it got dark. They could tell that the owners had tried to protect their investment, to include barricading the place. However, the front door had literally been smashed off its hinges, and the store had been badly looted. Inside the store they found two nine-year-old kids who couldn't speak English. The kids were taken to Juvenile Hall.

The 2-185th Armor continued their missions based on the Baldwin Hills Crenshaw Shopping Mall. There were several shooting incidents in the area, including one shotgun drive-by shooting directed at the one remaining undamaged window in the Broadway Department Store. They were never successful, but that one window seemed to be a powerful magnet to the gangbangers. The battalion sent patrols, both foot and vehicular, around the area to maintain a presence.

The 3-185th Armor was working out of Los Angeles High School, with their largest mission initially being protection of Koreatown to the east. The battalion scattered teams all along Olympic, Western and Normandie to make their presence felt.

The first concern of the troops was Korean shopkeepers, who were armed to the teeth. This made the soldiers uneasy, and they tried to convince the Koreans to put their guns away. The Koreans were reluctant because they had been targeted by gangbangers early in the riots when law enforcement was overextended. As a result, many Koreans had been injured, some seriously.

It came as no surprise that Koreans were very hesitant at first to trust the Guardsmen to maintain the peace, although this changed quickly. It helped that some of the older Koreans recognized the 40th Division's patch from the division's service during the Korean War. The division has a special relationship with Korea, helped by the fact that volunteers from the division built a now famous orphanage and school in Kapyong at the end of the war. Also, many 40th Division units have participated in military exercises in Korea since the Korean War.

In various parts of Koreatown, during and immediately following the riots, there evolved an implied division of responsibility. The Koreans secured the rooftops while Guardsmen patrolled the streets.

We were informed that George McCanley, agent-in-charge of the Los Angeles field office of the U.S. State Department, wanted guards for the Korean Consulate. The mission was passed through channels to the 670th MP Company. When they got there, they found the Koreans were greatly concerned about both the Korean Cultural Center and the Consul-General's residence. That was reported back to the 49th MP Brigade, and we approved Colonel Jerry W. Fields' recommendation expanding the mission to cover all three. The troops were given the Consul-General's guest house for the duration of the riots, and were treated royally by the staff there. They even did the soldier's laundry for them.

The curfew in Koreatown was comparatively well enforced. Night vision devices in 3-185th Armor were put to good use. At the periphery of their assigned area, the battalion strategically placed soldiers with night vision devices on dark roof tops to keep an eye on crack houses and centers of gang activity, generally to the south. The soldiers armed with sniper rifles and night vision scopes often saw gangbangers aim their weapons at Guardsmen, but withheld fire. As it turned out, the soldiers' restraint was well placed.

Some soldiers were assigned the mission of protecting the Ralph's Supermarket at the corner of Western and Olympic. This was the only source of groceries for miles around after others were looted or burned. Troops on the roof were fired upon, but they didn't return fire because they were unable to spot the source of the fire. In the morning they found the expended bullets where they had slammed into a wall.

Except for incidents like the above -- rare for our soldiers in Koreatown -- the assignment to protect Ralph's Supermarket was good duty. The people at Ralph's gave the troops cold drinks, "pogey bait" (snacks), and otherwise took good care of the soldiers assigned to protect them.

Troops from the 3-160th Infantry patrolling around the St. Francis Medical Center in Lynwood heard there were problems in the Emergency Room. When they got there, they found a room full of people with burns and other injuries waiting for help. The problems were being caused by a couple of nasty gangbangers who were only in the room to terrorize the people. The Guardsmen told them to get out. The gang members immediately backed off, saying "Okay man, no problem!" They left the hospital, and people in the Emergency Room spontaneously burst into applause.

Troops were rarely bored in Compton, which continued as a problem area. The original home of some of the oldest and most violent black gangs, a lot of troops were committed in and rotated through Compton.

Battery B of 2-144th Field Artillery was sent to Compton to replace Service Battery of the same battalion. They traveled in a convoy of buses with Hummers interspersed in between.

Heading down Central to make a turn on Compton Boulevard, they saw two young blacks on the corner holding large rocks about the size of softballs. Sure enough, they threw one through the windshield of the first bus. The driver told the troops "Welcome to Compton!" The black youths ran away as the convoy continued on. The unit traveled to the Ramada Inn which had been set up as a joint command center and EOC for the city of Compton. There the troops received their mission orders, and were sent to maintain security in Compton's Civic Center.

Artillerymen stopped a van with four Hispanics in it. They could see weapons, so they called police officers to arrest the men and take them away. Those same men were released later that night and came to a store in the area just a half block from where the troops were posted. It turned out that the men were a store owner and his employees coming to protect their store. They obviously harbored no ill feelings towards the soldiers. They fed the soldiers, gave them sodas and cigarettes, and invited them to sleep in the store.

About midnight, the 2-159th Infantry Battalion's Company C relieved some artillerymen in Compton. At that time, Captain Troy Armstrong assumed responsibility for thirteen checkpoints with the sixteen squads of his reinforced company. His soldiers from Redwood City in Northern California, like so many soldiers, faced a culture shock in this somewhat alien city. Buildings had bullet holes, and smoke still drifted around in some areas. They were extremely tense as they heard sporadic gunfire through the night.

Soldiers from the division artillery were still posted in the Target Center Mall in Culver City. Like so many scattered all over the county, they had a great many more people come by to

128

express their gratitude than to create problems. However, it seemed like there were gangbangers everywhere.

The police told troops at the Target Center Mall that the gangbangers harassing them were "wannabees" rather than hard core gang members. This was a term our soldiers heard everywhere. They found it very difficult to tell the difference between a wannabe and a gang member, but it probably didn't make any difference. Some police officers admitted that the distinction between wannabees and gang members was too difficult to define in any event.

Some kids were sent over from the housing projects to scout the situation for the wannabees or gangbangers. They would ask questions about how many bullets each soldier had, how many were stationed in the shopping center, what their instructions were, and how long they would be there. They didn't get much in the way of answers, but never seemed to get tired of asking. As seemed to occur everywhere, gangbangers would drive by to give soldiers the finger, shout taunts, make their gang signs, and promise to come back and kill soldiers later.

Just after dusk, the Culver City Police Department decided to send a message through one of the small groups of Hispanic wannabees who always seemed to be getting in trouble. They stopped a small four door Toyota right beside the shopping center. They pulled them out one at a time, frisked them, and had them sit on the ground facing their car with their arms and legs folded while their car was searched. The police lecture then went something like: "I'm disappointed in you guys. I thought we had an understanding, but you keep jerking us around. Have you guys any idea what's going on? Any idea at all?" After a short pause, they said "Turn around and look carefully."

The wannabees looked around as the Guardsmen emerged from hiding on the roofs and from behind pillars. It was obvious, as their eyes widened and mouths dropped open, that they had no clue there were that many troops guarding the mall. The police then told them "You have no business being here. Get out of here."

They did so, jumping quickly back into their car, heading north on Jefferson Boulevard and turning into the projects. The observation post on the roof kept track of them all the way back to their apartment building, which was a beehive of activity over the next several days. Shortly after the police made the stop, the officers came back and explained to the Guardsmen why they had done it the way they did. The police were convinced that at least two of the men in the Toyota had been involved in the looting earlier. They felt if additional problems were on the horizon, it would come from that group.

Once the group did gather and look like they were going to make trouble. The troops aimed a laser pointer at one gang-banger's toes, and then raised it to his chest. When the others spotted that red dot in their friend's chest, they all quickly scattered. The laser that the troops used was a training aid used to point at a projection screen. The troops also have other lasers, some of which are much more dangerous. The gangbangers couldn't tell the difference. The laser was used a couple of times more in similar situations, and they had no more trouble.

The 3-144th Artillery in Inglewood had to work hard enforcing the curfew in their area of responsibility. They were a little surprised at how assertive the police got when time came for citizens to get off the streets. Some of the officers were using profanity, and even had to physically push folks some times. The Guardsmen quickly found out why. It seems that some people, in some places, just like to stretch the law. The soldiers found out that if they also didn't push, and push hard, some of those citizens would quickly take advantage of them.

First Lieutenant Gary L. Beechum, owner of Air Improvement Resources of Santa Ana, had his soldiers posted on Avalon Boulevard. Avalon is the same street where the Watts riots of 1965 were started. His soldiers were constantly being tested. He heard gangbangers ask his soldiers if they really had ammunition. They were asked if they had lock plates installed (it was obvious that gangbangers listen to television too!).

A group of gangbangers was bragging about their AK-47 Kalashnikov automatic rifles to the infantrymen, until one of Beechum's soldiers had his fill of it. A weapons expert, he explained the thirteen reasons the American M-16 is more effective than the Soviet AK-47 to include range, penetrating power, and accuracy. The gangbangers also noted that our soldiers were equipped with the M-203 grenade launcher, a very imposing weapon. When those gangbangers heard enough, they said "Hey, our beef is with the cops, not you guys."

Soldiers were getting tired of being hassled by gangbangers. The 1-18th Cavalry sent a group of soldiers from the Long Range Surveillance Detachment (160th LRSD) to guard a liquor store at the corner of Martin Luther King Boulevard and Hillcrest Drive. Three young blacks asked if they could climb the fence and walk over to the Hillcrest Projects. When the cavalrymen asked why they didn't just walk to the gates in the fence at either end, they received a rather telling answer. The three told them they were afraid to go to the right because that

131

was a rival gang's turf and they could be killed if they went there. The police were to the left, and they were afraid the police would shoot them if they went that direction. The cavalry troopers let them climb the fence and go up the middle.

One of the three youngsters struck up a conversation with Master Sergeant Milo Cornelius, asserting that his gang members had better guns than the Guardsmen. Sergeant Cornelius pointed out that the LRSD soldiers are not only well armed, but are exceptionally well trained and ranger qualified soldiers that nobody should fool with.

The youngster returned a little while later with a friend about twenty years old, who the police identified as one of the gang leaders in the projects there. An LAPD lieutenant watched and listened as the two came over to talk to Sergeant Cornelius. The gang leader repeated almost the same spiel as the youngster, talking about how tough his gang was, and how much better they were armed. Cornelius finally had his fill of it. He said: "You guys need to understand something. This was going to be our first weekend off, and *YOU* destroyed it! Everybody is angry, and we're having to sleep in the streets. We're real angry, and you have to understand we're in a mood to annihilate anyone who gets in our way so we can get home to our families."

Cornelius's strongly worded statement had a large measure of what soldiers call "B.S.," but it also had the desired effect. The gangbangers got the message, and they left. This was just the kind of dialogue we had been discouraging. However, the police lieutenant told the cavalrymen it was the best thing they could have done. "What you did was throw down the gauntlet. Either they are going to come play, it is time to play...and if

132

not, they are just going to keep their tails home." The cavalrymen had no more problems in that area.

Other cavalrymen got a call for help shortly after midnight. They were dispatched from the Coliseum to the Vermont Knolls Convalescent Home on 83rd Street just off Vermont Avenue, which they were told was under siege.

Captain Alan J. Skidmore left with his first sergeant and twelve cavalry troopers in a Hummer and a truck. The trip was made through a pitch black area without any electricity. The only light came from burning buildings and the occasional spotlight turned on and then quickly off by police in a cruiser. They rarely saw any vehicles or people. They felt danger in the air, and described the situation the same way so many other Guardsmen did the first two or three days..."absolutely surreal."

When they arrived at the convalescent home, they found two very tired and nervous police officers, who left shortly after the Guardsmen arrived. Inside was a group of senior citizens, huddled in the lobby. When the Guardsmen entered, the relief was palpable. There were hugs and tears as the soldiers promised to stay with the old folks and not leave. This was a very special moment for our soldiers. One cavalryman described it as "instant gratification." He said "It was like all the years of training...all the pain you go through to become a good soldier, were rewarded all at once there...in that one night when we were so well received."

A detail was sent out to ensure the perimeter was secure. The building across 83rd Street from the convalescent home was burning, as well as several buildings across Vermont Avenue. The only light was from the flames. The team went around the building, and flushed several gangbangers who had

133

been hiding in the shadows. They took off running as the soldiers watched.

The manager of the convalescent home, Jewell Anderson, is a very special lady. She seems to have equal parts of strength and warmth, one of those people you automatically want to hug. When the soldiers talked to her, they found that her charges had endured an incredible ordeal. They were without electricity, and the neighborhood was burning all around them. The power pole in front even caught on fire. Gangbangers had climbed on their roof, banged on the doors and windows, and tried to get drugs from an adjacent office. The old folks kept the gangbangers at bay, though they got almost no sleep.

The Guardsmen kept some troopers with the senior citizens for several days until after they were federalized and told it was inappropriate. Even after that, they would go by the convalescent home at every opportunity, rattle the front door to ensure it was locked, and wave at and reassure any old folks who happened to be in the lobby.

Some have implied that the Guardsmen were heroes for rescuing the tenants of the convalescent home. The incident was even described that way by one speaker during the Republican Presidential Convention. However, the cavalrymen are the first to tell anyone that will listen that the real heroes were the residents of that convalescent home. Regardless, the troopers have adopted the senior citizens (or is it the other way around?) in a special relationship that exists to this day.

Company E, 2-160th Infantry from the farming community of Hanford (near Fresno) sent a reinforced platoon to relieve troops at the intersection of Crenshaw and Vernon. They were responsible for the intersection, which was critical to movement of emergency vehicles in the area, and for Liemert Plaza, a park

134

adjacent to the intersection. When they got to this scene of earlier heavy rioting, they found several buildings still smouldering. The Thrifty Drug Store there was completely gutted.

The sounds and smells of destruction impacted more on some Guardsmen than others. Vietnam veterans throughout the division were struck by the similarity of their emotions "in country" during that conflict, as compared to their feelings the first couple of nights in Los Angeles. These flash-backs of emotions appear to have been triggered by several factors. Most mentioned the unknown, and most especially, not knowing how to recognize the "enemy." Others vividly remember the burning buildings, bullet scars in some walls and buildings, smoke, smells, images of destruction, sounds of gunfire off in the distance, and utter chaos in some areas that so closely resembled combat. Many of these veterans had very mixed emotions as they worked to bring order out of chaos in their city.

By Friday night there was very little of what could be described as riot control occurring. Rather than riot control, troops found themselves deeply involved in law enforcement and maintaining law and order. What may have been one of the rare exceptions was at the corner of Crenshaw and Vernon. There the troops from Hanford confiscated at least one Molotov cocktail and chased away some gangbangers siphoning gasoline from cars.

Tension built up at that location as it grew darker. This was one of the areas where hostile citizens may have outnumbered the small number of friendly folks still on the streets. Sergeant First Class Toby Bogges described it as "people milling about the area, some hostile, some passive, few friendly." At about 8:00 p.m., a blacked-out Pinto went tearing by at high speed.

135

Sergeant Bogges locked and loaded his rifle. His soldiers hit the ground, and aimed their rifles at the Pinto. No shots were fired by those in the Pinto, so the Guardsmen held their fire. Tension in the area continued to be strained further by threats and insults yelled from dark side streets and alleys.

Other infantrymen were being tested also. Officials talking to the media about delays in ammunition had many gangbangers convinced there were Guardsmen in the street without ammunition. This kind of irresponsible talk put soldiers at risk. Those gangbangers who weren't sure whether we had ammunition tried to find out. Others didn't bother to find out, and continued to the daily testing of Guardsmen each night until some of the soldiers were actually assaulted Sunday night. In the meantime, Guardsmen all over the county were being questioned about their ammunition.

We continued to see the taunting and flashing of weapons by gangbangers all around the county. A couple of things were becoming increasingly clear. One was that there seemed to be a great many weapons, of all descriptions, in the hands of gang members everywhere in Los Angeles County. We knew that literally thousands of weapons had been stolen from gun stores and pawn shops during the riots, but the sheer numbers of weapons seen everywhere made it obvious that there were lots of weapons among gangbangers long before the riots.

The taunting was the other issue. Senior commanders traveling around the county clearly saw a common pattern to the baiting and heckling of Guardsmen, as well as the flashing of weapons. It was almost as though all gangbangers had attended a required course in "Gang Taunting and Teasing 101" to ensure all of them used a similar approach. The truth is that such behavior is probably cultural, and over the years they have repeatedly used that behavior on other gangs and individuals.

Generally the troops ignored the taunts and games played by gangbangers. On several occasions, when soldiers felt it was going too far, they would aim their rifles at the miscreants. The vehicles would usually then speed off.

Sergeant Everett E. Betts of 3-160th Infantry had four soldiers protecting the Sheriff's office and jail next to the freeway in the Civic Center about 2:30 a.m. He had just been relieved and laid down near what he described as an "earthquake bin," a very large, fully enclosed trash container. A bullet suddenly struck with what he described as a very loud "ping," followed by the report. That shot was quickly followed by two more that also hit very close.

"I thought...Oh s---! I jumped up, said to myself 'ah man,' (and yelled) 'Everybody keep your heads down! I just dealt with it from there. They were fired from the direction of the overpass." Although law enforcement responded immediately, they were unable to catch the perpetrators. Betts also remembers vividly the time a shotgun was fired at them in a drive-by from the freeway. There was no way a shotgun could be effective from the distance involved, but the troops all remember it sounding like a small cannon.

The streets clearly were still dangerous, as they are in some parts of the city regardless of riotous conditions. In addition to the impersonal gunfire Guardsmen heard off in the distance, some of it continued to be much more personal. Guardsmen were fired at on the northwest corner of 65th Street and Menlo Avenue. Automatic fire was aimed at soldiers on the corner of Redondo and Washington. Two rounds were fired by a sniper at Guardsmen on the corner of Crenshaw and 156th Street.

Military policemen at the corner of Pacific Coast Highway and Cedar Avenue were harassed by twenty to thirty rounds from an automatic weapon. A car tried to run over a Guardsman on Redondo Avenue. The Guardsman was unhurt, and the driver was quickly captured by police. Rocks and bottles were thrown at infantrymen in the vicinity of Firestone Sheriff's Station. A Molotov cocktail was thrown at Venice and Western, but without damage. Another arson attempt was made at Pico and Hoover, with the suspect captured and turned over to police.

As dawn approached, it was obvious the streets of Los Angeles were in a new phase. There had been no riots to confront. While the streets were still extremely dangerous, all of the Guardsmen were engaged in law enforcement duties, maintaining rather than restoring law and order.

The grim statistics continued to mount even though it was obvious the worst was over:

43 Deaths
1257 Injuries
5017 Structure fires (1172 for the one day)

CHAPTER SEVEN

Saturday, May 2nd, 1992
THE FOURTH DAY

The Intelligence Summary for Saturday reflected the changes that had occurred the previous day and night, plus what should be anticipated for the near term. There were still very serious law enforcement problems anticipated in the short term, but there had been no rioting on Friday. Fires were all but out, though many were smouldering. There was shooting at night, but that occurs *every* night. As a consequence of the return to relative normalcy, law enforcement officers were finally starting to catch up on their sleep.

Both the LAPD and Sheriff's Department were evaluating their operations. By mid-afternoon, Chief Baker of the Sheriff's Department announced they were "de-escalating" their operations as of this evening.

Senior military officers felt this was the end of the first phase. The next phase would involve what one colonel described as "basically buying back the streets and creating a sense of order...confidence on the part of the people that the streets are now safe." There was a massive troop presence on the streets, with helicopters overhead and Hummer vehicles everywhere. The situation in the streets felt very different from this point on.

139

Even though there were still no federal troops deployed, soldiers knew by this time they were part of a very sizeable military force. Soldiers very rarely ever see a full brigade "slice" (fighting troops plus their support, or between three to four thousand soldiers) all at one time, much less a full division. Sergeant First Class Toby Bogges said "This (military helicopters constantly criss-crossing the sky), coupled with the massive troop presence, gives one the impression of being part of a great effort." By this time, at least half of the 40th Infantry Division (Mechanized) was mobilized and in the area. This is particularly comforting to soldiers given dangerous assignments. They feel better knowing others wearing the patch (their division patch worn on the shoulder) are ready to lend immediate support if needed. In addition, they know that gang-bangers see the same massive show of force they do.

There was still concern about unauthorized Cinco de Mayo celebrations possibly escalating into violence. There also continued to be a general feeling of unease and desire by officials to carefully avoid inadvertently creating situations conducive to violence.

County officials closed some beaches as a precautionary measure. Beaches that were closed included Dockweiler State Beach in Playa Del Rey, Venice Beach, Will Rogers State Beach, and Cabrillo Beach. The Santa Monica beaches were open, but attendance was way down because the parking lots remained closed. However, one sign of returning normalcy was reopening of the Washington Golf Course. The southbound Highway 101 freeway off ramps at Alameda and Los Angeles streets were still closed.

There were literally thousands of troops in staging areas training and waiting for missions. The deployment of other military forces and law enforcement officers from neighboring communities under the mutual aid system as of six a.m.:

Requesting Agency	National Guard	Law Enforcement Mutual Aid Deployment
Los Angeles P.D.	3873	50 - Dept of Water & Power, plus Gas Escorts
Los Angeles S.D.	795	
Calif. Highway Patrol	30	
Compton P.D.	277	189 - (12 different dept.)
Culver City P.D.	150	
FAA (FBI)	10	
Inglewood P.D.	61	
Red Cross		22 (at various shelters)
Southgate P.D.		20 (Southgate Park & Mall)
Torrance P.D.		48 (Del Amo Mall)
Totals	5340	329

One particularly troubling intelligence report came from Fresno. The Fresno County Sheriff's Department notified their counterparts in Los Angeles that male blacks had bought an extraordinarily large amount of ammunition in Fresno on Friday. They brought two AK-47 assault rifles into a sporting goods store, and then bought magazines for the AK-47s and other weapons. They also bought large quantities of 7.62 mm, 9 mm, and .30 calibre ammunition before departing southbound with the weapons and ammunition loaded in a pickup truck with a wrecker boom in the bed.

Intelligence was received that the Revolutionary Communist Party had scheduled an "emergency meeting" for 11:00 a.m. in front of police headquarters at Parker Center to demonstrate against the Rodney King verdict. They were then to demonstrate in front of the Park Plaza Hotel at the corner of Sixth Street and Parkview, across from MacArthur Park. In the meantime, the International Committee Against Racism scheduled a noon march to City Hall. This group, closely related to the Revolutionary Communist Party, intended to demand jobs, "Death to killer cops," and "Communist equality." Another noon rally was planned by an anti-Castro group at the corner of Olympic and Beverly Boulevards.

The area was taking stock of the extensive damage that had occurred to the moral fabric of the community as well as the widespread destruction of the city's infrastructure. There were very few grocery stores left undamaged in the inner city, a situation that was becoming an increasing concern. Some of the destruction seemed particularly senseless. Even libraries had been extensively damaged. The Junipero Serra Library on Figueroa Street was burned down. The Wilshire, Felipe De Neve, Cahuenga and Vermont Square Libraries all reported damage.

Burnt and looted businesses and public buildings were everywhere. There were very few active fires, but hulks of buildings still smouldered, and broken glass, bricks, trash, remnants of looted goods and debris were scattered everywhere. Detectives canvassed the area and noted graffiti "tags" had been painted on some burned out sites to advertise gang roles in burning those locations.

The healing process seemed to really get started Saturday morning. At six in the morning, a Korean radio station was announcing to the Korean Community that residents should meet at Ardmore Street and Olympic Boulevard in Koreatown for a peace march. Throughout the city, thousands of citizens of every age, race and gender poured into the streets with rakes, brooms and trash bags to begin the cleanup. Volunteers directed traffic, furnished transportation for residents without bus service, and provided food.

More businesses were starting to reopen in the affected area. It wasn't always an easy process, as whenever a market or service station opened, they were immediately mobbed by customers. In several instances, business owners all but panicked. Sometimes troops or police officers would get involved, getting people into line, disarming people with weapons, and maintaining order.

One story that was making the rounds of law enforcement circles involved a Guardsman who had "abused his authority." He had been guarding an intersection with a service station on the corner. Cars were lined up to get gas when the station opened. When the owner saw the length of the line, he went to his gas sign, and started to raise the price from $1.19 to $1.99 per gallon. When the Guardsman saw that, he had a chat with the owner, who immediately lowered it to the original price.

The efforts to recover looted property moved into high gear this morning. Information on locations of looted property had begun to come in the day before. This morning, reports really began to flow into police and sheriff's offices all over the county. Some callers phoned on their own simply because their consciences were bothering them after they had succumbed to temptation during the earlier frenzies of looting. Many other people had their consciences triggered by ministers and others who appealed to their sense of right. However, a great many calls were triggered by a variety of motivations ranging from indignation to envy. Those callers, whether relatives, friends or neighbors, called the police with the addresses of quite a few looters.

As a consequence of some of these latter calls, the 40th MP Company had teams accompanying plain clothes detectives from the Newton Division as they went out to recover stolen property. When the detectives went into a building, the military police established a perimeter around the outside. They had to be careful no one got hurt by stolen property being jettisoned out of windows and doors. Most of it was in the original cartons. On just one side of one apartment house, the troops dodged four television sets, a video camera, and many smaller electrical appliances.

The total experience was great training for the military policemen assigned to Newton Division. The police taught the soldiers law enforcement techniques, and conducted critiques after each mission. The reciprocal arrangement ended up being a superb learning experience for these soldiers.

At 10:00 a.m., a meeting was conducted in the Sheriff's EOC to discuss military support issues. Attendees included Chief Myron (LASD), Sergeant Michael Woodings (LAPD), Colonel Zysk (National Guard), and Lieutenant Colonel Steve Parsons, who had been assigned to the EOC by the Joint Task

Force. It was agreed that federal troops would start replacing National Guardsmen. Missions were to be limited, and would include security for previously secured areas, building security at fixed (stationary) posts, and security for firefighters.

Post offices were again pressured by crowds, lined up as they had Friday for their mail. Rioting had made it too dangerous for the postal system to work normally in the area, so about 250,000 welfare checks weren't delivered the first of the month. Some post offices had as many as 1500-2000 people lined up on Saturday for checks. At several of the post offices there was pushing and shoving in the lines, with some troublemakers creating problems for police and postal inspectors. Every once in a while, a police team would come in and haul wrongdoers away.

Sergeant Alfred Reaza, a machine gunner from 1-18th Cavalry, is a postal mail carrier himself. He was sent with a team of cavalrymen to a post office where there were a lot of problems, and a great deal of tension. When the platoon of Guardsmen arrived, the people in line spontaneously applauded.

There were two police officers there. Sergeant Reaza said, "When we got there, she (one of the two police officers) crossed herself, and said she was glad we were there." The police left to handle problems elsewhere, and had no sooner left but when the Reverend Jesse Jackson arrived on the scene in his limousine. Reverend Jackson calmed the crowd, and shook hands with all the Guardsmen. The platoon then deployed, and talked to the people in the line.

The people told them that people across the street had been cutting into the line, greatly increasing the tension. The line was so long that it impacted on street traffic, so the Guardsmen also assumed the role of traffic officers.

When the situation outside was under control, Sergeant Reaza went into the post office to find out why the line was moving so slow. There he found that the post office had no electric power, and mail was being sorted by flashlight. The people in line were almost all Hispanic, so he explained in Spanish what the problem was, and appealed for patience.

When the people in line found that Sergeant Reaza could speak Spanish, they started calling for him to come over so they could explain their problems to him. One woman carrying a baby with a full diaper asked Sergeant Reaza if she could move to the front of the line, as she didn't have a diaper to change her baby. Reaza, who has five kids himself, decided to organize things. He went up the line (about two blocks long at that point) asking for diapers, and collected about twenty. He then redistributed them to those who needed them.

Sergeant Reaza, when he traveled up the line, had noted that many women were in advanced stages of pregnancy, and that there were senior citizens who had been in line a long time. The temperature was in the mid-eighties, and people were hot, tired, and thirsty.

He went in and talked to the postmaster and one of the inspectors, explaining the problem, and obtained approval for his next move. He then went outside and said in Spanish, "If you are pregnant or a senior citizen, you can move to the head of the line." There again was spontaneous applause by every-one.

After the line was reorganized, the troops arranged for drinking water to be available for anyone who needed it. Tension dropped off, and people became more friendly with the troops and each other.

Soldiers from 3-144th Field Artillery in Van Nuys were assigned to protect the Crenshaw Imperial Plaza on the corner of Imperial Highway and Crenshaw Boulevard. This is a very large shopping center with a Von's Supermarket. The Von's there had their butchers out with butcher knives protecting their store the night before, so they were happy to see the Guardsmen arrive.

That morning the artillerymen saw problems begin to develop at a "Checks Cashed" business on Crenshaw just north of the big shopping center. The small business did more than cash checks, also serving as a mailing address and a source of food stamps. About five hundred people were lined up to pick up their checks when the business ran out of money. The people quickly became unruly, so the police were called. They arrived, but more important was the arrival of an Arrowhead Water Company truck on that very hot day, complete with cups. The water was passed out, and the tense situation was defused.

Specialist Scott Traylor of 3-144th, a salesman for a family health plan, was on duty securing the Crenshaw Imperial Plaza. A young black in his early twenties started chatting with Traylor. He then offered Traylor two thousand dollars for his M-16 rifle, and showed him the color of his cash. Traylor saw fifty dollar bills, and it was obvious the man was serious, but he didn't take the man up on his offer.

The Korean Peace March that was called for early in the morning was expected to have only a couple of thousand marchers. They gathered at Ardmore Park at about 11:00 a.m., coming from as far away as San Diego. The numbers swelled rapidly, reaching at least 25,000 at one point. They included men and women of all ages, with some in traditional dress. The marchers carried signs ranging from those urging peace and understanding, to others requesting compensation for damages. Other marchers carried brooms and garbage bags, and fell out of ranks to help merchants clean up debris along the march route.

Sergeant David P. Tooley, a Guardsman from 3-185th Armor Battalion in San Diego, was posted along the march route. He was standing beside a young black teenager, and remembers the parade vividly, including one of the rare incidents that marred a very special event. "It was spectacular, reminding me of the peace marches of the sixties. It was peaceable, but one of the older Korean gentlemen started shouting degrading racial remarks at the black teenager. He (the teenager) started to move forward, but I put my hand on his shoulder, telling him not to take it personally. About that time, several people (marchers) grabbed the old guy and quieted him down.

"I explained to the teenager about the peace marches of the sixties, pointing out that there are people like that (the old man shouting racial remarks) in all races. We talked it out, and got to kind of understand each other a little bit."

Other Guardsmen marched with the parade to provide security. They were surprised by the sheer size of the crowd, and pleased by the warmth and peaceful attitude of almost all marchers and onlookers. The parade route covered literally miles, and turned out to be one of the more pleasant missions given to the soldiers. One of the few other untoward incidents during the march involved a sergeant who kept his eye on tall buildings along the route. Walking near the front of the parade, he noticed a man yelling racial epithets out of a third or fourth floor window. When it appeared as though he was getting ready to throw something, the sergeant told an LAPD officer. The police quickly got there to ensure no problem resulted.

The phones in the various Emergency Operations Centers began to hum as midday approached. The LAPD EOC was notified at 10:34 a.m. that a small group of Revolutionary Communist Party members were demonstrating at 6th and Parkview. At 11:05 a.m., about thirty members of the Revolutionary Communist Party were reported demonstrating in front of Parker Center. Gang members at 11:20 a.m. were reported to be filling beer bottles with gasoline for Molotov cocktails they evidently intended to throw at buses. At 1:30 p.m., about 100-150 skinheads were demonstrating between Second and Third Streets on Broadway, near the Civic Center and the L. A. Times Buildings.

The police department became concerned about the Gay Rights activists conducting a sit-in right in front of the L.A. Times Buildings on Broadway. There were lots of police, including mutual aid in the form of Riverside County Sheriff's deputies and California Highway Patrolmen. The media was there in considerable numbers, both on the ground and in helicopters overhead.

The Gay Rights activists had grown to about a hundred demonstrators, but about twice that many skinheads had headed that way to counterdemonstrate. The situation escalated, especially upon arrival of more media. Police arrested some of the demonstrators from both contingents, putting them on separate buses. They found a lot of handguns and knives, especially on the skinheads, as they searched the arrestees.

Second Lieutenant Frank E. Lum and his second platoon of the 649th Military Police Company were assisting the law enforcement officers. They set up road blocks at the four intersections in the area. People started harassing the police as they were arresting the lawbreakers, so Lieutenant Lum sent his last five people across to keep the people back. As he described it, "Two of them (my soldiers) were females, about five foot two, trying to stop twenty five to thirty people. A lot of TV cameras came down there, so that provoked the people even more in trying to get through my (five soldiers) people. I quickly got on the radio to the 40th Division, asking them to send me some infantry guys.

"They quickly sent me the one full squad they had available (in that area), coming down the street looking 'high speed.'" The Guardsmen were from 3-160th Infantry, and had been performing duties in the Civic Center. They came in a wedge formation down Broadway. This was done as a show of force, not to disperse any crowd. Lum continued, "They joined with my soldiers as the crowd built up to forty to forty-five people. And they were getting closer and closer. In particular, they were getting within arm distance of (the female soldiers). They were making racial comments...she is a very short Mexican girl. It looked like it was getting out of control, and law enforcement couldn't give me any help on that side of the street."

Sergeant Carvel Gay, owner of a towing business, had arrived with the 3-160th troops, and described the quick confrontation that followed. "The adrenaline was really flowing. We were given the order to fix bayonets...(we didn't have them fixed long, when an officer) quickly told us to unfix the bayonets. However, the protesters had already backed off." The troops stayed there about half an hour, then returned to the Hall of Justice.

About noon, a caravan of about twenty automobiles carrying Revolutionary Communist Party members paraded by the

150

troops at the Sports Arena and Coliseum. They flashed signs, threw out flyers, gave troops "the finger" and otherwise taunted the troops as they drove by.

One of the caravan of Revolutionary Communist Party members on MLK Boulevard harassing troops guarding the Sports Arena and Coliseum. (Photo Courtesy SFC Toby Bogges)

The caravan stopped right in front of the Hoover Street entrance to the Sports Arena. The Communists kicked their doors open, and jumped out with their flags on sticks. The troops were tired, on edge, and didn't like being trifled with.

The ominous sound of a bunch of rifle bolts being slammed home could be heard for some distance. The Communists immediately jumped back in their cars and took off in a hurry. Soldiers were increasingly finding out how effective a rifle's "lock and load" sound can be.

Troops from F Battery (target acquisition radar), 144th Field Artillery, were assigned as security for Raintree Plaza in Culver City. Sergeant Chris Wilson and Specialist Joe Rodriguez were posted in front of an Alpha Beta market near the Maytime entrance of the shopping center. Specialist Rodriguez was left alone a minute when Sergeant Wilson went around the corner to where their equipment was stored to get water.

While Rodriguez was alone, an Hispanic gangbanger rode up to him on his blue mountain bicycle. Dressed in green khaki pants, and a shirt, he was heavily tattooed on his neck, chest and arm. The gangbanger asked several questions about Rodriguez's weapon, and wanted to know whether it was loaded or not. When the gangbanger persisted, Rodriguez showed him a loaded clip. The gangbanger made it clear he was going to take the weapon from Rodriguez, and asked him to hand over his M-16 rifle. Rodriguez refused, so the gangbanger told Rodriguez, "How about you saying I took it from you, or beat you up?"

In the meantime, Sergeant Wilson had returned and was listening to the dialogue. As the gangbanger got more assertive, Wilson locked and loaded his own weapon and aimed it at the gangbanger. The gangbanger smiled...Wilson didn't. The 27-year-old gangbanger mumbled something in Spanish, got on his bicycle and rode a short distance away. There he pulled out what appeared to be a .25 calibre pistol. Rodriguez then also chambered a round in his own weapon. When the gangbanger saw that, he quickly rode his bicycle northbound towards Jefferson Boulevard.

Sergeant Wilson immediately notified the Culver City police. They shortly tracked the gangbanger down and arrested him about a mile away.

The Governor and his staff were putting in another busy day in Los Angeles, even though they had originally planned to return to Sacramento on Saturday morning. When they got up early in the morning, the Governor had changed his mind, so there was some scrambling to see who would stay, and who would go back to Sacramento. One participant described the group as "God-awful tired," but they headed out for another round of meetings and telephone conference calls with politicians, civic leaders, law enforcement officers and military commanders.

Among the miscellaneous policy issues that were decided in a series of meetings and calls between various officials:

1. The field force deployments would be lightened during the day, and strengthened during the hours of darkness. This would also include military deployments, starting on Monday.

2. There would be four officers or deputies in every squad car patrolling in the mall areas.

3. Current levels of EOC manning would continue at least until Wednesday.

4. Federal law enforcement personnel would return to regular duties on Sunday, May 3rd.

5. The State Office of Emergency Services assumed responsibility for ordering all law enforcement mutual aid with the exception of Orange and Kern Counties.

The Governor had noted in his discussions with mayors, business leaders and minority representatives that they all wanted the military presence to remain. The Sheriff wanted to quickly reduce the military visibility and demonstrate a "sense of normalcy" during the day, with an increased visibility at night. Chief Gates wanted to keep a military presence longer.

Unfortunately, two key players were too often omitted from some of these policy meetings and conferences. One was Robert S. Mueller III. He was an Assistant Attorney General sent out from Washington as the Senior Civilian Representative of the Attorney General, and represented the President regarding policy aspects of the use of federal forces. The other individual was Oliver "Buck" Revell, Special-Agent-in-Charge of the Federal Bureau of Investigation in Dallas, Texas. He was sent out to coordinate operational aspects of federal law enforcement deployments, including some F.B.I. SWAT teams, assisting in the effort.

It was about this time that some senior leaders recognized that they needed a "Super Emergency Operations Center" where key players could meet and make strategic policy decisions. A single geographical location for these kinds of meetings never was established. Military commanders especially felt the void, being used to relatively well defined hierarchical chains of command. There also wasn't a central clearing house to assist the press and issue press releases.

The Governor joined us for a short meeting on Saturday in our conference room at Los Alamitos. In attendance besides the Governor and I were Dr. Andrews, Generals Covault, Hernandez, and Stewart; representatives from LAPD and the Sheriff's Office, and several colonels and security officers.

154

The Governor was concerned about exposure to snipers and drive-by shootings. We pointed out that our only real defense was disciplined behavior of the troops. They had to perform as trained, and wear their flak vests and helmets. There was no way to avoid all vulnerabilities while we had troops in the streets. Interestingly, the law enforcement officers pointed out that they almost never catch snipers immediately after the act. If snipers are caught, it is only following good investigative work.

The Sheriff's representative, Commander Paul Myron, pointed out how pleased Sheriff Block was with responsiveness of the National Guard. Dick Andrews wanted to know what would happen if troops need help. We described our Quick Reaction Forces, capable of being rapidly flown in by helicopter anywhere in the county, day or night.

The only bullet to strike a soldier or marine in Los Angeles County was self inflicted on Saturday. A young private in 1-149th Armor Battalion of Salinas accidentally discharged his pistol when clearing (emptying) it. This, unfortunately, is a comparatively common occurrence when clearing automatic pistols. In fact, that is why every police station has a "clearing barrel" near the entrance. He shot himself in the leg, but it turned out to be a comparatively minor flesh wound.

About 4:15 p.m., the Marines became the first active duty federal troops to hit the streets as they arrived in Compton. Command Sergeant Major Bob Delaney and Master Sergeant Donald Fox of 4-160th Infantry, are both with the Santa Ana Police Department when not soldiering as Guardsmen. They pointed out to their Marine counterparts that they were making history together. They told the Marines, "This is the first time in history that the Army took the ground, and then turned it

155

over to the Marines to hold." The Marine Sergeant Major wasn't amused, but it is a story that spread around extraordinarily fast.

General Hernandez was surprised by the backlash from his own troops he began to feel as more and more of the Guardsmen were replaced by federal troops. None of the military commanders had been given a clue regarding the possibility that it would be weeks before the Guardsmen would be released so they could return homes to school or jobs. However, the undercommitted Guardsmen didn't like being replaced by other military forces. It became especially difficult when they were sent back to armories and staging areas to sit around without any missions to perform. It grew worse as time went by.

On Friday, Mayor Tom Bradley was beginning to think about the major rebuilding efforts that would be required in South Central Los Angeles. He was particularly hoping to persuade Peter V. Ueberroth to agree to spearhead those rebuilding efforts. Ueberroth is famous for organizing the financially successful Los Angeles Olympics in 1984, and has a proven track record. The Mayor reached him on Ueberroth's car phone as he was on his way home in Orange County. They agreed to meet Saturday in City Hall.

They met in the Mayor's office on Saturday, and Ueberroth agreed to head up what came to be called "Rebuild Los Angeles" (or R.L.A.). Mayor Bradley held a press conference shortly after 5:00 p.m. on Saturday. He announced Ueberroth's appointment and described briefly what they hoped R.L.A. would accomplish. The mission statement for R.L.A.:

To bring together the positive power and resources of the communities, government, and private sector to achieve change by creating new jobs, economic opportunities, and

156

pride in the long-neglected areas of our greater Los Angeles Basin.

Bradley also announced that President Bush had declared Los Angeles a disaster area, making the area eligible for federal disaster relief.

Troops were becoming more acclimated to the scattered incidents of harassment. Troops from 1-185th Armor Battalion were posted near the ABC Market on the corner of Vernon and Vermont. An old primer gray Chevy Malibu with two gang-bangers in it stopped right in the street, holding up traffic. One of the gangbangers, dressed in Levis, black jacket, and with a red bandana around his head (typical dress of a Blood), got out of the car with an Uzi submachine gun. He made signs with his fingers, and then threatened to come back that night and kill Guardsmen.

The above behavior was not unusual. Police had told Guardsmen to expect such behavior, and recommended troops not do anything unless a weapon was aimed directly at them. In this case, the leader of the twenty or so Guardsmen at the corner told his troops, "If he aims that (Uzi) at you, cancel his Christmas!"

An occurrence that *was* unusual occurred at the same corner, in the middle of the morning, and involved the battalion's chaplain. Captain Bob Field was standing in the parking lot, minding his own business, when a car with a female passenger stopped close to him. When she had his eye, she suddenly raised her blouse, exposing the chaplain to what Guardsmen in the area described as "an impressive pair of 38's!" Without a change of expression, she dropped her blouse and they drove off. The troops delight in telling this story about the nonplused chaplain.

157

Right up the street at Vernon and Figueroa was another company from the same battalion. A gangbanger with his young son pulled his car up next to the Ralph's Supermarket. They both got out of the car, the father carrying a "boom box." He played the tape "Cop Killer" and then got back into his car and left. The only thing that bothered the troops was the gangbanger involving his young son. The troops couldn't tell whether he was showing off in front of his son, teaching his son some obscure lesson, or merely babysitting and hadn't thought about the impact his behavior would have on his youngster.

The media continued to comment about delays in deploying troops on Thursday, talking about the lack of ammunition. It was obvious that many people on the street didn't think the Guardsmen had ammunition. Troops were constantly being questioned on the subject. Sometimes they were hassled by gangbangers, at other times the gangs sent their youngest members or wannabees to scout out the situation.

First Lieutenant Brian L. Hecht of 2-159th Infantry had troops at the corner of Compton and Central in the city of Compton. His story was typical. "We had groups of four or five kids between the ages of eight and twelve coming up and questioning our soldiers. They would say things like 'we've got a bounty on your heads,' and 'you won't live to see tomorrow.' They also said 'we know you don't have any ammo.' One of the sergeants pulled out a magazine and showed the cartridges to the kids and said, 'we're ready and waiting.' We had several incidents like this, Saturday and Sunday (during the day)."

A gangbanger came up to Master Sergeant Jim Sexton and said, "All you guys have got is 'dummy rounds' for that gun." Sexton responded, "We're saving them for dummies just like you!"

158

Intelligence continued to flow through the EOCs for evaluation and dissemination. An informant said that gangs from the area of 90th Street and Compton planned to loot the Carson Mall. Carson had been singled out because of the jewelry stores in that shopping center, and because no National Guard troops were on duty there. The solution was simple. National Guardsmen from 4-160th Infantry were immediately sent.

It was reported that the Rollin' 60s Gang intended to make false 911 calls and then catch police officers that responded in drive-by shootings. It was reported there were fifteen or twenty gangbangers making menacing gestures and threatening to climb the fence at Jefferson Boulevard and Kinston Avenue. An anonymous source reported a plot to torch the International Shopping Center at 8th Street and Alvarado. The media reported that Crips and Bloods they interviewed said they planned a drive-by shooting Saturday night, stating, "We are the Army." This, coupled with numerous intelligence reports that gangs intended to target military personnel, increased tensions.

Strategy meeting. Governor right foreground, then
counterclockwise around the table, the Director of Emergency
Services, the Adjutant General, and the author.
(*Photo: Author's Collection*)

CHAPTER EIGHT

Saturday, May 2nd, 1992
THE FOURTH NIGHT

The unit assigned to protect the small shopping centers and area around the intersection of Vernon and Figueroa dispatched a twenty man foot patrol as it started to grow dark. They headed west to Hoover Street, notorious gang territory (see Hoover Crips in Appendix 3), and then south down past 57th Street. They were thankful they hadn't scrimped on manpower as they patrolled through these tough neighborhoods in a show of force.

The patrol passed a group of forty or so gangbangers hanging around one house. The gangbangers made no effort to conceal their weapons. They had AK-47 assault rifles, and pistols in their pockets with the pistol butts sticking out. Radio scanners were blasting from inside the house as they monitored various police calls. As the patrol passed through, about ten or twelve of the gangbangers followed along, verbally accosting the soldiers:

"Get the f--- out of here!

"F--- you, white boy!

"When night comes, you mother f---ers are going to die!

"Hey nigger, what you doin' with those white guys?"

Our black soldiers took a lot of verbal abuse, which they generally tried to ignore. The patrol finished their route, covering about two miles, and then reported to police. When they told the police about the gang house with the scanners and weapons, the police acknowledged they knew the house very well. However, they also said they didn't have enough police manpower to go into places like that.

One of the two Marine Battalions arrived in Long Beach to relieve the 270th Military Police Company. They had been given specific guidance that there were to be no deployments smaller than a platoon. As a result, the incoming battalion could not cover nearly as much territory as the outgoing much smaller company, even though the situation had stabilized and was much quieter.

The riots were over, but the situation had not returned to normal. The term "normal" must be used advisedly, because so many parts of the county are dangerous during the best of times. There were a lot of fires that continued to smoulder, with some still burning. As a result, there was still smoke and the smell of burning in the air. There were also the sounds of shooting off in the distance from the sporadic gunfire that is endemic to South Central Los Angeles. The normal utilities services and garbage pickup had been suspended, so the garbage cans and dumpsters were really beginning to stink. There also was an occasional dead cat or other animal left lying around.

The curfew was still in effect, and generally being obeyed. There were military vehicles and lots of law enforcement sedans out. An occasional siren could be heard, but nothing like the constant screaming of sirens the first two days and nights. Tension increased as full darkness settled in. Soldiers particularly felt vulnerable then, as it was very difficult to see possible threats in the deep shadows. Cars occasionally drove by, sometimes with their lights out, which also made the troops jumpy. They felt very exposed, with too many alleys, shrubs and other spots where a sniper could conceal himself. In addition, the soldiers had not yet adjusted to reverse sleep cycles, finding it difficult to get used to nocturnal duty shifts.

When the curfew was in effect, the street people became especially obvious. The troops quickly became sensitive to the fact that a good many of the homeless simply have no place to go, so they let them "do their thing" as long as they didn't create problems. Each street person seemed to have their own special spot. For instance, one lady parked her shopping cart right in the middle of a vacant lot, and went to sleep with her two dogs providing security. They would bark long and loud if anyone got too close to her.

The hookers suddenly found themselves at a huge disadvantage. Their customers were all off the street, so the soldiers suddenly began to look increasingly attractive. They were finding no takers, so they tried different approaches. A couple of them told some of our troops from San Diego "We're sure happy you guys are here...we'll do anything to make your stay more comfortable. No charge!" Whether it was good discipline or good sense, no one seemed disposed to take them up on the offer. Master Sergeant Greg Welch of the Air National Guard was driving around in Compton visiting his Security Police securing various utilities when he stopped two hookers walking down East Compton Boulevard. He asked them where they were going, and they said they were going to visit the soldiers. Welch said "I don't think so," and sent them on their way. After a night or two, most of the hookers also decided to stay home.

Some soldiers were guarding the police station on 108th Street near Main when a man ignored the troop's order to halt.

Two police officers quickly came out of the station and carefully herded the man down the street. When the soldiers asked the police why they didn't arrest him, they said he was so "wired" (up tight) he probably would have exploded if they had so much as touched him.

First Lieutenant Erskine L. Levi Jr. of 1-18th Cavalry is a student at Cal Poly in Pomona. He is a former active duty military policeman, and also has civilian police experience. He was concerned most of all that his troops might shoot someone in error. "We did 'draw down' on people in the middle of the night. There were drunks and others doing dumb things." The streets were populated with quite a few derelicts who had mental problems, and others were high on drugs or alcohol. They sometimes would behave very strangely, so the troops had to exercise a great deal of restraint to avoid accidentally injuring an innocent person.

Some Guardsmen from 2-185th Armor were posted at an intersection when an old brown Monte Carlo came driving by. The gangbangers in it yelled taunts while waving an AK-47 in the air. About a block away they shot an entire magazine of ammunition into the air, scattering spent shell casings all over the street.

At that time, Sergeants Robert Matey and Duane Neynes were part of a special response squad made up of present or former police officers from the same tank battalion. They were patrolling in a Hummer north up Crenshaw Boulevard when an (another?) old brown Monte Carlo came up from their rear, obviously trying to catch up. As it started to pull up on the left beside the Hummer, all six soldiers in the Hummer went on full alert.

164

The window on the passenger side of the Monte Carlo started to roll down, and a female sitting in that seat started bending down to get something heavy. Sergeant Matey yelled, "She's reaching, she's reaching!" Everyone in the Hummer locked and loaded their weapon. It turned out she was coming up with an old fashioned video camera, complete with a pistol grip like a weapon. "It was a very tense moment as her eyes got real wide when she observed our reaction." She was no more tense than the Guardsmen, who breathed a huge sigh of relief. A couple of them shook as the adrenaline rush settled down and they reflected on how close they had come to shooting an innocent woman.

The troops' restraint was constantly being tested. In Compton, the 2-159th Infantry from San Jose had their fire discipline and restraint severely tested. The soldiers locked and loaded their weapons when a drunk driver ran through their checkpoint, narrowly missing them, and then ran right into a trash dumpster. This almost exactly duplicated an incident during the Watts riots when Guardsmen killed at least one person. In this case, like so many others during the 1992 riots, not a shot was fired.

On Vermont Boulevard, Guardsmen were walking their posts when some gangbangers fired a rifle in their direction, hitting a street sign above their heads. The rifle turned out to be a pellet gun. They did not return the fire.

Later Saturday night, troops from 2-159th Infantry were posted on Alameda Street just north of the Redondo Beach Freeway, State Route 91. Suddenly a car on Alameda weaved back and forth just like it was trying to run our soldiers down. The soldiers locked and loaded, then watched the car run right up onto a lawn. It turned out that a lady who works late simply

165

fell asleep at the wheel. When she woke up, bouncing over the curb, she was even more scared than the troops.

Private First Class Richard M. Nunez of the 132nd Engineer Battalion is a truck driver from Redlands. He was sent to Hoover Street to guard a church. He noted the transition they went through going from engineers to infantrymen. He said, "it was very different. It was the first time we ever had live ammunition while on the streets (in a city). Normally we only have live ammunition under very controlled circumstances, like on ranges. On the streets, we got very serious quickly." He admitted he was scared a couple of times. "They would drive by, sometimes without their lights on...sometimes taunting. They would say such things as 'we're going to kill you mother-f---ers.' Or they would say 'f--- the police,' or 'f--- the Army'...things like that. Other times they would just zoom by yelling at us, sometimes waving weapons in the air...but (they) didn't aim at us."

First Sergeant John B. Wood of 2-144th Field Artillery was walking the perimeter of their area near the Compton Civic Center with one of his squad leaders. Suddenly they heard the roar of a car engine. They looked up the street, and saw an orange Pinto Station Wagon come flying across what is called the "Blue Line," a modern light rail system serving the area. The car, going extremely fast, was literally airborne before it hit hard on the near side of the tracks with sparks flying. It kept coming towards the troops.

The troops kneeled down into firing positions, oriented towards the oncoming vehicle. First Sergeant Wood thought "Oh s---, this is it!" They could see a black female driving with a man in the passenger seat as they finally halted in front of the troops. Wood yelled "Hey, what are you doing?" There was a

166

long pause as the passenger looked at the driver, and she looked at him, obviously trying to figure out what would be an acceptable answer. Then, as Wood described it, "She leaned forward and looked at us. Finally she says 'I'm having a baby...I'm on my way to the hospital!' I said 'get out of here,' laughing as she drove off. That was real B.S.! Nights during the curfew were bizarre!"

The federal troops committed to the streets of South Central Los Angeles later had every reason to feel they were committed into a "hot zone," as almost all of them were unfamiliar with the area. The shots fired intermittently during the night, the taunts and sign flashing from gangbangers, all were typical of any night in South Central. However, the individual federal soldier or marine on a darkened street, seeing nothing but hostile faces at night (law-abiding people were off the streets), definitely felt threatened. They were feeling, although to a lesser degree, the tension experienced by their National Guard brethren earlier during the first several days.

There was a sizeable operation set up at the Washington High School on 108th Street and Normandie. There were about twenty fire units there, LAPD, the Sheriff's Department, California Highway Patrolmen, and a company from 4-160th Infantry. There were about two hundred vehicles total. The fire engines would be dispatched on missions, fight the fires, and then return to the back of the queue. The highway patrolmen had the escort mission for fire engines, but both the highway patrolmen and firemen felt more comfortable with riflemen along to suppress sniper fire. The Guardsmen therefore agreed to dispatch a truck or Hummer with the fire engines, and set up a perimeter while the fires were being fought.

The unit also provided security for the Lennox Sheriff's Station, not far from the Washington High School. Two Guardsmen were posted at a barricade set up on Acacia Avenue where it runs into Lennox Boulevard in front of the sheriff's station. They heard and then saw a vehicle tearing north up Acacia Avenue. At a considerable distance behind it they could see red lights chasing the vehicle. As it came closer, they could see it was a white van, and it also became clear that the driver intended to force his way through the barricade. Sergeant Daniel R. Alaniz warned his partner, and when it became apparent the van wasn't going to stop, fired a warning shot into the asphalt in front of the van. His partner did the same, and the van screeched to a halt.

They could see two men in the front of the van as a deputy sheriff from the Sheriff's Station came running out with a bullhorn. He yelled in Spanish and English for them to keep their hands up where they could be seen. They then had them dismount, searched them and found two handguns. The van was full of stolen property. The two rounds fired by these soldiers were the first two rounds "fired in anger" by the military.

The pace begin to pick up, typical for a Saturday night, even though the curfew was in effect. The LAPD reported officers were receiving fire from the Imperial Courts housing projects. It was also reported that gangs in Hawaiian Gardens were rumored to be planning to "shoot it out" with gangs from Artesia in El Dorado Park, a very large park (over two miles in length) along the border of Los Angeles and Orange Counties. A radio station had three death threats phoned in, threatening to kill employees if they didn't start reporting "the truth" about the Rodney King case. A large structure fire was reported at about 9:00 p.m. in businesses at Indiana Street and Olympic Boulevard.

There was a market at the University Village Mall on 32nd Street and Hoover just north of the Coliseum and the University of Southern California. This market had some troops from the cavalry squadron guarding it because it was one of the few markets in the area still open for business during the day. Intelligence had been received that gangs had targeted the market.

About 10:00 p.m. or so, a van very slowly cruised up and down the street about three times in front of the shopping center. One individual got out of the car and approached the parking lot. He then got back in the van and moved it a little further. The vehicle stopped again and the man got out to open the rear. Staff Sergeant Salvador Ramos (a State Department of Corrections officer and Vietnam veteran) advanced with his radioman and told the man to freeze. The rest of his squad then surrounded the vehicle.

Sergeant Ramos had the occupants of the vehicle dismount. The occupants tried to convince the Guardsmen they were college students, from U.S.C. across the street, doing a documentary on the riots. The police quickly got there and found a 10" Bowie knife, a .38 caliber revolver, and a .45 caliber automatic. They took the "students" away.

Colonel Bob Brandt was out visiting troops. He had heard about gangs targeting that same University Village Mall, so decided to visit the troops there. When Colonel Brandt arrived, he saw that the shopping center was completely dark, and there were four or five California Highway Patrol cars at Fire Station #15 on one edge of the mall. The troops had placed bundles of compressed cardboard around the perimeter of the parking lot,

169

but it was very difficult to see them. In fact, when he first got there, Colonel Brandt thought the shopping center was deserted. When Brandt asked the troops why they had the lights out, they said they didn't want to be good targets, and the CHP was concerned about drive-by shootings.

Colonel Brandt explained to the unit commander that the darkened shopping center might be good in combat, but this situation was different. The darkness was an invitation to loot, and the Guard was not there to entrap people. They turned the lights on, even though the highway patrolmen weren't happy with that, and moved the barricades back next to the buildings. Brandt then took the cavalryman across the street, and they looked back at the shopping center from the "enemy's" viewpoint. It was clearly much better. At the very least, if the troopers had a sizeable confrontation, they wouldn't have then had to retreat all the way across an open parking lot. In addition, no one could get close to them without crossing a well lit parking lot.

Troops did occasionally make mistakes they later regretted. One occurred in the university area. A platoon heard gunfire, and thought they had identified the apartment building that was the source of the problem. The troops emptied the building, but it was quickly apparent that the building contained ordinary folks, primarily Hispanic. The occupants didn't seem to bear the troops any ill will, but the troops nonetheless felt bad about the episode. The next morning the troops bought what they called "goodies," returned to the apartment building, and gave them to the people while again apologizing for the error.

Undersheriff Edmonds had phoned earlier in the evening, inviting Command Sergeant Major Jim Maxey and I on what is commonly called a "ride-along." He also asked us to invite

Major General Covault, and suggested we meet at the Carson Sheriff's Station. When I talking to General Covault's staff, I found he had been invited on a ride-along with Chief Gates, so I asked Brigadier General Bill Stewart to join us.

Bill Stewart and I got in the back of the Undersheriff's sedan, while Command Sergeant Major Maxey rode in the chase car that followed. We then covered a large part of the affected area, seeing it from a law enforcement perspective. Communications were conducted by both radio and telephone. Radio calls were being monitored over the radio, although Edmonds would occasionally be called on his beeper. He would then stop to use a public rather than a cellular phone for security reasons.

Large parts of the city were still without electricity, the city's Department of Water and Power having over 12,000 customers still without power on Saturday night. In some particularly dangerous situations, officers on the ground would wait until a helicopter illuminated the scene from the air. In one neighborhood, the only light came from an automobile that had been set on fire in the middle of an intersection. One of the stops we made was at the Firestone Sheriff's Station. There we found that literally hundreds of scofflaws had already been or were in the process of being arrested.

While cruising the area, we heard orders being broadcast to put federal agents in the cars. The reaction from various sheriff deputies was obvious in the tone of their voices as they responded over the radio. They weren't happy about it.

It was frustrating for both the police and sheriff deputies. The federal mutual aid personnel came in with very few vehicles, and very little equipment and radios. The various law enforcement agencies in Los Angeles County were already

171

overextended with inadequate equipment and too few properly equipped and undamaged cruisers. Most of the cruisers in the area already had a full load of four officers. As a consequence, many experienced officers from the area were asked to dismount from their vehicles so they could be replaced by federal officers who had been flown in from other cities.

A great many federal officers had been sent by the President to assist in Los Angeles. There were a total of 1717 agents available for duty:

- 346 Federal Marshals
- 109 Immigration and Naturalization Service Agents
- 461 Border Patrolmen
- 89 Alcohol, Tobacco and Firearms Agents
- 310 Bureau of Prisons personnel
- 168 U. S. Customs Agents
- 234 Federal Bureau of Investigation Agents

The Sports Arena and Coliseum were becoming by far the most populous staging area, as well as the most visible. The complex was, by Saturday night, considered "home" for literally thousands of troops. There were many hundreds, if not thousands, of military forces and law enforcement officers there at any one time. Those portions of parking lots not cordoned off for helicopter landing pads were full of police and military vehicles.

An interesting response was elicited when a UH-60 Blackhawk Helicopter with external fuel tanks landed at one of the helipads at the Sports Arena. The military intelligence officers got feedback that some gang members were concerned that the military now had "bombs" on some of their helicopters. They were worried that we might bomb them. It was easy to understand why they might think that way, as the fuel tanks do resemble bombs. But no soldier would purposely drop a bomb in any American city.

Commanders remembered Peter Luukko, the Regional Vice President of the complex, as a great host. The Sports Arena was hardly a hotel, with many troops sleeping between rows of seats on ground cloths sometimes stuck to old coke that had been spilled on the floor. But Mister Luukko offered all he had. The troops particularly remember the showers. Designed for basketball players on the Clippers team, the troops kiddingly said that the shower heads were so high the water was cold by the time it reached them. Mr. Luukko also provided much appreciated offices, telephones, fax machines and other support to the units there.

The Salvation Army on Saturday became a particularly welcome addition to the population at the Sports Arena. They arrived in force, providing hot coffee and food (non-GI). They also provided much-needed soap, razors, socks, and under-clothes. That great support won't be forgotten by the troops, many of whom wrote a check to the Salvation Army after they returned home.

The Sports Arena was becoming home to the troops by Sunday. The troops were settling in, sleeping more and getting better rest each night (or day).

Just prior to midnight, reports came in regarding problems in Pasadena. There were several hundred people causing a disturbance at the corner of Los Robles and Woodbury. A helicopter sent to the scene was hit twice by high powered rifle bullets, with a pilot receiving minor shrapnel injuries to his face and neck. The pilot flew back to the heliport, and returned in another helicopter. He was fired on again, and made an

173

emergency landing based on the mistaken belief he had been hit again.

Police on the ground engaged the perpetrators. One of the police officers had a bullet hit his helmet, causing a concussion. However, the "bad guys" got much the worst of it, including one death. There also were two wounded individuals and four suspects detained, for a total of six arrests. The incident had started at 12:49 a.m., and concluded at 3:26 a.m. The police in Pasadena insisted that this had been a normal Saturday night.

The 2-160th Infantry's Company E was directed to relieve a platoon at the Manchester Post Office. This was in a hostile area where the troops had suffered through a great deal of sporadic sniping and harassment by gangbangers. The incoming company therefore made a tactical insertion, using formations much like a unit in combat prepared to react to hostile fire. They were hopeful that the show of force would prevent additional sniper shooting in their direction. They set up their security and waited, listening to the sporadic gunfire in the area. No gunfire, as best they could tell, was directed at them. There were the occasional taunts from gangbangers, and one lady drove near their position in an erratic manner, but the troops held their fire.

Shortly after midnight, a local television talk show host had a caller phone in who represented himself as an "O.G. (old gangster)," gang member. He warned that because the National Guard was a "real gang" that had invaded their neighborhood, the Crips and Bloods planned to unite and kill Mayor Tom Bradley, Chief Daryl Gates, and Judge Joyce Karlin.

Too many outsiders don't understand how dangerous the streets in some parts of South Central L.A. are. A couple of Army Times reporters had flown out from Virginia. They had rented a new Oldsmobile and were following Colonel Metcalf around as he visited troops from his brigade. They were in the middle of Watts, on 108th Street between Main and Central, about 2:00 a.m. They were getting tired, and wanted to return to their motel in one of the beach communities. Their car was about out of gas, and they naively told Colonel Metcalf they were going to stop and get gas on the way back. They didn't know that there are some places where you don't stop for any reason, period. Colonel Metcalf didn't want to take any chances on their safety, so he directed two of his soldiers to hold the reporters there. He then found a police cruiser to escort them to safety.

Artillerymen from 3-144th Field Artillery stopped a little pickup at the corner of Imperial Highway and Crenshaw Boulevard around 2:00 a.m. The driver said he was from Redondo Beach, and worked for a petroleum company. He looked like he was a teenager, but turned out to be in his thirties. When they asked him what he was doing, he merely responded "Oh, you know." They searched his truck. They found he had taken tennis balls, stuffed them with cherry bombs, put a long fuze in each, and then taped them with electrical tape. He had a Wrist Rocket sling shot to propel the homemade bombs into stores. He also had smaller explosive devices which were very powerful. They exploded one and could feel the concussion all the way across the street. The police arrested the man and took him away.

In the same area, four young gangbangers kept coming around even though the curfew was in effect, and even though they were repeatedly told to go home. When it was clear they were looking for trouble, they were stopped. One of them was heavily tattooed. The police later told the Guardsmen they were Broadway Crips. One gangster had crack cocaine in the battery compartment of his small pager, others had huge wads of money.

Soldiers from the same battalion were posted at the intersection of Century Boulevard and La Brea. The manager of the Viva Market had left it open so the soldiers would have some shelter and access to a rest room. About 2:00 a.m. the troops heard a noise from the area of the dumpster next to the market. When they investigated, they found that someone had jumped into the dumpster, claiming that he was looking for food. This was a particularly fishy cover story, because he was very well dressed, and was carrying both a screwdriver and a very long flashlight. The police decided not to arrest him, pointing out that they already had too many in jail already. They only had room to arrest serious criminals.

Staff Sergeant Robert S. Thompson of 3-185th Armor in San Diego is an aidman (medic) for the unit and a medical technician in civilian life. He was supporting troops on Western Avenue when his medical skills were put to use. A red Datsun 260Z had smashed in reverse through a cinder block wall. The injured couple inside turned out to be from the West Indies, and had been drinking heavily. Thompson monitored their vital signs until a paramedic arrived a couple of minutes later.

It was about 2:30 in the morning when Thompson and others heard a woman across the street running back and forth yelling and cussing. They went over to see what the problem was, and she led them to two men around the corner that she said were ripping her off. It turned out to be a drug deal gone bad. The police got there very quickly, and found rock cocaine. She obviously was not one of the brightest drug addicts on the streets, and had needle marks on her arm. All three were arrested.

Sergeant Thompson had many street adventures like the two described above. However, like so many others in his battalion, they particularly remember one of their own soldiers. Specialist Cesar Zamora was losing weight during the riots. He also was experiencing stomach cramps. The pain grew worse each day but he refused to be relieved from duty. Finally it got the best of him. After two weeks and losing thirty pounds, the pain finally got so bad he asked to have it checked out. Thompson took him to a hospital. After a series of tests, they eventually diagnosed Zamora's severe cancer of the stomach and liver. He was admitted to the hospital and died in less than a week.

It was a shock to the soldiers to lose someone they knew so well, especially losing him so quickly after sharing the dangers in the streets with him. They saw a lot of death and destruction during the riots, but it struck close to home when they lost one of their own.

Warrant Officer Steven Schrieken is an Intelligence Officer for the 40th Division Headquarters. He went off duty at 2:00 a.m., and decided to stop by a Laundromat he owned in Carson. He headed out on his Honda Goldwing motorcycle, stopping on the way to visit with some marines in the Lucky Supermarket parking lot at the corner of Main and Carson Street in Carson. He found them extremely bored, having seen no action of any kind all night.

Schrieken ended up with his own action after riding the three blocks to his business. As he approached, he saw men going in and out of the liquor store next door. Thieves had attached a chain from a car's bumper to the grate in front of the store, and pulled it off. About fifteen looters had then broken the front window glass, and were hauling merchandise out by the armload. They were all males, from kids up through men in their mid-forties. Schrieken recognized some of them as residents of the Ha' Penny Inn across the street, and there was a trail of bottles and debris across the street to the motel. Some of the looters were his own customers.

Right after Schrieken pulled up, one guy stepped over the front window sill with his arms loaded. Schrieken told him to put everything down and go home. The looter said "Oh, f--- off...you're National Guard, and they won't let you shoot." Another guy came out of the store as Schrieken pulled his personal Smith and Wesson out of his glove box. The second looter was one of his customers. Schrieken pointed his weapon and told them, "You have a choice, either go home or to the hospital." His customer responded, "He'll shoot. He owns the laundromat...we had better leave." Some still came out with their hands full, but they all left. As several of the men got into two cars and left, the rest went across the street to the Ha' Penny Inn.

Schrieken went into the liquor store and searched for the owner's phone number. He had no luck, but phoned 911. The Sheriff's Department responded, but they also were unsuccessful in contacting the owner, so Schrieken decided to camp right there. The Korean owner, In H. Lee, came in about 6:15 a.m., carrying a revolver. He was distressed at the amount of damage that had been done to his store, but thankful it wasn't worse. Lee had put everything into the store since coming to this country a few years ago. He was deeply thankful that Schrieken had saved much of his store, and gave him a big hug.

Mister Lee was missing about a quarter of his inventory. The looters had ripped the videotape out of Lee's security camera, although they hadn't damaged the camera itself. For some reason, the security alarm hadn't gone off. Lee was particularly unhappy because they had taken his television set. He normally watched television, primarily religious programs, when he didn't have customers. When Lee had finished surveying the damage, he wanted to follow the trail of bottles to the Ha' Penny Inn. Schrieken couldn't talk him out of it. However, they couldn't tell which apartments the trails led to, though they did hear a lot of laughing and partying.

A Marine unit came to the Carson Sheriff's Station to relieve the 4-160th Infantry's Company E from Fullerton. This particular National Guard unit had set up in the parking lot across from the Sheriff's Department for the two days they had been there. When they heard the marines were coming, they moved all of their gear to one corner to make space for the incoming troops. The executive officer and first sergeant of the incoming unit came in for a tour and mission orientation. Although the Guardsmen suggested the marines sleep in the same place they had used, the marines made it clear they didn't want to sleep on the asphalt. Instead they chose a grassy knoll on one end of the lot, even though it was very uneven and troops would have to sleep on a slant. The hand-off of missions from the National Guard to the Marine Corps was to occur at one minute after midnight.

Both units were in place when the hand-off occurred. The marines had brought a considerable amount of gear with them, which was laid out with them on the grassy knoll. Both the soldiers and marines were sleeping. First Lieutenant Jeffrey D. Smiley (normally a federal special agent at Vandenburg Air Force Base), Company E's commander, and First Sergeant Jim Brown (vice president of a contracting firm in Buena Park)

179

were sitting in their Hummer shortly after midnight. They suddenly heard screaming from the direction of the marines.

Sprinklers on the grassy knoll, evidently controlled by a timer, had suddenly been triggered. No one was using water that time of night, so the shower heads that popped up were spraying under *great* pressure. Young marines were yelling, cussing, grabbing some of their gear and running for the asphalt. Others were dancing around trying to step on the sprinkler heads to stop the shower, but the force of the water was much too great.

After watching this for a few moments, First Sergeant Brown suggested using traffic cones over the sprinklers to protect the troops. Lieutenant Smiley said "I can't take it any more!" He put three of the orange cones under his arm, and ran across the asphalt and grass yelling "watch this!" He dropped each one on top of a sprinkler. It worked, so the marines quickly followed suit, and finally got the situation under control.

As dawn broke, those awake stole glances at the grassy knoll. Others looked that way as soon as they woke up. As much as anything, all the orange traffic cones scattered around made that knoll look much like a pumpkin patch! It was a sight to behold, and took the tension off of a situation that could have happened to anyone. As the sun came out, uniforms were spread out to dry.

Those of us in a reflective mood noted there had not been anything resembling a riot to quell since Thursday. We now had 6950 troops deployed, not including support troops, with 2730 standing by. All of our soldiers were now engaged in law enforcement missions, not riot control. In that regard, commanders were struck by the fact there were so many criminals

180

obviously still in the streets even though many thousands had already been arrested and remained incarcerated. If troops didn't appreciate the tough job law enforcement had before, they certainly did by now.

The toll for the riots by this time had made the Los Angeles riots of 1992 the deadliest in the nation's history. There were a couple of bodies found in the rubble that involved deaths that had occurred earlier in the riots, so the new totals:

47 Deaths (only two occurred on Saturday)

2,116 Injuries (211 critical)

5,534 Fire responses

8,601 Total arrests (County custodial facilities were near capacity with 23,527 inmates)

3946 LAPD arrests.

2787 LASD arrests.

1868 Other arrests.

*Military Police Hummers in front of famous Grauman's Chinese
Theater on Hollywood Boulevard.
(Photo by SSG Alan Zanger)*

182

CHAPTER NINE

Sunday, May 3, 1992
THE FIFTH DAY

Intelligence Summaries on Sunday morning noted that it appeared as though certain of the gangs had declared a truce. Gang alliances were reported, with some of those gang members wearing white hats. Blue and red bandanas had been found tied together as a symbol of solidarity. Various law enforcement agencies became increasingly apprehensive as reports were received noting that some Crips and Bloods that were normally mortal enemies were seen together. A few of the gangs, having looted gun stores, had a lot of weapons to spare. It was even reported that a Crip gang had given some captured weapons to their rivals as a show of good faith.

Informants tied certain gangs to specific businesses that had been looted. Among others, they mentioned Weatherby's Gun Store, plus the Western Surplus Store and pawn shops near Manchester and Western Avenues. The police found many emptied gun boxes all along 109th Street after those lootings.

Intelligence officers received more reports that parole and probation offices were to be targeted in an effort to destroy records. There were also increasing threats to kill National Guardsmen and white police officers through drive-by shootings and sniper attacks. Some of the reports, as usual, were conflicting. A few hot heads were exhorting fellow gangsters to immediately retaliate against police for such incidents as the recent wounding of three LAPD officers and one suspected "83

183

Gangster" associate during a shoot-out at Manchester and Vermont.

Other gang leaders were counseling restraint, suggesting they would be better off waiting until the curfew was lifted. Their movements and actions would then be much less obvious, covered by the normal activities of innocent people. The military and law enforcement officers could be expected to be less alert when the curfew was lifted, and therefore less of a threat. Gang informants also noted there had been talk about waiting until the military left before retaliating against the police.

The Intelligence Summaries advised that both Friday and Saturday had seen much less activity than the previous Thursday, and in most areas, much less crime than is normal for the region. Troops were nonetheless admonished to constantly remain alert, and reminded of the wide variety of weaponry in the hands of gang members. A variety of scheduled events was included:

-- Former Soviet President Mikhail Gorbechev was scheduled to visit Los Angeles sometime during the day. This ended up being cancelled because of problems in the former Soviet Union, not Los Angeles.

-- Presidential candidates Pat Buchanan and Bill Clinton were both due in town.

-- The Reverend Jesse Jackson had scheduled another full day of visits in the area.

-- The Rapid Transit District planned to reinstate some bus service into the affected area.

-- Los Angeles International Airport phoned the EOC to confirm they were resuming normal operations.

-- The California Highway Patrol intended to reopen the Harbor Freeway (I-110) off ramps at 1:00 p.m.

-- A commemorative Cinco de Mayo march was scheduled for 9:30 a.m. from Belvedere Park to Salazar Park.

-- State Senator Diane Watson scheduled a rally for 2:00 p.m. to demonstrate and march for solidarity and justice.

-- A Black Muslim event, scheduled prior to the riots, was planned for 2:00 p.m. at Muhammad Mosque #27 on Western Avenue. Louis Farrakhan was listed as a possible speaker.

Military chaplains were seen everywhere their troops were deployed. They were available for the soldiers who had problems on the home front, and were often asked to lead troops in a prayer before they went out on patrol, regardless of the day or night. This being Sunday, each battalion's chaplain was making himself available to conduct services any place a group of military men and women could pause for a while. Sometimes this was a parking lot, sometimes a school building or auditorium, sometimes just a street corner.

Chaplain (Captain) Ralph Martinez and Chaplain Candidate (Captain) Steve Sexton had just completed services for their own troops at a high school between territory claimed by the Crips and the Bloods. A Red Cross shelter had been set up there for the homeless and victims of the riots, so the Red Cross leaders asked the chaplains if they would provide services for their charges. The two chaplains obliged with a bilingual service, complete with communion.

The 1-185th Armor Battalion of San Bernardino is served by Chaplain (Captain) Bob Field, and his Chaplain's Assistant, Staff Sergeant Joe Sanders. Sergeant Sanders arranged for a joint service with the Mount Moriah Baptist Church on Figueroa Street. The Reverend Doctor Melvin Wade brought fifty members of his choir from his black church to sing for the

185

soldiers who weren't on duty, about a hundred primarily white and Hispanic soldiers. Both Pastor Wade and Captain Field preached. The choir sang (beautifully, by all accounts). One choir member collapsed while they were singing, and some of the soldiers immediately went for their weapons as the lookouts attempted to locate where the shot came from. Chaplain Field knew that the choir member had merely fainted, and quickly put the soldiers at ease. Finally they all sang the Battle Hymn of the Republic together while soldiers and choir members held hands. This was a very special time.

The services and sing-along were conducted on the parking lot of the Ralph's Supermarket at the corner of Figueroa and Vernon. This was the same corner where the 40th Military Police arrived in the middle of the rioting as the first contingent of National Guard troops on Thursday afternoon. Afterwards Chaplain Field and Sergeant Sanders returned with the pastor and choir to the Mount Moriah Baptist Church. Both of them spoke for a few minutes to the congregation, and expressed their appreciation.

The Carson Sheriff's Station is on Avalon Boulevard in Carson. This is where the Marine unit had gotten so wet the night before. Two days before, community leaders had arranged for a special meal to be shared this Sunday at 10:00 a.m. with the National Guardsmen there. The people of the area brought in a great buffet. The marines were invited to join the Guardsmen, and put the embarrassment of their soaking behind them. They all shared the outstanding food, and the camaraderie that always exists when military men get together, regardless of service. The soldiers and marines were particularly touched by the special warmth and gratitude that had been shown by Carson's people.

186

One of the churches the Reverend Jesse Jackson was scheduled to visit was on the corner of Alondra Boulevard and Central Avenue in Compton. The crowd was too large to fit in the church, it was hot outside, and Jackson was running late. The National Guardsmen from the 2-159th Infantry Battalion were responsible for security at that location, and grew increasingly nervous. This was because the crowd outside grew to several hundred, and had become very restive by the time Jesse Jackson arrived about an hour late.

Reverend Jackson's arrival quickly defused the situation. He was immediately sensitive to the problem, and talked from the church's steps for ten or fifteen minutes to the people who had been waiting outside, before he went inside. He pointed out that the National Guard was not their enemy, but people from their own community protecting the community. He particularly complimented the Guard for their patience and restraint.

Things were are not always so pleasant, and there were incidents to mar otherwise enjoyable interludes. Staff Sergeant Gary Ayala of the 40th Military Police Company remembers one particular incident. The troops were getting used to friendly folks waving at them, as the great majority of people they saw were friendly. Sergeant Ayala remembers driving by a church in the Newton district as a couple came out. The man had a bible in one hand, and started to raise his other hand. Ayala said, "I got ready to return his wave, but he gave us the finger! He said: 'F--- you! Get out of here, whitey. G--damn National Guard!' It certainly caught us off guard..."

A similar incident occurred near the Compton Civic Center. Lots of people were out, and people were waving at the field artillerymen posted there, or giving them a "thumbs up." However, a sergeant described one exception to the norm. "Once a

187

car came by with a little guy, maybe two or three years old, and his mother. He was waving at us, and we were waving back. Then his mother grabbed him and formed his hand so he was giving us the finger." Little happenings like that were not easy to forget.

Two Hummers from the 40th Military Police Company and a police cruiser from the Newton Division were patrolling that area about 10:30 a.m.. They had been asked to back up a Bureau of Alcohol, Tobacco and Firearms officer heading out to pick up looted weapons. They were driving in the area of Jefferson High School when they heard gunshots nearby. They quickly arrived at the scene of an automobile accident at the corner of 41st Street and Hooper Avenue. Two automobiles driven by Hispanic men had an accident. A female in one of the cars was bleeding. It turned out, when all the facts had been sorted out some time later, that the driver of the other car tried to flee the scene, and was restrained by the first driver.

While the second driver was being restrained, a 21-year-old black male from the neighborhood took his money. When the other men in the two automobiles, along with the first driver, tried to stop the thief, the thief pulled a gun and fired several shots. The thief turned out to be a convicted felon who lived very close to the corner of 41st and Hooper.

When the police and soldiers pulled up at the scene, the thief, dressed in a blue and white jogging jacket, took off running. The police repeatedly yelled at him to stop. He turned around once with the pistol in his hand just as he ran around the corner, and fired one round. Two shots were quickly fired by one corporal, and one each by two other military policemen. He threw his weapon away as he ran off, but was quickly captured. They found the weapon after a quick search. The

188

felon fired a total of between six and eight rounds, the Guardsmen fired four. Incredibly, no one was hit.

Specialist David P. Andrews belongs to a Glendale unit of the 3-160th Infantry Battalion. When the riots started he was an Emergency Medical Technician and a nursing student. He is an outstanding soldier, and according to many people, quite a guy. Among other things, for several years he spent his off hours providing medical treatment to homeless youngsters and runaway kids he used to find under freeway overpasses.

Even though he is an infantryman, he was being primarily used as a medic in his unit. He remembers the fires and smoke when they were first committed on Thursday night. He also remembers watching their city burn, and the frustration in not being able to do anything about it. His most vivid memory was being shot at, but that came later.

Some soldiers reported for duty who were sick or injured. One had particularly bad scrapes on his arm that he was trying to conceal. The soldier didn't tell anyone, as he wanted to stay with his squad. He kept his sleeves rolled down over the bandages to conceal the problem. Finally, after five days, the pain got to the point he had to take his problem to Andrews. Unfortunately, by that time it was infected. Andrews described the wound. "His bandages were stuck, so I had to peel back his skin. I finally had no choice but to send him to Daniel Freeman Hospital for treatment."

On Sunday a Hummer was patrolling through the Mission District, loaded with several soldiers from the unit, including Second Lieutenant Peter Strada, Sergeant Carvel Gay, Corporal Ernie Caraza, and Specialist Andrews. As they approached the intersection of 5th and Wall Streets, they saw a body laying in the street.

As they got closer, they got a better look at the situation. There were a lot of street people and what appeared to be gangbangers kind of milling around in the area. A police officer was getting back into his sedan, getting ready to leave. As the Hummer arrived, he got out of his sedan and yelled, "Get out of here! Get out of here!" The Hummer started to go by, but Andrews could see that the man in the street was bleeding, so he asked the driver to stop. He went back to the man and saw that his face and right hand were bleeding.

While Specialist Andrews started treating the man, the Hummer stopped in the crosswalk across the street. The police officer, obviously concerned about the belligerent attitude of the street people in the area, walked up and grabbed the injured man by the shoulders while telling Andrews to grab him by the feet. He started to drag the man, and said "come on, let's throw him on the sidewalk and get out of here!" Andrews said "No, I can't do that. I'm a medic, I'm here...once I start I can't abandon the guy."

Lieutenant Strada jumped out of the Hummer and came over. The police officer was increasingly concerned about the explosive situation, and urged the platoon leader to leave the injured man and get out of the area. The lieutenant looked at Andrews, who insisted "No, we've got him here, let's finish with him!" The driver, Corporal Dave Dillon, radioed for back-up as the police officer did the same.

Specialist Andrews put on rubber gloves, and started to work on the injured man in earnest. Andrews is a large man, and a weight lifter who can bench lift over 300 pounds, and dead lift over 600 pounds. He nonetheless had a very difficult time holding the injured man down, even though he wasn't particularly big, as he tried to stabilize him. The man tore one of Andrew's gloves, so he had to put another pair on.

Specialist David Andrews of 3-160th Infantry ministering to a PCP user after the crowd was dispersed. (Photo courtesy Spec. David Andrews)

They later learned from a friend of the victim that he had been smoking PCP-laced cigarettes (sometimes called "Sherms" by people on the street). Andrews was having a very rough time treating the man at the same time he was holding him down. As Andrews worked on him, the injured man, obviously

191

in pain, yelled "No me mata! No me mata! (Don't kill me! Don't kill me!)." He then yelled "Ayuda me! Ayuda me! (Help me! Help me!)." The crowd seemed to consist primarily of the homeless, winos, and probably a few gang members. They yelled at Andrews to leave him alone, and started to close in around him. Andrews heard bottles breaking in the background, just as Corporal Dillon pulled the Hummer up right beside Andrews and the victim.

Sergeant Gay and the other soldiers dismounted, held their rifles at port arms, and pushed the crowd back while forming a perimeter around Andrews and the injured man. Some of the crowd explained later how the man got hurt. A car had come through the area, and for whatever the reason, some of the people were throwing rocks and bottles at it. The driver got scared, and raced off, but hit the man as he tore up the street.

Specialist Andrews continued to work on the injured man until more police officers and an ambulance showed up. They put the injured man on a gurney and hauled him off to the hospital.

Specialist Andrews is a man who gives a lot of himself to others. He repeatedly demonstrated his courage and humanitarian instincts during the riots. Unfortunately, he was on duty so long during the riots that he lost his standing in the nursing course he was attending with his wife at Pasadena City College. He was required to recycle and repeat the classes a year later.

People generally responded well to National Guardsmen. There was however, a significant exception, and that was people from El Salvador. The reason is obvious, but Guardsmen didn't even think about it until they were faced with a Spanish-speaking individual who was acting very frightened for no apparent reason. Salvadorans were used to being severely harassed and beaten by the Guardia Nacional in El Salvador. A Salvadoran taxi driver in Los Angeles explained it to me rather pungently. "In this country, soldiers do what the President tells them. In El Salvador, the President does what the soldiers tell him." He then, to explain his own fear, related a story about soldiers beating him in his former country for little or no reason.

Guardsmen learned that when a Spanish-speaking person acted very frightened of them, they should quickly get them in the hands of policemen. They would then relax if they were a Salvadoran, and those who acted frightened for no obvious reason almost always were.

The Huntington Park area is heavily Hispanic, including Salvadorans. Elements of 2-144th Field Artillery were posted in the area when a police car came screeching to a halt in front of them (the troops said the police there did everything at top speed). They had four Salvadorans handcuffed in the back seat. They pulled two of them out of the car and brought them up to the Guardsmen. The police then said, "See these guys, these are National Guard troops. You do stupid things like you've been doing...I don't want to shoot you, in fact, I can't shoot you. It takes too much paperwork. These guys here, they don't have to do any paperwork." They put them back in the car and took them away.

The Guardsmen knew that they had just as much, if not more, paperwork to complete if they were involved in a shooting. Anyhow, when they saw one of the policemen later, they asked him what he told the Salvadorans. He explained they were trying to get the Salvadorans to behave without incarcerating them, and said, "I told them to be sure and tell all their friends. They are very scared of the National Guard."

The police were also telling gang members that the National Guard was, in effect, a much, much bigger gang. They felt those were terms the gang members could relate to.

The problems with Salvadorans again surfaced while some troops of the 2-160th Infantry were relaxing at the Sports Arena. Sergeant Jay Clark is a police officer with eighteen years of service with the Porterville Police Department. He ordered some Domino's pizza for his troops. Sergeant Tom Harmon then drove him to the Hoover Street gate to meet the deliveryman. Just about the time he had a hundred dollars worth of pizza carefully balanced in his lap, Second Lieutenant James M. Martin came running over and said that a woman had just asked for help. She had come running up the street saying there was a man with a knife threatening her at her store down Hoover Street.

The lieutenant grabbed two soldiers and jumped in the back of the Hummer. As they sped the block and a half down Hoover to the Mom and Pop Grocery, a police sedan raced after them (the police often did this during the emergency when they thought the military might be responding to some crisis). When the Hummer got there, they did a U-turn and pulled up in front of and just south of the store. The Guardsmen deployed, and Lieutenant Martin and Sergeant Clark started into the store. About that time the police pulled up and asked what was happening. Clark told them "We've got a '4-15' (disturbance in progress) man with a knife." The LAPD officer then said "I think we've got your guy already." He was handcuffed in the back of the sedan.

It turned out that the perpetrator (a Salvadoran) had seen the Guard coming, and hid behind a car. The minute the police car approached, he ran out in the middle of the street in front of

194

the police car. He was waving his arms, with the knife still in his hand, telling them "I surrender! I surrender!" He obviously much preferred being arrested by the police, and told them "I don't want anything to do with the Army guys!" About that time, the lady who owned the business got back, out of breath, and still rather hysterical. The pizza was cold by the time the troops got back to the Sports Arena, but they had another interesting tale to tell their buddies.

A soldier from 1-185th Armor was on Wilshire east of Vermont, not far from the I. Magnin store. He dropped his gear to the concrete, which made a louder noise than he intended. A Salvadoran about fifty yards away freaked out, put his hands on the wall and yelled "Don't shoot! Don't shoot!" When the soldier heard the Salvadoran yell that, he assumed someone else was getting ready to shoot the Salvadoran, and quickly swung around with his rifle to cover whatever problem there was. When the Salvadoran saw that, it unfortunately scared him even more.

Another incident, involving the same battalion, occurred on the corner of Vernon and Vermont. As already pointed out, this is a rough part of town. The soldiers noticed some suspicious activity involving a yellow Cadillac and a light blue Chevy Impala parked next to a building. The Chevy had its trunk open, with a lot of weapons showing. That car pulled out and sped away, while the Cadillac pulled out and stopped right on Vernon. One man got out, only to see about twenty soldiers with weapons pointed right at him. He literally wet his pants. This embarrassed him, but embarrassed the soldiers also. They found one weapon, and sent the men on their way.

Soldiers relating an incident like the above remember them well, but did not see them as funny in any way. If anything, they considered them rather poignant.

The Guardsmen, did however, feel that some other incidents were rather humorous. Artillerymen from 2-144th Field Artillery were getting a little fed up with the constant taunts and signs from gangbangers. Some of them were at a stop light when a car full of gang members pulled up beside them. One of the gangbangers signed the Guardsmen, curling his index finger to about one inch from his thumb, forming a "C." This was typical finger signing for the Crips. A soldier in the back of the Hummer responded with his own taunt for the gangbangers. He said, "Oh, that's too bad...mine's about like this," holding his hands about nine inches apart. The gangbanger looked confused, while the Guardsmen all laughed. Soldiers will be soldiers!

First Lieutenant Jeff Smiley of the 4-160th Infantry clearly remembers a similar incident involving a Ford Torino that pulled up beside their Hummer at a stoplight. A gang member pointed his finger like a pistol at Smiley and said "bang, bang, bang!" Soldiers and marines all over the county remember gangbangers doing this quite often. There was even a rather crude flyer that was widely reproduced and distributed using the phrase "bang, bang, bang". In this case, Smiley turned around to one of his soldiers in the back and said, "Show him what we can do. The soldier pulled both fingers like John Wayne, pointed them at the gangbanger, and went 'rat-tat-tat' like two machine guns. We all laughed and drove off."

This kind of repartee was relatively common until the curfew was over, and law-abiding citizens returned to the streets. The troops then returned to much more professional and circumspect behavior.

Sunday had its share of shooting incidents. Marines suffered one drive-by and two sniper attacks during the day. They didn't return the fire. Every marine was very conscious of the sad experience of the Marine Corps in Beirut in 1983 when over two hundred marines were killed by a terrorist. Even some of the Guardsmen drew parallels between the hardest hit parts of South Central L. A. and Beirut, but that was based more on devastated appearances, smoke, and bullet scarred buildings. In addition, most of the marines were veterans of Desert Storm. They took their duty in Compton and Long Beach very seriously.

Some of the businesses scrambled on Sunday to get ready to reopen the next week. A few, like the Target Mall on Jefferson Boulevard in Culver City, even opened on Sunday. It was quickly very crowded, with wall to wall people. There was considerable cruising by carloads of gang members and wanna-bees, engaging in "staring contests" and other typical gangbanger behavior. Former gangbangers in the Guard units often oriented fellow unit members on how to handle that. In addition, any time gang members started to accumulate, troops would slowly drift their way, whereupon the gang members would leave.

The big Baldwin Hills Crenshaw Mall took longer to open. Right on the edge of gang territory, a large swap meet and a Marie Callendar's Restaurant close to the mall had each been targets of at least two fire bombings by the gangs. The troops cracked down, and caught two groups of at least fifteen people. Those groups included kids, gang members, and complete families. This was particularly difficult for the troops, who didn't have any trouble handling gang members, but they found it very difficult having to detain kids and families.

The large Lucky Store at the Baldwin Hills Mall had a lot to do before reopening. The store had been a particular target of gangbangers for several days, but the troops of 2-185th Armor carefully guarded it until the store reopened on Monday with its own added security. On Sunday several truckloads of perishables were hauled away from Lucky's while four or five truckloads of durable goods were dropped off. Lucky's Western Manager provided the troops with pies and goodies from the deli, and invited the battalion's chaplain in to load a cart up with shaving cream, cigarettes and other items for the troops.

Infantrymen of the 2-159th Infantry were guarding a K-Mart store when a car stopped at 59th and Menlo. Young gangbangers got out and fired several shots in the direction of the Guardsmen with a pistol. Platoon Sergeant Charles D. Culver, a systems analyst in civilian life, described what happened next. "They drove off laughing. We had a couple of guys on the roof, and they watched where they went, which was just a couple of blocks away. We notified the police, and they picked them up. One was 14-years-old, the other was fifteen. The pistol turned out to be a .22 caliber target pistol." They told the police they "just wanted to see if the Guardsmen really had bullets."

The ammunition issue refused to go away. It was being discussed every day in the media by the Governor, his staff, and others. The Governor told David Brinkley on ABC on this day that "Someone's head may very well roll" when discussing the original delay in getting ammunition to the soldiers.

Vikki Vargas of Channel 4 television told her audience "Unlike the National Guards (sic), the Marines have orders to shoot when necessary." One Marine spokesman told an interviewer that the only difference between the National Guard and the Marines was the fact that the Marines had real bullets.

The constant talk about ammunition, interspersed with thoughtless comments like the foregoing, put all of the troops, soldiers and marines alike, at great risk. Civilians rarely could tell the difference between soldiers and marines when they were in their field gear and flak jackets. Troops all over the county were constantly being asked if they really had ammunition. It was clear that a great many gang members did not believe they were fully armed. Others felt that if Guardsmen did have ammunition, they were not permitted to use it. Staff Sergeant Norman Vogel from 2-144th Field Artillery, expressed the feelings of many Guardsmen. He said, "Why did the media say we had no ammunition? That scared our troops, and we were already scared. They (our troops) could pull the trigger in a heartbeat. Noncommissioned officers kept cautioning the soldiers to use restraint."

The situation was complicated by an edict that came down shortly after the federal troops were brought in and all National Guardsmen were federalized. The Joint Task Force changed the Rules of Engagement regarding Arming Orders (shown in Appendix 2). Before federalization, we gave subordinate commanders great latitude regarding Arming Orders. The general guidance was "listen to your law enforcement counterpart, they know the territory and the threat." We had no reason to regret that policy, even though Guardsmen quite often went to a modified AO-5 (Arming Order number five). This involved weapons ready, loaded magazine inserted, round not chambered, safety on, and without bayonet attached. The reason we didn't regret that policy? In the two days prior to federal-

199

ization, the most dangerous period during which the riots were brought under control, Guardsmen didn't fire a round. Not one bullet was fired.

The order out of Joint Task Force-Los Angeles was very specific. It read "The Mission Arming Order Posture is 'AO-1' for all assigned elements. Upgrading of unit's AO requires JTF-LA Commander's approval."

When questioned about it, the JTF-LA leadership explained that order should not be interpreted literally. Common sense was to prevail, and if a higher Arming Order was appropriate, the commander on the scene should so order and then notify higher headquarters. That was all well and good, except that soldiers are trained to specifically obey orders. In addition, staff officers were sent out from JTF-LA to ensure soldiers and marines in the field were all at AO-1 unless specifically authorized another Arming Order.

This revised policy resulted in some heated exchanges out in the streets between National Guard commanders and JTF-LA commanders and staff. We finally met with folks at JTF-LA, who explained again that what the order said was not what they really meant. We pressed for them to revise their order to say what they meant. They promised to do that, but their Staff Judge Advocate officers (military lawyers) were "still working the issue" some days later when the 7th Infantry Division returned to Fort Ord.

Some felt that the order read like it did as what soldiers call a "Cover Your Ass (CYA)" measure just in case someone killed somebody in error. We will probably never know for sure. What was clear was that the change in Arming Orders exacerbated the ammunition issues and placed our troops at even further risk. Before the revised order, gangbangers

200

thought that the Guardsmen might not have ammunition in their weapons, or if they did, they weren't permitted to use it. The revised Arming Orders required Guardsmen to walk the streets without even having magazines in their weapons. If there was any question before whether they could quickly respond to threats, now it was obvious to everyone that they were at a decided disadvantage.

The revised rules were particularly galling to our military police. They have always been permitted to carry loaded weapons, even when no one else is. Besides, as pointed out before, a great many of them have civilian jobs in law enforcement. Some commands only sent out volunteers after this point, not feeling it was appropriate to order their soldiers out under the revised guidelines. Other commands exercised selective indiscipline in the face of what they considered a dumb order that unnecessarily put troops at risk.

Most important of all, the revised Arming Orders may have had just the opposite effect from that which was intended. Remember first of all that there were no significant shooting events until the Arming Order rules were changed. That may have been coincidence, but if so, probably only partially so. The weapons without magazines may have encouraged gang-bangers. On the other hand, the troops certainly felt more vulnerable, and at a time when they were feeling increasingly tired. Did that change their behavior or response? Were troops more inclined to quickly lock and load or shoot when threatened? After all, they didn't know if other soldiers even had a magazine in their weapon. Behavioral scientists may be the only ones who can provide answers to these questions.

It may have been coincidence, but most of the bullets fired by the military would be fired on Sunday night, even though the riots had been brought under control some days before.

CHAPTER TEN

Sunday, May 3, 1992
THE FIFTH NIGHT

By Sunday night, soldiers and marines found themselves engaged exclusively in law enforcement work. There was good reason for this...there simply were no more riots to control. In fact, there hadn't been for a couple of days. However, servicemen were finding out just how dangerous streets can be, especially at night, in a large megalopolis with serious crime problems. They also were finding that their Intelligence Summaries, warning of increased threats of attacks from gangs, were accurate.

At 5:55 p.m., at 71st Street and Compton Avenue near the Firestone Sheriff's Station, marines reported they were fired at by several black males. The marines did not return fire, and there were no injuries or arrests. An hour and a half later, several male blacks in a red and white Chevy Blazer with off road lights on top came by the same intersection. They fired several rounds, again with no hits. Sheriff's deputies found the stolen vehicle abandoned a few blocks away.

At 6:00 p.m., scouts from the 2-160th Infantry reported several shots fired at their location. At about the same time, south of Dodger Stadium, Guardsmen were taunted by four or five Hispanics armed with shotguns and pistols.

At 6:30 p.m. Guardsmen near the intersection of Gage and Western Avenues were threatened by individuals in a compact light blue Celica. They brandished a weapon and said they

would come back and "get them at seven." The troops also
reported that several males in a white Cadillac made threatening
gestures.

*A looting suspect being held by soldiers from the 3rd
Battalion, 160th Infantry of Inglewood, prior to
being searched by police. (40th ID Photo)*

At 6:39 p.m., in the vicinity of 21st Street and Pacific Avenue, four or five persons in a black Ford Ranger harassed marines. A short time later, there was a report of seven or eight unidentified gang members near the Los Angeles Forum brandishing automatic weapons. At 7:00 p.m., Marines from the 1st LAI battalion were fired on from a light blue truck.

There were continued problems and threats emanating from the housing projects. Jordan Downs, Imperial Courts, and Nickerson Gardens are all dangerously gang-ridden housing projects that the police avoid whenever possible. First Lieutenant Jeff Smiley's Company E, 4-160th Infantry had been relieved by marines from the mission at the Carson Sheriff's Station, so they were assigned an area security mission at the Nickerson Gardens Projects on Imperial Highway a half mile east of Wilmington. They were reinforced with some soldiers from the battalion's Scout and Mortar Platoons, giving them about a hundred soldiers total.

First Lieutenant Gary Beechum was one of Smiley's platoon leaders. He was with a group that made a vehicular reconnaissance before it got dark. Beechum, who is black, commented on what they found in Nickerson Gardens. "It was flooded with people, many of whom made comments and taunts. Even the little kids were making gang signs, and pretending they were shooting soldiers. The troops were disturbed by the kids being lost to the gangs, although Nickerson was the only place we saw this." Other troops, did however, see this phenomenon elsewhere.

The members of Beechum's platoon were primarily from Orange County, and had very little experience with street gangs. He had his one soldier who is a former gang member, and very familiar with Nickerson Gardens, orient the others.

205

This really spooked the troops, who were very uncomfortable heading into the dangerous housing projects. They ended up talking it through, making sure each Guardsman was committed to taking care of his buddy. They also made sure each Guardsman thoroughly understood how the platoon was going to handle various gang reactions and threats.

They were particularly concerned about the possibility of hurting innocent people, and repeatedly cautioned each other that their bullets could go right through walls. They were understandably concerned about being shot at from windows or doorways. They had been taught how to react during their training to fight in urban terrain, but that military training assumes that any occupant of a building is enemy.

While they were discussing how they were going to secure Nickerson Gardens, the police officer assigned as liaison to them heard them talking about entering the projects on foot. He told them if they were going in on foot, he was not going in with them. He pointed out that the police were always getting sniped at when they went in the projects, even in vehicles. They convinced the police officer to accompany them by pointing out that never again would the police have so much firepower in support. He went in with them until about 3:00 a.m., but from that time on the troops "soloed."

At about 6:30 p.m., the company deployed as planned into Nickerson Gardens simultaneously from all four corners. Almost immediately there were a series of what they described as "crazy" radio calls, as the gangs tested the Guardsmen to see what they would do. The police advised that a 911 call came in saying that fifteen gang members wearing Los Angeles Raider jackets were coming in with AK-47 assault rifles to kill National Guardsmen. Lieutenant Smiley responded "I don't have enough manpower to handle a big rumble." Within five minutes about a hundred law enforcement officers came rolling in with lights and sirens screaming. They all formed a skirmish line and went through the projects from one side to the other. The Scout Platoon then patrolled on foot through the projects the rest of the night.

First Lieutenant Stephen P. Rowan from Headquarters Company was assisting Company E, along with seven soldiers. They were patrolling the northern perimeter of Nickerson Gardens at approximately 11:00 p.m. when they heard several gunshots close by. They couldn't see the flashes from the weapons being fired, and weren't sure where the shots originated. They quickly got help from one of their partners who was perched on the roof of a church with a night vision scope. The night vision scope helped him spot the individuals who were causing most of the problem, shooting and then running from building to building.

The team called for help, and had two helicopters and several police cars respond within a very short time. Using what soldiers call "bounding over-watch," the Guardsmen then lead the police into the projects while receiving radio guidance from the rooftop regarding reactions by their quarry. They quickly cornered a total of four suspects for the police to arrest.

They could hear shooting about every fifteen minutes somewhere in Watts. In addition, from midnight to about 4:00 a.m., someone in the projects would shoot off a clip load (about twenty rounds) of ammunition on full automatic at least once an hour. It was difficult to tell where the shots were coming from, so First Lieutenant Jeffrey W. Roach put a small team from his first platoon up in another church steeple. The team had a radio and night vision devices. They finally spotted the shooter when he fired off a clip at about 4:00 a.m. They called in a police team, and pointed out the door. The police smashed in the door, arrested the man, and seized his Mac-10 automatic weapon.

Company C of 4-160th Infantry was assigned a similar mission at the Jordan Downs Housing Projects about a half mile east of Jordan High School. Captain Jeffrey M. Bygum, an engineer with an environmental site remediation firm, commanded the unit. His younger brother Matt works for LAPD, and called him on Jeff's personal cellular phone to warn him of the dangers in Jordan Downs. He told Jeff about the threats from snipers on roofs, and the darkness due to bulbs being removed or shot out. Matt described how gangbangers congregate in the projects for meetings and parties, considering the projects gang territory.

Company C got a later start than Company E, so didn't have time to make a leader's reconnaissance before it got dark. The unit, did however, gather up all the night vision devices they could borrow from other units.

They stationed one soldier with a night vision telescope (AN/PPS-5) and a radio in a church steeple to keep tab on the roofs. By the time Captain Bygum had briefed his operations order back to battalion, it was well after dark. The unit was to be on site by 8:00 p.m. Each platoon started from a particular intersection, and branched out from there. The plan called for them to ignite blue chemical lights as they cleared the zone. Any place a soldier saw a blue chemical light (called "chemlites" by the troops), he knew at least two Guardsmen were posted there.

They apprehended and then freed fifteen or twenty persons. Most were women with children going between apartments.

They had one man stabbed by his wife during a marital dispute, but one of the unit's two medics quickly patched him up. Unlike Nickerson Gardens, Jordan Downs ended up being much quieter than they expected. For that matter, it was much quieter than a normal weekend night.

The troops speculated that the police wanted the Guardsmen in the projects as a power play to show the residents that the military could come in at any time and completely shut down the projects. Many people in the projects, during the two days they were there, commented they were happy to see the National Guard there. But it was also quite obvious to the residents that the Guardsmen were not there to stop drug dealing and other such offenses, but merely to keep the peace.

Famous Pico Boulevard, named after the last Mexican Governor of California, runs through the older part of downtown Los Angeles. Pico Boulevard changes character just south of Koreatown. The signs are primarily in Spanish in that almost exclusively Hispanic area of small stores with apartments upstairs. The area normally has a lot of foot traffic during the day, with sidewalk vendors and people selling fruit out of the back of pickup trucks. In the period before and during the riots, the area was claimed by the Playboy Crips. Drug dealing occurred all along the area, day and night. As a result of the riots, there was more than the normal graffiti and broken glass. There was some destruction, looting, and bullet holes in plate glass windows. At night the street was rather dark in places, as street lights had been broken or shot out by the gangbangers to make it more difficult for law enforcement to do their job.

Patrolling along Pico Boulevard was one of the missions given Lieutenant Colonel John Gong's task force from the

CALTRANS parking lot in Little Tokyo. The Guardsmen here, like everywhere else, heard a lot of taunts. According to an officer in the unit, gangbangers said such things as "Nice gun, wait until dark, we'll show you apes! We'll cut you up! You ain't sh--, you don't even have ammo!" Most of the Guardsmen, who were primarily mechanics from the 40th Support Battalion, had heard this type of taunting before.

Victor Rivas was a Playboy Gangster well known along several blocks of Pico Boulevard. He had told some of the National Guardsmen during the afternoon that he was coming back in the evening to kill them. Unlike so many taunters, Rivas was serious.

The Guardsmen were posted along Pico Boulevard to preclude looting, and maintain road closure when the curfew went into effect. They had been expressly warned about drive-by shootings. At about 7:40 p.m., after the curfew was in effect, Rivas came east on Pico Boulevard at a very high rate of speed in his dark blue 1974 Datsun 240Z. The troops were scattered along the street enforcing the curfew when Rivas tried to run them down along the four blocks between Catalina Street and Vermont Avenue. The soldiers were yelling for him to halt when he hit his brakes, reversing his direction with a screeching "wheelie," and tore back west on Pico at a high rate of speed.

The soldiers were leaping right and left out of his way, ducking behind telephone poles and automobiles while others yelled for Rivas to halt. Almost all of them escaped untouched, but one soldier was hit on the right leg, although not seriously injured.

Not a shot was fired, and Rivas turned north up Catalina Street. Three sergeants ran up to several of the agitated soldiers, settling them down, and returning them to their posts. A short time later Rivas returned southbound on New Hampshire at a very high rate of speed, and without his lights on. He turned left on Pico as soldiers again leaped out of the way while yelling warnings to other soldiers and civilians.

As Rivas continued trying to run people down, three of the Guardsmen opened fire. They initially fired at the tires and rear of the car, flattening one tire. The car continued in a threatening manner in spite of the fact ten rounds had been fired from three rifles. Several witnesses confirmed later that the Guardsmen were obviously shooting down, trying to stop the vehicle without hitting the driver.

The driver continued trying to run soldiers down, so the Guardsmen applied lethal force. They missed with one bullet that hit a window post, but then hit him with one bullet in the shoulder, and two in the head. The car came to rest near the intersection of Pico and Vermont Avenue.

The police arrived very quickly, put up barricades and crime scene tape, and initiated an investigation. Two Los Angeles Police Department investigating teams from the Ramparts Division arrived, one from homicide, and one from internal affairs. One of the LAPD officers who arrived on the scene took one look and said, "Well hell, that's the guy that tried to run us down two weeks ago!"

Colonel Brandt was not far from the area when the shooting occurred, and arrived there shortly thereafter. He found lots of police, and some media, including helicopters overhead. The media contingent rapidly grew in numbers. Some of the initial television flashes repeated something like "Gang member tries to run down Guardsmen, dies with three bullets in head." The initial impression was that he had been hit with three rounds in the head because one of the two bullets was tumbling after penetrating the window.

The police found three bags of suspected drugs in the car. The decedent was not carrying a driver's license. The car had no license plates, and rather interestingly, had *rusted* bullet holes. This was obviously not the first time the car was a target. In addition, the decedent had been arrested three times the previous year on felony charges.

There was an intensive investigation conducted by LAPD immediately following the shooting. In addition, the National Guard's 170th Criminal Investigation Detachment conducted a collateral investigation. The military investigators checked the facts, and also made sure the soldiers were familiar with the Rules of Engagement prior to the confrontation.

It was found that four residents of the area knew the deceased as a local drug dealer. One said that he was mad because this area was his drug territory, and the National Guard's presence had adversely impacted on business. Two commented that Rivas was a "Vato Loco" (crazy guy). One had seen the deceased threaten other people in the area, including pointing a gun at people.

Several of the soldiers had seen Rivas driving erratically during the middle of the day, at a high rate of speed, and not stopping for pedestrians. Later during the day he was seen losing his temper because the car in front of him was going too slow. He was obviously agitated, banged his front bumper into the rear of the other car, and pushed it around a corner. Two soldiers also commented that Rivas was laughing as he tried to run them down during the confrontation.

The police took the three soldiers who had done the shooting to the fire station on Vermont Avenue one block up from Pico. One police officer went out and got each of the three soldiers a big meal of steak and prawns. Two of the soldiers were obviously hungry. Colonel Brandt, who accompanied them to the fire house, said they "dove right in, eating up a storm." Brandt asked them if he could do anything for them. One said "Well, you can get us some more ammunition so we can get back out in the street."

No one should assume the soldiers took the incident lightly. Two of the three soldiers did not seem particularly upset emotionally immediately after the incident, but that did not mean there were no emotional problems later. The third soldier, however, was visibly shaken by the events. Brandt said, "He was very upset...started to eat just a little. But he then had to rush out of the room to upchuck." The picture shown in the Los Angeles Times on Tuesday showed an obviously distressed Guardsman, with one hand covering his eyes in anguish. This is a typical reaction from all but the most calloused soldiers, even experienced combat veterans. One Guardsman involved in the incident even had to be hospitalized for a short time with emotional problems.

The news quickly spread about this first application of deadly force with a killing involved. The news wasn't only repeated on television, it was disseminated through military channels. As one Sergeant put it, "We hear the word...a Guardsman has shot and killed a civilian. We prepare for round two." Tension increased markedly among troops out in the streets.

Tension also increased in various military headquarters. On Sunday there were more than the normal media reports regarding Guardsmen and shooting. A couple of reports inaccurately stated that Guardsmen had been hit. An Army general now had overall command, but most of the troops were Guardsmen, and their lives were very precious to commanders at all levels. A commander can select subordinate leaders very carefully, train his troops hard, and plan operations with great care. Sometimes, however, commanders are unable to impact on tactical situations in the field.

Many of us normally do most of our praying early in the morning. On this night, what with the media reports, we were particularly concerned about the safety of our soldiers. Some of us therefore did some intensive praying on their behalf.

Just after 8:00 p.m., Angel, 28-years-old; and Yolanda, 27-years-old; went to use a telephone at the corner of Century Boulevard and Vermont Avenue. When they finished using the phone, the two Hispanic women started walking south on Vermont towards their home. A 32-year-old black male walking north stopped them and asked a couple of general questions. He then said "I've got a gun. If you scream, I'll kill you. I'm not afraid of police or the National Guard. I'll kill them too."

Fearing for their lives, the women did as they were told. As they walked down Vermont, the kidnapper saw two soldiers from the 4-160th Infantry standing at a post. He got between the two women and told them to hold his arms so they would look like a threesome. When they put their arms through his, he clamped their arms tightly against his body. Several times he repeated his threat to kill them. Then they walked towards the Guardsmen, who thought the women looked scared. Angel silently mouthed "help" as they walked by, while Yolanda was gesturing with her head.

The two Guardsmen at the post were Sergeant Jimmy L. Hathaway, a squad leader from Coronado, and Specialist

Clinton Rees. They locked and loaded their weapons, and separated the women from the kidnapper. When Hathaway asked the kidnapper what they were doing, he responded that they were just getting gas for their car. Sergeant Hathaway, who someday wants to be a police officer himself, kept asking him questions until they spotted a Sheriff's sedan from Lennox Station coming down the street. They flagged down the deputy sheriffs as the women dissolved in tears. It later turned out that the kidnapper was a registered sex offender and convicted kidnapper who had just been released from state prison on parole the previous March.

At about 8:20 p.m., Firestone deputies pursued a vehicle that failed to stop for traffic violations. Suspects inside tossed unknown contraband out of the vehicle during the pursuit. When the vehicle was finally stopped, a 9mm pistol was found that had been reported stolen from a looted Western Surplus Store. Two suspects were detained, both from an 83rd Street Crips gang.

At 8:40 p.m. at the intersection of Santa Fe and Walnut, two Hispanics tried to run down four marines. The marines apprehended the individuals and turned them over to deputy sheriffs. A short time later, Guardsmen in the Fox Hills Mall received sniper fire.

At 9:00 p.m., most of the federal mutual aid resources supporting the county were released. In the meantime, many Guardsmen were moving into new quarters in response to the decision to return to business as usual on Monday. Schools had to be reopened, and that impacted on both the military and law enforcement. For one battalion however, the requirement to move out of school yards turned out to be an advantage.

The 3-185th Armor from the San Diego area was one of those battalions that had to move out of a school, so Sergeant Dennis M. McClary phoned the local Scottish Rite Temple on Wilshire Boulevard. The Shriners welcomed them, and invited the entire battalion to move in. They did.

The Scottish Rite Temple had suffered one attempt to burn them out. A couch inside had been set on fire, and one marble wall broken. Sandbags were set up in front, and the presence of the Guardsmen guaranteed security for the Temple. But the Guardsmen came out much better for the deal. Not only did they have beautiful accommodations, the Shriners turned out to be very gracious hosts.

The Scottish Rite asked what the troops needed. They didn't need much. The next thing they knew, a hundred cases of soda were delivered, plus the same amount of bottled water. Sergeant McClary said, "They brought in cookies, cakes, you name it. A lady across the street baked every day, all day long, and brought us great baked goods. They provided USO-type shows. They brought in the Comedy Shop, Dave Phillips, a rock band, and a couple of singers. Royal Dano had just flown back from a show in New York. He threw a show for us. They (the Shriners) provided us free haircuts."

Guardsmen were scattered all over the county during the emergency, but there wasn't a happier group than the tankers from the 3-185th Armor Battalion at the Scottish Rite Temple. Hosting the Guardsmen was obviously very expensive for the Shriners, but it also was very much appreciated by the troops.

Interestingly, the Shriner's Sovereign Grand Inspector General had to go to a meeting in Turkey just a day or two after the National Guardsmen moved in. The meeting held in Turkey involved various Eastern Bloc countries where Shriners were just getting restarted after many decades under repressive governments. They couldn't understand why the Shriners in America permitted the military inside the Temple. It was discussed for two days. It is difficult to explain to foreigners that the National Guard on the one hand are soldiers, but also are neighbors (and sometimes Shriners) from the local community.

The demonstrations sponsored by the Nation of Islam at 45th Street and Western Avenue continued well into the night. Louis Farrakhan had not shown up as advertised, but Minister Khallid Abdul Muhammad spoke on his behalf. Speakers were scattered throughout the neighborhood to widen the impact. The Department of Justice dispatched some agents to monitor the demonstrations after hearing there were seditious appeals. Speeches to the demonstrators (as many as five hundred at one time) called for guerrilla warfare against whites, and denounced anyone calling for peace. The Fruit of Islam, the Nation of Islam's security force, was reported to be providing security for the gathering.

It was 9:47 p.m. when troops from the 3-160th Infantry Battalion guarding the Civic Center had a scare. Shots were fired in a drive-by shooting from the direction of the 101 Freeway. Sergeant Carvel Gay had a 2 1/2 ton truck, loaded with sodas, ice, food, candy, magazines, newspapers, writing material and other items donated by Glendale merchants for their Guardsmen. Specialist David Andrews was in the back of the truck riding "shotgun" as they were starting on rounds to distribute the items to the troops. Andrews was standing near the truck's muffler, so he didn't hear the shots fired.

The truck had just started forward when troops and Sheriff's deputies ran by aiming or pulling their weapons, yelling, "Shots fired!" Specialist Andrews described what happened next. "Sergeant Gay put it in reverse, setting a speed record in the process. I was thrown off my feet, ending up with my butt in one of the ice containers with sodas. As I finally extricated myself, Sergeant Gay hollered for me to follow him. We went running across the street (across from the Hall of Justice) and set up firing positions with other cops and soldiers. There were apartments in the background, so we couldn't return fire.

"The MP's set up a perimeter on the other side of the freeway, as about six motorcycle cops responded. They couldn't find the sniper. We were set up behind a three foot wall, ready to fire, but couldn't. We didn't see a target, and were concerned about the apartments."

The litany of incidents reported in the Emergency Operations Center continued:

-- At 10:20, near 21st Street and Pacific Avenue in Long Beach, two unidentified males threw bottles at marines. There were no injuries, and both men were arrested by the police.

-- At 10:35 p.m., an anonymous phone call was received warning that gangs were heading for Nickerson Gardens to "jump" Guardsmen there and take their weapons and uniforms.

-- At 10:45 p.m., near Main Street and Aliso, military police reported seeing a white Cadillac with individuals flashing automatic weapons.

-- At 11:04 p.m., at the corner of 26th Street and Vermont, Guardsmen were fired upon.

-- At 11:14 p.m., the Los Angeles Fire Department reported that the Arco Refinery plant was set on fire. No suspects were detained.

-- At 11:50 p.m., the Department of Justice reported that two Compton police officers were wounded when they responded to a call that a man was on the roof of Compton High School.

-- At 12:10 a.m., near Normandy Avenue between Second and Third Streets, shots were fired at LAPD officers. No arrests resulted.

Soldiers of the 2-159th Infantry's Scout Platoon were patrolling in Compton. They constantly reminded each other to exercise restraint as they kept facing unusual situations. They might suddenly come across strange people in the streets, such as the "Crack Mama" stinking of urine, who was lost in the dark and came stumbling up on them for help. A little later there was the young couple whose car ran out of gas on the Highway 91 freeway near Alameda Street. They were scared and had no money. The soldiers drove to a service station and bought a can full of gas for them, and then gave them a lift to their car. The young girl was shaking uncontrollably, so the Guardsmen asked her if she was cold. She said, "No, I'm just real scared. I have never seen so many guns in my life."

Company C of this battalion had a little 8-year-old boy come up to a group of their Guardsmen. He asked them to please shoot up a crack house in the neighborhood. When they asked him why, he said, "Because it makes my mommy sick."

The 2-185th Armor Battalion's attention was drawn to another crack house this early morning. They had a patrol mounted on Hummers in the vicinity of Martin Luther King Boulevard and Western Avenue. They saw a crack house, all boarded up, but with a lot of men hanging around. They dismounted and sent patrols around each side of the house. They found one .25 calibre pistol, and sent everyone home, explaining that a curfew was in effect. When they turned the pistol over, the police said, "It's a shame we didn't hear a lot of 'rat-a-tat-tat' while you were up there (at the crack house)." The crack house obviously was an infamous and continuing problem to law enforcement. Sergeant First Class Leonard W. Formosa, a former marine, said, "It was clear they wouldn't have been disappointed if we removed the problem for them..."

Military Policemen from the 649th MP Company were supporting the Sheriff's deputies at the Hall of Justice and Jail. Second Lieutenant Lum was accompanying a deputy sheriff in a ride-along as he was making rounds in the area. A black Nissan pickup truck "low rider" with a camper top fitted on the back ran a red light. The sheriff chased him with lights and siren down Spring Street. The pickup finally stopped in a little burned out area which was dark and deserted.

Lieutenant Lum covered the deputy with his M-16 rifle, first from behind a telephone pole, then a mail box, and then from a doorway. They were having trouble seeing into the pickup through the tinted glass. They could see three men sitting in the front, and assumed there were more from the way the truck was rocking from guys moving around in the back. The deputy, who was Hispanic himself, yelled at them in English and Spanish to get out.

It was beginning to look like a standoff, so Lieutenant Lum used his hand held radio to request assistance. They saw the three men (they assumed, although it was very difficult to tell how old they were) lean over in the front seat of the pickup. This worried them, so the officer very forcefully yelled at them a final time, but they still didn't respond.

What happened next was almost like it had been scripted for a movie. As described by Lieutenant Lum, "All of a sudden, one Humvee (Hummer) came from the rear, around the corner to the rear of their (pickup), and the other came to the front of the (pickup)...with two people in the hatches, and three inside of each vehicle (Hummer). Bodies came out of that truck! The three Hispanics in the front came out, and laid on the ground. Six people came out of the back." They ranged in age from 17 to 22-years-old. The military policemen searched them and found one 9 mm automatic, and two Mac-10s, among a total of eight or nine different handguns. They also found two sticks of dynamite which they said they had gotten from a construction site, and quite a collection of liquor. The military policemen put flex-cuffs on them, and were ready when a sheriff's van came by to haul them away.

At 3:58 a.m., two Compton police officers responded to a domestic dispute, accompanied by marines. They had just gone up to the door when two shotgun birdshot rounds were fired through the door, hitting the officers. One yelled "cover me!" to the marines, who then laid down a heavy base of fire. One officer pulled the other one to safety. The man in the house, undoubtedly even more frightened than the police after the heavy gunfire, refused to surrender until members of the SWAT team arrived, along with many other law enforcement officers.

The police officer had not meant "shoot" when he yelled "cover me" to the marines. The term "cover me" meant the same to him as it does to Army (or Army National Guard) soldiers. That is, point your weapons and be prepared to respond if necessary. However, the marines responded instantly in the precise way they had been trained, where "cover me" means "provide me with cover *using firepower.*"

The problems with terminology brought to mind an old joke that continually recirculates around the Pentagon. It starts with the command "secure the building." To a soldier, that means occupy the building so no one can enter. The Navy would turn off the lights and lock the doors. The Marines would assault the building, capture it, and defend it as necessary. The Air Force, as the story goes, would take out a lease with an option to buy!

The incident in Compton was another lesson learned the hard way. The response to "cover me" involved a total of over two hundred bullets fired into that house. When this was discussed with the police later, they said considerably more than two hundred rounds may have been fired. Some of the holes in the wall were large enough for several bullets to pass through. When the man surrendered, the police found that there were kids in the house along with the parents. Fortunately, in spite of the hail of bullets, no one in the house was hit.

Sunday night seemed like a war zone to many of the soldiers and marines. They were all struck by the number of weapons in the streets, and the belligerent attitude of the thousands of gang members. It therefore came as a considerable surprise to the military when the Compton police announced how pleased they were that the crime level had dropped to only 40% of normal. Sunday night's incidents, may however, have almost matched pre-riot levels of lawlessness in some areas.

The total number of people in custodial facilities as of Sunday now totalled 25,199, establishing a new record for the county. The toll by the fifth day and night had now reached:

    51 Killed
 2,383 Injured (221 Critically)
11,113 Fires
10,904 Arrests

CHAPTER ELEVEN

Monday through Wednesday, May 4-6, 1992
RETURN TO "NORMAL"

"It is the joint intent of civil authorities and myself (the Commander, JTF-LA) to hasten the return to civil stability within the greater Los Angeles area by enhancing the profile and visibility of civil law enforcement agencies while continuing to gradually realign the role of military forces to one of less visible backup and reinforcement capabilities." That was wording in the "Intent" subparagraph of the "Execution" paragraph of the JTF-LA Operations Order issued effective 7:00 a.m. Monday morning.

The Operations Order made it clear that the military was to extract itself from law enforcement missions. The order also reflected increasing concerns for the safety of soldiers and marines. In the words of the JTF-LA commander, expressed separately, "We are just providing targets for the gangs." Examples of what JTF-LA listed in the Operations Orders as inappropriate missions included:

-- Isolated patrols or security missions which are incapable of being rapidly reinforced or are outside of tactical communications range of higher headquarters or a response force.

-- Traffic Control Points, roadblocks, traffic direction activities.

-- "Ride-alongs" with civil law enforcement agencies.

-- Mission (sic) which lead to a perception that military personnel are assuming a law enforcement role as opposed to assisting civil disturbance operations.

-- Mission requests from private citizens, business enterprises, or institutions.

The order also required daily revalidation of missions. This sometimes took as long as eight hours, as they were being checked by legal officers as well as senior commanders.

This was all more than a little confusing to subordinate commanders, especially the National Guardsmen who had been on the streets from the beginning. The civil disturbances had ended several days before. As a consequence, any missions performed by the military were therefore *de facto* law enforcement missions. The Guardsmen had been doing just about anything that law enforcement officers asked them prior to federalization, but that rapidly began to change.

The Intelligence Summary distributed to the military forces included what was becoming a routine listing of worrisome gang activities. An Inglewood Police Department captain informed the troops that 1100 guns had been stolen Sunday from a gun shop in West Los Angeles. Over 800 empty cartons for those stolen guns had been found in Inglewood. There were increasing reports of troops being scouted by gang-bangers. There rarely was much of an attempt to conceal these activities. The gangbangers would often be out in the open, obviously counting soldiers, and then phoning in their reports on cellular phones. They sometimes would fake mechanical problems with their cars, or make multiple slow vehicle passes.

The Intelligence Summary noted the many capabilities of the gangs, summarized their previous activities against military forces, and noted the many threats to target military forces and law enforcement officers after the curfew was lifted. It was not clear when that would occur, but there was a listing of fifteen gangs thought to have unified in attempts to attack the police and military forces. Early Monday morning, death threats were again received against Mayor Bradley, Chief of Police Gates, and Judge Karlin.

The streets were rapidly returning to normal, complete with traffic jams. Schools, colleges and universities were open, buses were running, and the shopping malls were open again. Business was normal, although the sale of alcohol, ammunition and gasoline in containers was still prohibited. Thousands of those who had been put out of work when businesses burned were lined up at state employment offices around the county. Many thousands would end up applying for unemployment benefits.

An order had been sent out early in the morning to get the military troops off the streets during the day to enhance the appearance of normalcy. This also served to provide commanders the opportunity to regroup and reestablish accountability for the widely scattered troops. Normal military doctrine is for commanders to control subordinate units down through two levels. In other words, division knows where battalions are, brigades know where companies are, and so forth down to the lowest levels. However, as is often the case, politicians and even some senior military commanders weren't comfortable unless they knew where every patrol and post was.

Federal commanders were also uncomfortable unless they felt that orders would be instantly obeyed down to the lowest levels. This was very difficult in many parts of the county where communications were rather limited, and troops were widely scattered. The National Guard commanders were more comfortable working within the tenets of "commander's intent," trusting subordinate commanders with a great deal of latitude. This is understandable given the fact that most Guard commanders had known each other for many years. Regardless, the order to pull back, issued early Monday morning, had been generally accomplished by six in the morning.

Members of the Korean-American community met to develop a strategy for helping their members rebuild. In addition, several banks announced programs to help both businesses and homeowners in the affected area. In the meantime, harried court employees and lawyers struggled with the normally routine processing of arrest cases. The system was grossly overloaded by this time.

There were a great many tips phoned in regarding the location of stolen property. Police officers could often tell that gangbangers were greatly irritated at having some hiding places revealed to the police. By this time it was also difficult to tell when merchandise was stolen unless the item was still in the original carton, or had a price tag.

There was some violence continuing on the streets, but it was considered normal for the areas involved. At noon, shots were fired at LAPD officers on Normandie Avenue between Second and Third Streets. The suspect fired a shotgun as he fled the scene of an accident involving a stolen automobile. He was not immediately apprehended.

The 40th Military Police Company, supporting Newton Division of L.A.P.D, in the late afternoon got word that several hundred gangbangers were creating problems for the police in South Park. When they got there, they saw what they described as "hard-core type" gangbangers, right in the faces of police officers. They were making their finger signs, and gener-

226

ally being obnoxious. The military police went tearing across the grass in their Hummers. The military police dismounted, dropped the face shields on their helmets, and went into a line formation with their rifles held at high port. The gangbangers backed off and drifted away. This was another of the very few times any troops actually went into any kind of crowd control formation.

Major General Covault provided a Commander's Assessment to his next higher commander at Forces Command as of 2:30 p.m. on Monday. He pointed out that he had just finished a conference call involving the Governor, the Mayor, the L.A. Chief of Police, the County Sheriff, and the "SCRAG" (Senior Civilian Representative of the Attorney General). He commented that there were incoming calls from all over the county expressing concern over the military leaving. He said that all involved in the conference call agreed:

-- Monday night would be the critical time, being the first night when the curfew was no longer in effect.

-- The military had been drawn into law enforcement work and that's not the military's job.

-- To respect General Covault's Arming Order requiring magazines be kept in the pouch.

Chief Gates confided that he was getting increased intelligence that the gangs intended to avoid taking on the military. The military was not only well armed, it would be "bad public relations" for the gangs to fight the troops. There were more threats that the gangs would take on LAPD after the military left. There was graffiti appearing that said "Don't Screw with the Ninja Turtles." The military was being described as the Ninja Turtles because of our appearance in Kevlar helmets and flak vests. At the same time, more graffiti reading "ACMD" (All Cops Must Die) was being noted.

During the conference call, it was suggested that the military establish more Quick Reaction Forces that could immediately respond to emergencies. This ended up being done using two sources. Military police units from the 49th Military Police Brigade were organized to provide several Quick Reaction Forces to respond on surface streets. In addition, the 7th Division's 2-7th Brigade organized a Quick Reaction Force for possible airmobile insertion from the Whittier Narrows area to specified landing zones within the area of operations.

Some troops from 2-144th Field Artillery were posted in Compton. Like many others, they were up tight, having heard intelligence reports about Guardsmen being targeted. Every time they heard shooting off in the distance, and they heard it reasonably often, they were afraid some of their buddies were being shot at. They were in no mood to fool around when a gangbanger across the street started kicking in some glass. A sergeant went across the street. He found the tough-looking gang member was heavily tattooed, complete with a spider web on his neck. The sergeant told him to stop kicking in the glass and sit down, but the gang member responded, "No comprende" (I don't understand). The sergeant then chambered a round in his weapon, a very distinctive and impressive sound in an M-16 rifle. He immediately and forcefully said "Sit down, *now!*" The gangbanger suddenly understood English, and quickly sat down. He stayed there until the police arrived to haul him away.

First Sergeant Vernon Snodderly's Company B of 2-160th Infantry was patrolling on foot in a residential area late at night. First Sergeant Snodderly had three soldiers with him going

228

down a dark alley when they suddenly came across three individuals sitting against an old shed. There was a rather rancid smell in the area, a combination of stale beer and marijuana being smoked. One of the three was a lady behaving rather strangely. She had her leg in a cast, and constantly talked to herself, or anyone around her. The three of them got up and ran (as fast as her cast would permit) the short distance into an old house near the corner of Wadsworth and Florence. It was a crack house, broken down and partially boarded up.

Five or six other people came out of the crack house in a couple of minutes, and started giving the troops a rough time. When the troops peeked in between the slats, they could see drug paraphernalia and booze, and smell a mixture of odors, including the distinctive stink of marijuana.

They secured the perimeter of the crack house. Snodderly, who is the principal of a Continuation High School, is familiar with the drug culture. He recognized that most of the occupants were drugged out. They continued to give the troops a rough time, calling them names, and using a lot of obscenities. A truck arrived with reinforcements, and the addicts all went back into the crack house.

The police arrived when called. They didn't want to deal with the problem for a couple of reasons. One was that the jails were already full. In addition, they said there are thousands of crack houses in Los Angeles, and if they arrested all of the occupants, there wouldn't be enough room for them all even if they started with empty jails. They left after making a note of the address, and said, "We'll get it someday."

Some of the troops were in a retaliatory frame of mind, and disgusted with the situation they had found. They walked around the house every once in a while, rapping on the windows, and calling , "Want to come out and play?" Some of the troops were hoping for a response that would permit them to clean out the mess there. Finally, around 2:00 a.m., the troops were told by their leadership to knock it off. They weren't as contrite as their leaders would have liked. They were also finding that most habitues of crack houses were not as aggressive as typical gangbangers. Looked at another way, consumers of drugs tended to be less combative (although there are notorious exceptions, such as PCP users), than those that provide the drugs.

The 1-184th Infantry Battalion, which is stationed from Madera in the south to Auburn above Sacramento, had arrived Friday afternoon. The battalion then was split into three task forces. One of the task forces was placed under the command of Captain Mark A. Dodd and sent to support LAPD's Pacific Area. When they originally were brought into the area, just south of Santa Monica, the two companies were escorted into the area with two police units in front, one in the middle, and two in the back. Captain Dodd checked in with the Pacific Area of LAPD on Culver Boulevard. They were then taken into the neighborhoods. The soldiers were up tight, but not as nervous as the people on the streets, who immediately went inside their homes. The drug dealers cussed as the Guardsmen arrived, but also got off the streets.

On Saturday, the older folks in the neighborhood told the police that they would keep things under control in the neighborhood, and the Guardsmen weren't needed. They kept their word.

There were ongoing problems at the Penmar Recreation Center in the park about a block from the southwest corner of the Santa Monica airport. Gang members would go by flashing their weapons, everything from handguns to Uzis. The Guardsmen decided to help keep the Penmar Recreation and Day Care Centers open. In a few days the park itself was full of kids. Some of the parents told the Guardsmen it was the first time their kids, as old as eight, had been able to play in the park. Some of the troops joined the folks in the Recreation Center taking aerobics classes.

On Monday, Dodd's task force was asked to provide security for a mini-mall at the corner of Lincoln Boulevard and Sunset Street. The mini-mall had a Smart and Final Drugs, and several small businesses. The police department had set up a command post behind the Smart and Final Drug Store, and Dodd had soldiers posted on the roof to provide security. The troops kept seeing cars right across Sunset. They said it looked like they were primarily college students, buying drugs.

Then occurred an incident which unfortunately was repeated, more often than could be proven, in various places around the county. Troops on the roof saw the incident from start to finish. It involved a business near the corner of Lincoln and Sunset, across from the shopping center. The story was related by Sergeant Neal Fine of LAPD's Pacific Area (and Command Sergeant Major of the 40th Division's First Brigade when National Guard requirements override needs of the police department). "What they saw...they saw him (the businessman) enter the business through the front...they saw him go out the back. They saw him walk around to the front, and then the business was on fire. The (Los Angeles) Fire Department determined it was arson, and he (the one the Guardsmen saw) was the only one who was ever in the location. They believe it was for insurance.

231

"There is no doubt that if they hadn't been there, this man would have gotten away with it, because there were no police officers in view of that business. Although we (the police) were within a hundred yards, we were in back of the Smart and Final. There's no doubt that they (the troops) prevented insurance fraud, and they captured an arsonist."

The troops moved across the street to protect the burned out business. Their new location, however, was an impediment to the drug dealing that normally occurred there.

Finally, after a couple of days, the drug dealer approached Captain Dodd. The drug dealer told him the troops along "his street" were costing him six figures a day (Undoubtedly an exaggeration). He offered Captain Dodd a large bribe to move his troops back across the street. Dodd responded, "No way!" He was being a good soldier. However, for the rest of his life, he will remember being offered six figures to move his soldiers back across the street to the place they started from.

The toll as dawn began to break on Tuesday had risen to 58 killed. In the months to follow, this figure would be revised down to about 54 as it was determined that some of the killings were not related to the riots. The revised total also reflected bodies later found in the rubble of burned buildings. The arrests totalled 13,212 by this time.

The law requires that arrestees for felonies be formally charged within two days. Police officers were finding it all but impossible to get all the paperwork processed while spending almost all of their time in the streets protecting the populace. Fortunately, the courts had been closed, in effect extending the 48-hour deadline. The glut of cases was more than the court system could handle, so legislators in Sacramento were scrambling to get a bill written and passed extending the arraignment requirement for the L.A. riots to seven working days. If it didn't get passed, the authorities in Los Angeles would be forced to turn all of those accused felons back out onto the streets.

Military and law enforcement officials were relieved that comparatively little violence occurred Monday night, the first night without a curfew. The Intelligence Summaries on Tuesday morning noted that Mayor Bradley, Chief Gates, and Judge Karlin were targeted for assassination a third time since the riots erupted.

On Tuesday the City of Long Beach announced they were lifting the curfew. There were no more curfews in effect anywhere in the county. All federal agents brought in for the riots were released except for 114 U.S. Marshals and some FBI SWAT teams. In addition to the FBI's Los Angeles SWAT team, there were a total of forty SWAT team members from Denver, Phoenix and San Diego. The FBI's Hostage Rescue Team also remained in Los Angeles. None of these federal agents was deployed as of Tuesday morning.

Scheduled events for Tuesday included a rally planned for 10:00 a.m. at the Federal Building on Wilshire by Queer Nation and Act-Up L.A., two homosexual organizations. Demonstrations also continued to be scheduled and conducted at the Simi Valley Courthouse where the "Rodney King Four" were tried.

Troops were going through shift changes, with most of them being pulled back into assembly areas to reduce the daytime military presence. Sergeant First Class Ardilla of 3-185th Armor had just relieved the troops at Midtown Center, when he saw a head pop up at a burned out Union Station on Pico Boulevard. They crossed the street and found a thief taking copper pipe for its scrap value.

The LAPD was going through their shift changes also. They brought coffee and donuts to share with the Guardsmen at Midtown. The troops were standing there chatting when an RTD bus screeched to a halt on Pico heading west. The people aboard were screaming.

Sergeant Ardilla was closest to the bus, and described what happened then. "The lieutenant and Wilkinson (First Lieutenant Gregory V. DeBarnard and Sergeant Randy Wilkinson) and I were closest, so we ran to the bus. We started to get on the bus, but the crowd on the bus were throwing this guy out." Evidently a street person, he was described as slim, black, in his mid-twenties, long hair, dirty and scroungy looking, with several layers of clothing. Sergeant Ardilla, an experienced law enforcement officer, threw an arm lock on the man, while Lieutenant DeBarnard grabbed his other side. "We searched him, but the only weapon was a pointed piece of glass six inches long in his gloved hand.

"We then got the story. He got on the bus, and then started ranting and raving. He then threw a bottle at the driver, hitting him in the head, while the bus was still moving...and broke a window. When he started after the driver again, the crowd grabbed him. The driver had a cut on his head. The guy kept telling us 'I know the King of the Mafia and Elizabeth Taylor, and I'm going to have them get you.' The paramedics came and checked the driver out...patched him up."

The Lynwood Home Savings and Loan was robbed in the morning, shortly after a National Guard unit that was there was relocated. At 10:12 a.m. there was a firebombing of a private mailbox service in the 600 block of South Lincoln Street in Venice. One person was reported injured.

The military was having great difficulty disengaging. The military commanders were trying to get permission to send the troops home, while civilian authorities pressed to have the military remain as long as possible. Major General Covault, the JTF-LA commander, had coordinated with Buck Revell, in charge of federal civilian assets. They both wanted to get troops off the street at night as well as during the day, and get law enforcement officials to rely on Quick Reaction Forces.

General Covault told higher headquarters that he was unable to do that unilaterally, and that the Governor, the Mayor, the Chief of Police and the County Sheriff all must be heard. He advised that Buck Revell was drafting a letter to come down through FBI channels, with a similar letter desired down through top military channels. He ended up his report clearly expressing his concern. "At this point the military is providing 10,000 targets for the type of activity going on in the streets (i.e. pure lawlessness versus civil disturbance). The potential downside to continue in the law enforcement mode is enormous (not trained and ready to do so)." General Covault was unable to persuade political leaders and law enforcement officials to pull the troops off the street Tuesday night.

As usual, the violence picked up as darkness set in. At 7:00 p.m., the troops were warned that two gangs may have been deploying snipers on rooftops on Shenandoah Street, Garth Street, and Sawyer Street to target troops and police at La Cienaga and 18th Street. The Marvin Street Gang and the Rolling 60s were particularly mentioned. Their ammunition was said to have been purchased in Bakersfield by female friends of the gang. A few minutes later, it was reported that a California Highway Patrolman had his patrol van window shot

235

out as he was traveling west on the 101 Freeway in the vicinity of Alvarado Street.

A marine liaison officer at the LAPD EOC produced a supplementary flyer on "Increased gang activities and indications." It discussed the gang truce indicators of red and blue bandanas lying or tied together, and the wearing of white hats or headbands. There was great concern over the number of stolen uniforms (both police and military), and weapons in the hands of gangs. The threats of assassinations, sniping attacks, and drive-by shootings were repeated.

Another information paper on gangs noted that the Black Muslims were involved in uniting the Crips and Bloods from the housing projects, with meetings on three successive nights. Representatives of both types of gang were in attendance first at Jordan Downs, then at Imperial Courts, and finally at Nickerson Gardens. Sheriff's deputies from a gang detail stopped a car with three Grape Street Crips in their purple colors leaving Blood territory at Nickerson Gardens. The Crips told the deputies they could then go into any project, as a truce was in effect. They told them that they didn't know about other gangs, but the gangs in the projects had called a truce.

Informants told law enforcement that cooler heads in the gangs had prevailed, and they would wait to declare "war" on the police until after the military left and things returned to normal. Then police cars would be responding to calls for assistance with only one or two officers. However, some gang members were determined to continue the fight without letup, and promised to lure law enforcement personnel where they could be ambushed.

There were continuing threats of sniper attacks and drive-by shootings directed against the military and law enforcement officers. These in fact occurred, but it was obvious they were scattered, and gangbangers were taking very few real risks facing up to military firepower.

By this time it was noted that over half of the arrestees during the riots were Hispanics. Interestingly, over a thousand of those arrested were illegal immigrants. Law enforcement authorities, as previously mentioned, were concerned that the more serious criminals might have to be released Tuesday night if a bill was not passed in Sacramento extending the time allowed for arraigning those accused of riot-related felonies. The District Attorney for Los Angeles, Ira Reiner, finally got the word that the bill extending arraignment time to seven working days had passed the State legislature. In fact, it passed both houses of the legislature unanimously, and was being flown down in an Air National Guard aircraft.

The aircraft landed at Santa Monica airport as the deadline approached. Governor Wilson met the aircraft, and signed the bill into law on the hood of a car.

Soldiers from the Madera unit of 1-184th Infantry were posted in the area of Santa Monica Boulevard and Western Avenue. There were several posts in that area with both Guardsmen and police officers. Just before 10:00 p.m., there was a minor traffic accident at the corner of Santa Monica Boulevard and St. Andrews Place, with a blue Nissan Pathfinder rear ending a white Volvo. The two vehicles pulled over, with the Nissan hitting the Volvo a second time. The Nissan's driver acted nervous as he kept revving his engine and looking around. A police officer went over to conduct what is called a preliminary investigation, when the Nissan driver decided to flee.

When the driver started to flee, he ran over a police officer, and then broke through a barrier tape. He headed at high speed and erratically for one of two Guardsmen in the immediate area, as four or five people yelled for him to halt. The two Guardsmen each fired one round through the door of the Nissan Pathfinder, which sped down St. Andrews Place, and then turned left onto Sierra Vista Avenue. The suspect stopped his pickup there and tried to flee on foot. If he didn't know it before, he quickly found that he was missing some key body parts. The police then caught up with him.

Two ended up going to the hospital. The police officer went to Cedars-Sinai Hospital for his injured hip. The suspect, an adult Hispanic who appeared to be intoxicated, was hit by bullet fragments in the buttocks and testicles. He also was taken to the hospital, where tests showed an alcohol blood level of 0.179. He had two bags of amphetamines in the back of his car. The police did a records check on the suspect, and found that he was on felony probation for fifteen years due to a vehicular manslaughter in Florida. He obviously was an individual not averse to running people down and killing them with his automobile.

Later in the night (early in the morning), between five and seven rounds were fired at Guardsmen from 3-185th Armor at the corner of Jefferson and Hauser Boulevards. This incident involved six soldiers, with Sergeant First Class Richard E. Montee in charge, securing the Goodhew Ambulance Service, Inc. Goodhew is an extremely large company, with about three dozen ambulances at this one location. The ambulance company is located in an industrial area. In fact, railroad tracks run right in front of the company, between the fence enclosing their compound and Jefferson Boulevard. There is a Nabisco warehouse on one side, a Bekins Van and Storage across the street, and apartment complexes off in the distance.

Sergeant Montee had three soldiers on the roof, with one soldier and his RTO (radio-telephone operator) at ground level. He was able to communicate with that radio all the way to his battalion headquarters in the Shriner's Temple on Wilshire. It had been a quiet night, with very little street traffic, when the serenity was shattered at about 4:00 a.m. They suddenly heard bullets tearing through the trees over their heads, followed by the sound of shots. A total of three or four quick shots rang out, followed almost immediately by three or four more.

The Guardsmen almost simultaneously yelled, "Shots fired! Shots fired!" as they all hunkered down. The shots were obviously fired using a semiautomatic weapon from one of the two apartment complexes north of the ambulance company. One bullet landed in a telephone pole next to Sergeant Montee, others hit a wall of the ambulance company. Almost a year later, the little craters made by the bullets were still visible in the wall.

Sergeant Montee radioed his report in to his battalion headquarters. The police came by shortly afterwards, followed quickly by Lieutenant Colonel Ronald B. Flynn, the brigade executive officer. Lieutenant Colonel Flynn, a highly experienced veteran of Vietnam and former Special Forces officer, dismounted and assumed what he kiddingly calls his "Patton-like pose." He asked Sergeant Montee, who remained hunkered down close to the telephone pole, what had occurred. Montee told him. Flynn then asked where the shots came from, and where they hit. Sergeant Montee told Colonel Flynn that one bullet struck the telephone pole right about where Flynn's head was. Colonel Flynn, nobody's fool, instantly went from his "Patton-like" pose to a hunker-down position beside Sergeant Montee.

Command Sergeant Major Jim Maxey and I were sometimes accompanied by the State's Command Sergeant Major, Ramon (Ray) Thompson in our nightly rounds. We particularly remember two locations in Compton that we returned to several times. One was an intersection with two service stations on it. One service station was broken into and completely stripped. A squad was assigned there, headed by Staff Sergeant David Brown, an infantryman from 4-160th Infantry. They guarded that intersection, night after night, from the roof of the devastated service station.

Across a vacant lot from the service station they occupied were apartments with quite a few gangbangers. Catty-corner across the intersection was a service station that was doing a lot of business. Cars were coming through there all night long, every night. Some were even buying gasoline. It was obvious that the station sold something other than fuel. On the other hand, we were told that the stripped service station occupied by the troops was legitimate, and it was obvious why they were looted and the other one not. There was considerable tension each night for Sergeant Brown's young troops as shots were fired, weapons flashed, and taunts thrown around that intersection.

The other location was the Gateway Plaza Shopping Center at the corner of Central and Rosecrans in Compton. This shopping center was anchored with a Blockbuster Video at one end and a Boy's Market at the other. Sergeant David McGill and his fire team (half of a rifle squad) were responsible for this mall. All the stores had been broken into, and several were burned. Gang headquarters was right up the street. This young

240

Desert Storm veteran, along with four other Guardsmen, protected that shopping center night after night. He always had two or three of his soldiers sleeping on the floor but close at hand in case of an emergency. They were in Anna's Linens, which had been completely stripped but not burned.

They were tested several times by gangbangers in the area, and stood up to it. Sometimes gangbangers threw rocks and bottles at them. Other times gang members would drive a car into the shopping center, lights out, taunting and testing the soldiers in various ways. The young Guardsmen in that shopping center always maintained their discipline and exercised restraint.

The gangbangers were one thing, the decent folks another. As happened elsewhere, the Chinese Restaurant and Tam's Burgers refused to take their money. Sergeant McGill only had twenty dollars, but he couldn't spend it. The troops in Compton also felt very good about what they were doing. They told us one man told them it was the first time in twenty years that his wife could safely walk to the market.

Law enforcement in South Central Los Angeles was pleased that lawlessness and violence for this day and night had been much lower than normal. It wasn't so obvious to the troops who kept hearing gunfire off in the distance, and for those troops who had been the targets of snipers and drive-by shooters, it still seemed like an extremely violent area.

The Intelligence Summary on Wednesday announced that President Bush was due to arrive in the city that night at 8:30 p.m., with the President touring the riot-torn areas Thursday, and leaving on Friday. Mayor Bradley was scheduled to tour Koreatown. It was also announced that students at Jordan and

241

Locke High Schools were planning a walkout at noon in an effort to rekindle rioting.

Warrant Officer Steve Schrieken, who we met earlier catching thieves looting a liquor store next door to his laundromat, was sent out to pick up AWOLs. He was accompanied by Staff Sergeant Walter Fiske, also assigned to the Headquarters Company of the 40th Division, and who normally works for the California Department of Justice.

They were supposed to pick up a black female member of the National Guard who hadn't reported in when the troops were mobilized, and hadn't phoned in. When they got to her home near 53rd Street and Avalon, they went up and knocked on the door. She promptly opened the door, and responded affirmatively when asked if she was in the National Guard. She told them she didn't have a phone to notify the unit that she was scared to leave her home and report in. Many blacks were scared to report in, but more on that later. Schrieken and Fiske then asked her if she had a uniform, and she assured them she did. They then advised her to get into uniform while they waited in their vehicle.

They went out to wait in their vehicle, the military version of a Blazer, while she dressed. It was a longer wait than they anticipated, and considerably more tense. They were leaning against the side of their vehicle, when they realized they were becoming the center of attention for a growing crowd of gang members. All had blue bandanas hanging out of their right rear pockets. Some were holding one hand behind their back. Little kids from the neighborhood also began to gather.

Warrant Officer Schrieken encouraged the youngsters, assuming the gangbangers would not jeopardize their own kids. While they were talking to the little ones, the gangbangers

242

were, as Warrant Officer Schrieken described it, "jiving, and making their signs." Eventually a couple of hundred gathered, which hardly improved the troops' comfort level. The two Guardsmen offered the kids "Army water" from their canteens, and let them each wear their heavy Kevlar helmets, but only for a minute. They were in a hurry to get their protective helmets back on in case things got violent.

They were extremely glad to have their fellow soldier finally join them in the vehicle. As they quickly drove off, they asked her what took so long. They found that she had taken a shower before getting dressed in her uniform and joining them for the ride back to Los Alamitos.

General Covault continued pressing to get the military released, but without success. He appeared to be somewhat uncomfortable with the civil disturbance role he had been given, especially since there had not been any rioting since his arrival. A very professional soldier, his concerns were understandable. He was pushing hard to get his federal troops released, returned to Fort Ord and Camp Pendleton, and back to more familiar missions. In his update, he described his intention to coordinate this evening for Guardsmen to assume again all of the military missions.

In spite of a series of shooting incidents that night, the police in Newton Division told Guardsmen that things hadn't been so quiet in the Newton area for at least ten years. Several "car trains" were reported this evening. At the corner of Alameda and East Laurel, the car caravan at 11:40 p.m. consisted of eight vehicles with lights out, and most without license plates. Another car train with fifteen vehicles was reported en route to the Bonaventure Hotel to create havoc with protesters and police. Troops from 3-185th Armor at

243

11:10 p.m. requested police assistance at 5505 Wilshire Boulevard. Shots had been fired at the troops by a sniper on the roof across the street.

The 670th Military Police Company was securing the perimeter of the LAPD Police Academy in Elysian Park, not far from Dodger Stadium. They caught what they described as a "nut case" with a handgun late this evening on a ridge above the academy. He turned out to be a convicted felon on probation. He acknowledged he was a gang member "looking for trouble."

The troops considered their assignment to the Police Academy good duty. They had good quarters, and even had a Jacuzzi available for their use. One of the military officers assigned there said there were two commands he never thought he would have to give in combat. One, not at all funny, was "Fix bayonets!" The other, much funnier, he was forced to use at the Police Academy. "You guys in the Jacuzzi, keep it down...we're trying to have a staff meeting!"

The troops at the Police Academy also had access to the Academy's Dr. Wayne Gayton, a stress management psychologist. This was a great help to troops that got involved in some of the more serious action.

The Adjutant General, Major General Bob Thrasher, had requested an opportunity to present the Military Department's side of the story of National Guard deployment delays to the Governor's Office. As his Military Field Commander, he wanted me immediately available to accompany him to the Governor's Office when the call came. So I could get to Sacramento quickly, he had sent a T-42 twin-engined Beech aircraft to Los Alamitos. The two pilots and aircraft sat there on standby. After several days it had become clear that the call would never come, so General Thrasher released the aircraft for other missions.

The soldiers in Joint Task Force-Los Angeles were trying to posture themselves to disengage and turn all law enforcement support duties back to the California National Guard. In the meantime, Undersheriff Edmonds had expressed his concerns about renewed violence during a discussion we had at about ten in the morning. The press was discussing the departure of troops, which could encourage criminal elements. Edmonds was also concerned about the trial of a police officer accused of shooting two Samoan brothers, which he felt could serve to ignite the riots again. Alfred Skiles, a Filipino police officer in the Compton Police Department, was on trial for allegedly shooting the Tualelei brothers in the back after responding to a domestic disturbance call. The trial had been ongoing for some time in the Compton Courthouse, and the Sheriff's Department had been told (inaccurately as it later turned out) that a jury decision was imminent.

There was concern that Samoan gangs would be involved if the trial outcome wasn't what they anticipated. Intelligence officers, who had just finished providing information on Hispanic and black gangs, scrambled to obtain information on the other types of gangs in the area.

The threatened ambushing of law enforcement officers had become more than a threat late Wednesday night. A carload of gangbangers provoked Sheriff's deputies into a chase. Two Sheriff's sedans chased the suspects, who pulled into the Imperial Courts Housing Projects, and then jumped from their car and ran into a crowd of 150-200 P. J. Watts Crips. The deputies left the area without any problem, but it appeared to them that the whole incident had been a carefully contrived setup.

It was also becoming increasingly apparent to law enforcement officials that radical black religious groups were increasingly involved in organizing black gangs, including letting gang members use their facilities as a focal point for meetings and social gatherings. There was concern that the radical black religious groups were trying to further inflame racial tensions.

More reports were coming in regarding suspicious persons and vehicles following individual police officers when they left their police stations for home. Officers were admonished to be particularly wary, and vary routes going to and from work.

CHAPTER TWELVE

Thursday & Friday, May 7-8, 1992
POLICE AND TROOPS INCREASINGLY
FRUSTRATED

Intelligence Summaries Thursday morning again commented on the continuing unusually low level of shootings and open drug dealings in the streets. Direct confrontations between gangs and the troops were becoming particularly infrequent. Feedback from the gangs described their concern about the troops having an advantage because of their night vision equipment. Informants also said the gangs believed the military had machine guns and would use them if provoked.

The American-Korean Coalition received death threats after they gave their phone number to the media to publicize their needs and ask for assistance on behalf of those affected by the riots. The Korean community planned to again demonstrate outside of the Bonaventure Hotel, requesting reparations for damages to Korean businesses. President Bush was scheduled to again tour the riot-torn areas, and then visit firefighter Scott Miller in the evening. Miller was the firefighter shot in the face during the riots.

It had been a very quiet morning. At 8:52 a.m., the 3-144th Field Artillery reported that two Hispanic males attempted to break into the Fallbrook Mall. The 3-17th Infantry from the 7th Division reported a few minutes later that a firebomb exploded at 8526 Grape Street in Southgate, just twenty minutes after troops left the building.

Reports were growing regarding black civilians confronting black soldiers in an attempt to turn them against whites. Every day we knew that many of our black soldiers were being given a rough time by other blacks for being in the military and on the side of law enforcement officers, but this was the first time we felt there was any kind of organized effort to coerce black soldiers.

Reacting to the riots and the duty that followed was tough for black soldiers. Many of them live in areas heavily dominated by gangs. Just getting to the armories after they were alerted turned out to be quite a challenge for some. Many, before the riots, had been afraid to wear their uniforms in primarily black neighborhoods. When the riots started and they were alerted, some hunkered down in vehicles out of sight as friends drove them to armories. Others brought their uniforms with them, and didn't put them on until they got to the armory.

Their problems were quite different as they left some areas and crossed through or approached areas that were more effectively policed. There they faced very tense law enforcement officers who often tended to assume a car with blacks in it during a riot were probably up to no good. If they were in uniform, blacks rarely had a problem. Otherwise, negotiations tended to be strained as they scrambled for military identification cards and sought to convince the police they were on the same team.

Black soldiers were also frustrated by the hassling from non-military blacks after they started patrolling the streets. There were literally hundreds of anecdotes to illustrate the problem. There was the lady who kept telling soldiers from the 3-144th Field Artillery that they were traitors for being in the National Guard. Some soldiers were asked if they would really shoot civilians. If anyone wonders whether the term "Uncle Tom" is still being used, black Guardsmen can assure them that the phrase is not obsolete.

Command Sergeant Major Charles J. Dorsey is the senior enlisted soldier in the Second Brigade of the 40th Division, and a black. He took a certain amount of heckling himself, in spite of the fact he is a very tall, imposing soldier. Like so many senior sergeants, he spent a great deal of time out visiting his soldiers in the streets, counseling and encouraging them. Many of the soldiers were very concerned about returning to their home neighborhoods after the riots.

A veteran of the Watts riots, Command Sergeant Major Dorsey was able to make comparisons for his troops. He felt a great sense of pride in how much better the fire discipline and restraint were in 1992. He was extremely proud of his sergeants, regardless of color or seniority, and the discipline they as leaders maintained while ensuring no innocent people were hurt by Guardsmen during the 1992 riots.

Soldiers kept asking each other if they had heard any news about when they were to be released. Just before two in the afternoon there was a breakthrough, although only a hint was provided regarding releases. Colonel Tucker in Sacramento phoned regarding the results of a conference call involving the President, the Governor, and many other officials. Several key issues were discussed during the conference call:

-- The planned dispositions of the federal troops were discussed. There were no surprises, as the discussions matched what we had already been told.

-- The National Guard was to remain in federal status until at least Saturday.

-- The Governor felt that Friday and Saturday nights would be critical. He wanted to keep the National Guard in the streets.

-- Both Los Angeles Police and Sheriff's Departments said they didn't want federal troops. Too often the federal troops refused missions. The protection of fire departments and trucks was specifically mentioned.

-- The Marines and Army were to return home Friday.

-- Mayor Bradley said he needed the federal troops. General Covault's response, as described by Colonel Tucker, "That's baloney."

-- It was agreed that nothing would be said about defederalization until a joint release by the President and the Governor on Saturday.

There had been frustration on the part of Guardsmen as a consequence of federalization. Operationally, changes in mission guidance and Arming Orders tended to further complicate an already complex situation. The lines of authority were very clear at the highest levels. All missions were theoretically flowing through the County Emergency Operations Center as they were from the beginning. In practice, that agreement was often circumvented, and complicated by a lot of officers, both civilian and military, in advisory roles.

Law enforcement officers, however, were even more frustrated. Particularly baffling was the increasing arbitrariness in approving and disapproving missions. This was especially frustrating after several days of having National Guardsmen willing to perform any mission that law enforcement officers gave them. After federal troops were brought in, and the National Guard was federalized, only about ten percent of missions were approved.

Guidance from JTF-LA to their liaison officers regarding reducing mission support even further had an immediate impact. On Thursday afternoon we got a phone call, asking for an appointment. Shortly afterwards we were visited in Los Alamitos by Commander Bayan Lewis and Captain Keith Bushey of LAPD. On behalf of Chief Gates, they described the frustrations experienced by their department, and appealed for help. They simply did not understand the criteria being applied for mission approval. They weren't alone, as many military commanders didn't fully understand either. We also discussed disengagement strategies.

We agreed that the problem of missioning criteria was serious, and something was needed to provide clarification for both the military and law enforcement officials. It was agreed that the Sheriff's Department also had to be involved, and we needed a small task force to address the issues. Commander Lewis agreed we could have Ross Moen from his department to serve on the task force. Lieutenant Colonel Ross Moen is a Guardsmen, and understands our system. Just as important, Ross is a senior detective in LAPD, knows police work and enjoys their confidence.

After the meeting broke up, we contacted Undersheriff Edmonds, reaching him on his car phone. We explained the issue and how we were determined to attack the problem. He readily recognized the problem, as the Sheriff's Department had experienced the same frustrations as LAPD. Commander Paul Myron was much too senior to ask for, so we had another man in mind to represent the Sheriff's Department.

Lieutenant Richard E. Odenthal is from the Sheriff's Emergency Operations Bureau. He runs their Emergency Operations Center and is an officer the Sheriff has great confidence in. The

251

National Guard does also. He was one of the best intelligence officers we ever had in the 40th Division. Unfortunately, he is a big bear of a man, and then-Captain Dick Odenthal had to leave the Guard because he didn't meet the required height/weight profiles. Regardless, he is very smart, and ideal for the task force. We asked Bob Edmonds if we could have Dick Odenthal for our task force. You could almost hear him gulp after the tough question was popped, but he did agree.

The Future Operations Task Force. From left: Major Jim Thigpen, Lieutenant Colonel Ross Moen, Lieutenant (LASD) Dick Odenthal, and Major James O'Neill.
(Photo: Author's Collection)

As believers in "the fewer the better" (as long as you have the right few), we pulled in just two more people. One was Major James G. Thigpen. He was a Future Operations Planner from the G3 Plans Cell of the 40th Infantry Division, and would represent the interests of the division commander. The fourth soldier was Major James P. O'Neill, an attorney in civilian life, and an armor officer from the Post Detachment at the Los Alamitos Armed Forces Reserve Center. We felt an attorney was needed because of the many legal issues the task force had to wrestle with. He gave us someone half steeped in military tradition (and as an armor officer, having the needed aggressive approach to military operations), but at the same time highly experienced in legal requirements.

We gave the team a wing in the building they could call their own. We also assigned Captain Daniel W. Smith, an outstanding young officer who commanded a National Guard Military Police Company called up for Desert Storm, to assist with administrative requirements. The "Future Operations Task Force" quickly went to work.

A special Intelligence Summary was issued early Thursday evening. It commented that the gang truce seemed to be holding, and only one exception had been noted in the past twenty-four hours. That involved a gang fight in the Carson area. The summary observed that a large number of gang members were moving on the streets, many sporting white hats and the ACMD acronym. Informants passed information that the publicized withdrawal of troops was being discussed and anticipated by the gangs, with plans to then hit law enforcement agencies.

Troops from 1-185th Armor were back at the Ralph's Market at Vernon and Vermont. Leaks about troops leaving had been discussed by the media, which shouldn't have been a surprise with so many federal troop convoys headed down the highway for Tustin and El Toro. Captain Keith D. Lochner recalled a particularly poignant incident that occurred at the supermarket this Thursday evening. "A woman came up to me, hugging her three and four-year-old in her arms, and crying. She grabbed my arm, and kept saying 'Don't go! Don't go!' I told her we weren't going anyplace. She settled down, and said this was the first time in some years she felt safe going out...and that kids could play in their front yard." Lochner then said, "She and her mother came back at about 2300 hours (11:00 p.m.), and brought us coffee and pies."

Troops in the vicinity of the projects were told by local citizens that gangs were meeting in the projects to discuss possible reactions to the trial being held in Compton. They expected a verdict on Friday. Their sources were no better than ours.

Just before 11:00 p.m., a brown Toyota sedan northbound on Stadium Way shot at a 670th Military Police Company Hummer. The Hummer was hit twice by very small caliber rounds. Slightly later, a late model green Dodge sedan with three black gangbangers threatened Guardsmen from Battery C, 1-144th Field Artillery posted at the Carson Mall. They yelled "We will be back to kill you!" and then sped off.

A Situation Report was sent via facsimile at 11:05 p.m. from General Covault to General Burba at Forces Command in Georgia. He commented on the attitude of the troops, characterized as, "We've done our job so why are we still here?" General Covault was continuing to have difficulty in gaining consensus for withdrawal of troops. He noted that Governor Wilson was uncomfortable with the move of the troops to El

Toro and Tustin. Covault's report said, "(the Governor) won't challenge. It's done." He noted that the Governor reluctantly agreed to the defederalization of the force. It was unclear (and still is) if the Governor was uncomfortable because the State of California would have to again begin picking up the bill, or there were other motivations involved.

General Covault's Situation Report noted that "Governor Wilson wants 'a string' on 'brigade size force' (sic) from Camp Pendleton. 1st MEF Commander informally reached and agreed." He informed General Burba that the Governor and others agreed at 7:30 p.m. to release the 7th Infantry Division so they could return to their home station on Friday. Their intention was to travel by bus with impedimenta carried by truck.

Sergeant First Class Toby Bogges from 2-160th Infantry talked about their duty assisting Newton Division on Thursday night. "We patrol the area and guard Bower's (gun store). Mounted patrol is about the only excitement left in the streets. Although the curfew is off, and we hear of scattered shooting around South-Central, our area is calm. Now and then, a gangbanger will sign us or run from us. We sign back by aiming at them. Driving the streets, one can feel the hostility in the air. People look at us with a hardened, indifferent gaze. I believe they see us a temporary impediment to the crime in the streets, nothing more. As we seized the streets when we arrived, the criminals will take it back when we leave. It seems the whole place is a violent ecosystem in which humans are in the food chain."

The State Office of Emergency Services provided a comprehensive report of damages that had been attributed to the riots.

Among the figures:

-- 59 Killed (As discussed previously, this eventually was reduced to 54 killed).

-- $717 million was the preliminary damage estimate for Los Angeles County.

-- $ 35 million was the preliminary damage estimate for Los Angeles City.

-- $ 3.235 million in damage to over two dozen state facilities.

The Red Cross estimated that 32 homes were damaged or destroyed. There were 276 apartment units destroyed, with 60 additional units sustaining some damage. They advised that emergency shelter operations were shrinking, with 22 people housed at Belmont High School, and 108 at Dorsey High School.

Arson investigators announced that their best estimate was that 565 arson fires were set in Los Angeles during the riots. Thirty individuals had been arrested to date for arson, including 21 blacks, 8 Hispanics, and 1 white. Their ages ranged from 12 to 41-years-old.

There were no organized patterns of arson recognized in the 565 arson fires. However, it turned out that 55 buildings of the first 57 fires investigated were owned by Koreans.

By Friday, May 8th, Intelligence Summaries were getting shorter. There simply wasn't much to report, as violence on the streets had now been quieter than normal for a full week. It was reported that students at Long Beach State University planned to riot for the "ACMD" campaign, and the Police Reserve unit at the university received death threats. Informants from another area advised that gang members were planning disruptions in Westwood Village. Later there were several reports regarding possible breakouts at juvenile detention facilities throughout the region. The primary focus on Friday morning, for both the military and law enforcement, however, was the presence of President Bush.

President Bush had stayed at the Bonaventure Hotel at 5th Street and Figueroa. He had endured a series of demonstrations at his hotel. One of the larger groups was about a thousand Koreans that peacefully demonstrated in front of the hotel for many hours. The hotel had also been host to a demonstration by about fifty members of "Act-Up L.A."

The troops had known for some days that their Commander in Chief intended to meet and speak with them at the Sports Arena/Coliseum complex. The planning became intense on Thursday. It was decided that the group representing the military for the President's speech would consist of 800 National Guardsmen, 100 Regular Army, and 100 Marines.

The 1-18th Cavalry Squadron was detailed to assist in hosting the President. Some of the officers thought the duty was rather routine, and delegated some of the tasks to subordinates. They were thoroughly chagrined later when the President went out of his way to shake hands with the Squadron's staff and some of the cavalrymen who organized the effort.

Captain Ned Lee's 670th Military Police Company was given the Presidential Security mission. They took twenty military policemen who ended up very close to the President. Captain Lee said, "I was surprised they let our guys with ammo get that close to the President. He gave two of our soldiers autographs, and signed their helmets. He asked one of our soldiers what the flex-cuffs were that he had hanging from his flak vest. He (the military policeman) demonstrated their use."

The President's remarks to the troops were warmly received. The President said, "I first would salute *all* that participated in keeping the peace, guaranteeing the peace, and fighting against those who wanted to break the peace. We've seen the worst human beings can do...and then we've seen some of the very best."

President Bush, flanked by General Covault, addressing troops and law enforcement officers at the Sports Arena/Coliseum complex. (Photo by SFC Jim Ober)

The President described as "heroic" the response of all those who fought the riots. He told the troops, "I think the very fact

258

that the military was here, prepared to do what was necessary, served as an enormously inhibiting factor to the hoodlums that wanted to disrupt the civil tranquility of Los Angeles...indeed of our country." He went on to say, "You did what was right, and you did what was demanded of you. I came really just to thank each and every one of you who worked around the clock to restore order."

The troops cheered the President as he left. On his way he stopped for more pictures and autographs.

In the meantime, the federal troops had actually left the city, and the Joint Task Force headquarters was working hard on making the transition so they could disengage and return to Fort Ord. Lieutenant General Glynn C. Mallory, Jr., Commanding General of Sixth U.S. Army at the Presidio of San Francisco, had sent liaison teams to Los Alamitos some days before, preparatory to assuming responsibility for defederalization processing of the National Guardsmen.

This was much more of a challenge than many people had anticipated. Normal federalization of reservists anticipates several days for administrative processing. That includes everything from checking inoculation records to ensure shots are current, to making sure each soldier is comfortable with his last will and testament. It also includes detailed briefing of family members so they can take advantage of medical, commissary, post exchange and other benefits while their Guardsperson is away. None of this was accomplished for the riots. All National Guard men and women were federalized at the stroke of a pen, without having time to extend their families any of those benefits normally associated with active duty.

When the time approached to discuss defederalizing the troops, Washington originally insisted that all administrative minutiae be accomplished. This included lengthy administrative outprocessing, including lengthy forms attesting to their total military service. One was the same form (DD Form 214) that is used by a serviceman after a complete tour of duty to prove eligibility for benefits as a veteran. Complete medical and dental examinations were to be conducted, and legal counseling provided.

Brigadier General John R. (Jack) D'Arajuo of National Guard Bureau phoned to see if we were pushing for the lengthy outprocessing. We assured him we weren't, and expressed some of the frustration with what we considered onerous requirements. He helped fight the battle in Washington, and got some of the most burdensome requirements lifted. The medical and dental requirements were changed to verbal screenings, with doctors and dentists made available if that was what the soldier preferred. We still had to have federal forms (DD Forms 214), which required dozens of personnel clerks working for thousands of man-hours under Sixth Army's supervision. A big lesson was learned, and the Department of the Army agreed to do it differently next time.

In the meantime, the 40th Military Police Company was tasked to provide six security teams to accompany medical crews heading out to screen the troops. Guidance was also provided for actions to be taken by each unit when they received the demobilization order. Guardsmen assumed they couldn't be far behind the Army and Marines in being released. They were to be disappointed.

Federal troops were seen leaving the county on both Thursday and Friday. Their departure was made more disconcerting to citizens because the National Guardsmen charged with continuing to assist law enforcement had been told to maintain a low profile during the day. Citizens thought they were being abandoned. Phone calls were placed to political leaders pleading for assurances that Guardsmen would remain "until the streets return to normal," or were "one hundred percent safe."

Television reporters headed out to sample Angelenos' feelings about the military presence. One lady, when asked if she felt safer with troops around, responded, "Naturally, I can't help but feel anyone would, because they are here to protect everybody." Another acknowledged the troops' "ominous appearance," but recognized it was a false sense of security. As she put it, "the troops have to go sometime." In the Crenshaw District, one man said, "I think they should be here...until things settle down." Another lady said she felt much safer with the troops around. "We have a lot of kids who are 'off track,' and my son is one of them...and I feel safe with them (the troops) around."

Anticipating the return of control to the National Guard, General Thrasher sent a letter order to General Hernandez, naming him Military Field Commander as soon as the Guard was defederalized. Permission was explicitly given to return to many of the missions the National Guard had been performing prior to federalization. Those missions included:

-- Traffic and circulation control operations.

-- Static area security operations.

-- Detention facility security operations.

-- Patrols accompanying and augmenting law enforcement officers.

-- Providing security support for vital public utilities including firefighter support.

In the letter, I was named as the Adjutant General's "personal representative and liaison with political and law

261

enforcement officials...responsible for coordination and resolution of all policy issues." In effect, the letter codified what we agreed should have been the arrangement at the start.

Colonel Zysk phoned advice that the Sheriff's EOC intended to discontinue operations at 4:00 a.m. on Sunday, May 10th. In a separate call, we were told that the National Guard would be returned to state status at one minute past midnight on Saturday night.

The special Future Operations Task Force had worked through a good part of the night. They had identified a couple of things they were to accomplish, and wanted reassurances they were on track. One requirement was spelled out in big letters on the wall. It read "Prepare a one page summary of tasks for National Guard troops in support of civil disturbance control activities that will clearly define those which are appropriate for troops under *State* and *Federal* control. The task force was taking a two-pronged approach. They were addressing issues to make things work better between law enforcement and the military immediately, and they were also working to improve responsiveness if the National Guard was called for a civil disturbance in the future.

Later in the morning we had a joint meeting of the 40th Infantry Division's leadership and the task force. The task force presented their proposed one page Mission Tasking Guidelines. We then discussed how best to posture ourselves to respond if we were required again. It was emphasized that for any future civil disturbances:

    1. Mutual Aid would be in place before the National Guard is called.

    2. The Los Angeles Sheriff's EOC would be in charge of taskings.

3. The California National Guard is, in effect, the *last* step in Mutual Aid.

There was a far ranging discussion about the complexities in providing military support to a county with 43 different city police departments, and more than that many cities counting on the sheriff for protection. It was agreed that steps needed to be taken to reduce response time, be able to mass forces, and sustain that mass. The law enforcement officers in the meeting briefed how they felt their command structure would best be utilized in a similar emergency. They also emphasized the point that the mere presence of tactical military vehicles on the streets has a significant psychological effect.

It was agreed that the system would work best if continuing relationships were established between designated National Guard major commands and counterpart law enforcement agencies. It was generally agreed that the system would be more responsive if authority was delegated to the lowest level possible. Senior military commanders, for instance, should have the authority to call their troops to duty in an inactive duty status for a short period. That would speed up assembling the troops while formal requesting channels were being energized.

After the meeting broke up, copies of the draft Mission Tasking Guidelines were sent to affected commanders for comments and concurrence. The final product was a matrix designed to assist everyone in determining what missions were appropriate when the troops were in state status. Most were appropriate. When the troops were federalized, there was the same degree of flexibility *as long as the troops were restoring law and order*. However, if the troops were merely *maintaining* or *preserving law and order*, there were very few missions that were appropriate for the military. The matrix they produced looked like:

CIVIL DISTURBANCE
MISSION TASKING
GUIDELINES

APPROPRIATE	STATE	FEDERAL	
		RESTORE LAW/ORD	PRESERVE LAW/ORD
1. MAN TRAFFIC CONTROL POINTS	X	X	
2. PROVIDE BUILDING SECURITY	X	X	X(-)
3. ESCORT EMERGENCY EQUIPMENT	X	X	
4. PROVIDE AREA SECURITY/AREA PATROLS	X	X	
5. PROVIDE SECURITY AT CUSTODY FACILITIES	X	X	
6. PROVIDE SECURITY FOR EMERG WORK CREWS	X	X	X(-)
7. PROTECT SENSITIVE SITES	X	X	X(-)
8. TRANSPORTATION LAW ENFORCEMENT PERSONNEL	X	X	
9. SHOW OF FORCE	X	X	
10. DISPERSE CROWDS	X	X	
11. EMPLOY RIOT CONTROL AGENTS	X	X	
12. PROVIDE VIP PROTECTION/ESCORT	X	X	
13. PROVIDE RESERVE/QUICK REACTION FORCE	X	X	
14. JOINT PATROLS/RIDE ALONGS	X	X	
15. OTHER MISSIONS MUTUALLY AGREED UPON	X	X	X
INAPPROPRIATE			
1. HOSTAGE NEGOTIATION	X	X	X
2. BARRICADED SUSPECT	X	X	X
3. EVIDENTIARY SEARCHES	X	X	X
4. CRIMINAL INVESTIGATION	X	X	X

The planning pace really began to pick up. The same players met shortly after noon, with some additional staff officers. General Hernandez provided his "Commander's Intent" so both the Future Operations Task Force and the division staff were working in the same direction.

The Los Angeles Police Department's Foothill Division is located out toward the City of San Fernando. Home of the officers involved in the Rodney King incident, the station had been the target of obvious surveillance and drive-by threats. There also was a comparatively far-fetched intelligence report that gangbangers said they were going to bomb the station from the air using a private aircraft.

The 2-159th Infantry from Northern California was sent in to improve security around the Foothill station. The previous military there were not infantrymen. These infantry troops had the infantryman's typical esprit and conviction that no one, but *no one* could do that kind of a mission better. They then went on to prove it wasn't arrogance.

The Foothill station, like almost all police stations, is designed to be visible and accessible to the public. That, however, also means the station was vulnerable. This especially seemed to be the case at Foothill. The police had placed a school bus in front of the station to provide a barrier between the street and the station. The troops didn't think much of that.

First Sergeant Bruce E. Bay from Company D, 2-159th Infantry is a Production Machinist Mechanic at McClellan Air Force Base, and a former Marine. He didn't want the bus with all of its glass windows and flammable fuel around his troops. He said, "Anyhow, we got it organized. We put up a perimeter (of defense, around the station), and about 2000 sandbags." The troops quickly renamed the installation Fort Apache, and felt much better after they had constructed their fortifications, complete with gun ports.

The unit was billeted in a crowded Marine Corps Reserve Center, but went scouting for better quarters. They found them at the Veterans Administration Hospital. There they were very well cared for, to include having access to a gymnasium and showers.

An intriguing document was surreptitiously distributed to various agencies. The document was purportedly a joint demand from the Bloods and Crips, designed to solve the problems of Los Angeles. At least portions of the ten page document were provided to the media.

The first part of the proposal was designed to give Los Angeles a face-lift. It called for two billion dollars above existing appropriations. Every burned and gutted structure in the county would be removed. Community centers and career counseling or recreation areas were to be constructed in specified locations. Lighting was to increased in all neighborhoods and alleys. New trees were to be planted, existing trees trimmed, and there were to be no weeds. Proper pest control was to be implemented in the neighborhoods, with all vacant lots and trashed areas to be cleaned up.

The Bloods/Crips educational proposal had a total price tag of seven hundred million dollars. Three hundred million was to be spent upgrading schools, with two hundred million to be donated for computers, supplies, and adequate books for every student. No teacher in the district was to be paid less than $30,000 a year. There would be a special election of all Board of Education members. Every bathroom in the school district would have a bathroom monitor, who would sell low-cost freshen-up toiletries to support the salary of the bathroom monitor. Tutoring would be made available for every student, in every subject, after normal school hours. Students whose grades are up to par to be provided federally funded bonds applied to their college education. High achievers in specified academic disciplines, fifty per school, would be granted free trips to another country for an indefinite period each year.

The Bloods/Crips law enforcement program called for a "buddy system." They would be former gang members trained in law enforcement. They would be provided uniforms, video cameras and vehicles. All patrol units were to notify a buddy so they could be present in the event of a police matter, with each police matter videotaped. This part of the program had a six million dollar price tag.

The Bloods/Crips economic development proposal involved twenty million dollars for low interest (4% maximum) easily obtained, no collateral small business loans. The Small Business Administration was to provide expert assistance, from beginning to end, in developing business plans.

Their human welfare proposal called for one billion dollars. There would be three new hospitals built in the area, forty additional health care centers, plus dental clinics no more distant that ten miles from each community. All services would be free. All welfare was to be eliminated except for invalids and the elderly, and replaced by work programs. All parks were to have complete face-lifts, with activities, programs and security all through the night.

The total bill was estimated to total $3.726 billion over and above present appropriations. The demands were well written, using sophisticated language, although some financial estimates seemed extremely low. In return for meeting the demands, the Bloods/Crips committed to:

1. Request L.A.'s drug lords to invest their monies in Los Angeles.

2. Encourage drug lords to stop the drug traffic and use the money constructively. The document read then read "We will match the funds of the state government appropriations and build building-for-building."

3. Match funds for an Aids Research and Awareness Center in South Central and Long Beach that would only hire minority researchers and physicians to assist in the Aids epidemic. (It was not clear whether this was one center or two, or what funds were to be matched in what amount).

The document concluded, *"Meet these demands and the targeting of police officers will stop!!"* Seventy two hours were given for a response and commitment, in writing, to support the demands. Implementation was to begin within thirty days. All construction, including the hospitals, to be completed in ten years. Discussion about the document seemed to stop almost as suddenly as the document appeared.

Captain Bruce D. Pulgencio is a commander and helicopter pilot with the 1-18th Cavalry, and a firefighter with the City of Costa Mesa. He had been using his OH-58 helicopter, the military equivalent of the Bell Jet Ranger, for what he called "ash and trash" flights. That is, hauling people and supplies, being helpful any way possible.

He had taken Lieutenant Colonel Charlie Arce, Executive Officer of First Brigade, to Los Alamitos for a meeting with the division commander. Senior officers of the division had met to decide how to handle the annual training period. There was great concern about the number of days the Guardsmen were spending away from work. On the other hand, the combat readiness of the division was also of great concern, because the division felt itself in competition with other divisions for retention or elimination as part of the downsizing of the military. If they missed annual training, readiness ratings would suffer. They ended up making some complicated compromises.

Well after dark, Captain Pulgencio was landing in the Coliseum parking lot. There were shots fired just as they landed, from a drive-by down Martin Luther King Boulevard. The blue detachment of the Long Range Surveillance Detachment of the squadron immediately reacted along the perimeter, but no one was injured, and no holes were found in the helicopter.

He had a similar experience one afternoon four days later. He dropped off some passengers in the California Highway Patrol area of the Coliseum and was in the process of repositioning the aircraft to his own landing area. He took off, going about four hundred feet in the air to ensure he cleared all power lines, and crossed over a residential area in the process of repositioning. Suddenly shots rang out. Sergeant Pitts, his Aeroscout, saw and heard the shooting. The police responded very quickly, complete with a helicopter overhead. In spite of the quick response, and guidance from both the ground and Pulgencio's air-to-air radio, the sniper got away.

The JTF-LA Situation Report from General Covault to General Burba of Forces Command again emphasized that Friday night was extremely quiet. The night was extremely quiet in spite of predictions that the pace would pick up for the weekend. The JTF-LA headquarters was directed to maintain a presence at Los Alamitos in the event federal forces needed to be redeployed. General Covault assured National Guard leadership that he "had no intention of looking over their shoulder...(maintaining a headquarters there was) not a 'Big Brother' action."

269

While the action was extremely quiet for the military, the police were still feeling threatened. Shortly after midnight, two LAPD officers were dispatched to the area of 58th and Normandie. They were fired at by two suspects about a block away. They returned fire, hitting one of them in the groin, and arresting the other.

At 4:45 a.m., an LAPD officer in the San Fernando Valley area heard shots being fired at his home. He went outside and felt projectiles pass by his head. No suspects were caught.

A little later, three motor officers on their way home reported being followed by two vehicles at extremely high speeds up the San Diego Freeway. Two of the officers took the Highway 14 off ramp. The two vehicles continued to follow the third officer, who increased his speed to 110 m.p.h. The two vehicles stayed with him, so he took an off ramp, pulling his weapon as the two vehicles swerved slightly toward him. He got the license number of one of the vehicles.

Although they were isolated incidents, it was apparent that law enforcement was being targeted by some criminals. On the other hand, the military seemed to be facing little or no organized targeting by criminal elements.

CHAPTER THIRTEEN

May 9th through May 26th, 1992
TRANSITION AND DISENGAGEMENT

The Intelligence Summary for Saturday morning confirmed that 1,179 firearms, including a sniper rifle, had been stolen just from Western Surplus. Less than fifty weapons had been recovered in the next week. Troops were advised that the Revolutionary Communist Party planned to demonstrate at City Hall at 11:00 a.m. About fifty turned up, with ten then arrested for failing to disperse. The remainder dispersed and headed to their headquarters where their leader was scheduled to speak to them at 2:00 p.m.

Just before noon we met with General Covault. He advised that at 12:58 a.m. Eastern Daylight Time, Undersecretary of Defense Donald J. Atwood signed a paper which was then faxed to him authorizing defederalization and termination of JTF-LA. The Marines said they could have 3,000 troops back in two hours. Just to be safe, the 40th Division was doing their planning based on a three hour recall time. There was no shortage of troops, as the division had only 176 troops committed, 1,781 troops immediately available, and over 8,000 Guardsmen sitting around in armories and staging areas without missions.

At 12:48 p.m. we made a call to Lieutenant General Mallory in San Francisco. Generals Covault, Hernandez, Stewart, Thrasher and I were in the room, plus a half dozen others. We used a speakerphone to advise General Mallory that we had

271

agreed on defederalization to take place at midnight, and discussed various transitioning requirements. It was agreed that administrative responsibilities should move from JTF-LA to Sixth Army at 3:00 p.m.

Dr. Richard Andrews of OES, Buck Revell of the FBI, and Bob Mueller, the SCRAG; joined us at 1:00 p.m. It was decided that a conference call was necessary to include those who had previously been involved in such calls, but especially the Mayor. Dr. Andrews was concerned that Mayor Bradley, who initiated involvement of the federal troops, be comfortable with disengagement plans. The technique for announcing the plans was also discussed, and Dick Andrews started drafting a press statement.

A few minutes later, Undersheriff Bob Edmonds joined what was becoming a crowded conference room. He expressed concern about the trial verdict involving the police officer who shot the Samoans. He wanted to ensure the National Guard was available until it was clear that situation had been handled. Bob Mueller noted that timetables had to be adjusted because the defederalization administrative processing was going much faster than anticipated. The meeting began to break up just before 2:00 p.m.

Undersheriff Bob Edmonds and Lieutenant Dick Odenthal met with me after the meeting to discuss EOC staffing and the chain of taskings. We agreed to keep it the same, and just use a smaller staff.

Just after 3:00 p.m., the players reconvened in our conference room, joined by Governor Wilson. A conference call was placed, adding Anton Calleia to represent Mayor Bradley, and Chief of Police Daryl Gates. We had all of the senior military officers, plus Undersheriff Edmonds representing

272

Sheriff Block. There was pressure to say the transfer had already taken place, rather than say it would occur at midnight, to keep criminal elements from then testing the system. It really made no difference to the military, as we were fully prepared for a transition.

General Covault pointed out that it was unnecessary to layer a single headquarters over another headquarters, especially after the marines had left. He pointed out the 40th Division had been executing all missions for some time, and that it is dysfunctional for two headquarters to do the same thing. Undersheriff Edmonds emphasized that he had no apprehensions about the transition. For those not familiar with the issue, he discussed the trial involving the police officer who shot the Samoans, and described the Samoan communities in Carson and Compton.

The Governor asked if 176 was all the troops we really had committed, and what they were doing. We assured him the figure of 176 was accurate, and described their activities as area security plus response forces. Bob Edmonds pointed out that he wouldn't feel comfortable unless we had a quiet night or two without troops visible. The Governor agreed with that, and then left at 3:44 p.m. to make his press statement. His staff called it a press statement. It more accurately could have been described as a gross understatement:

"What it means is that we've had more Army, Marine and Guard troops than required. The regular contingent came very quickly. We were very grateful to receive them. Now it is time for them to return to their normal duties. We have, I think, *more than sufficient troops remaining* in place in terms of the Guard troops (emphasis added)."

The Governor's caravan left about 4:00 p.m., and we immediately joined the Future Operations Task Force in their wing of the building. Major Jim Thigpen and Sheriff's Lieutenant Odenthal briefed the group. The group involved most of those who had been meeting earlier, less the Governor and his staff, and included the federal military and civilian representatives. Joining the group were Command Sergeants Major Ramon Thompson (the State Sergeant Major), Jim Maxey (my Sergeant Major), and Rolland Alexander (40th Division).

The Missions Tasking Guidelines matrix was briefed as fully coordinated and ready for implementation. They then briefed the concept for future operations. Undersheriff Edmonds pointed out that the Sheriff's Office would be prepared to provide escorts to quickly get our troops anywhere they were needed. We discussed the fixes needed to ensure we could properly communicate throughout the county. We also discussed ways to posture the troops so they would be less visible yet quickly available if needed. We finally broke up at 5:25 p.m., and our future planners went back to work.

A meeting was conducted this evening among gang members and Jim Brown's group "American" at the Los Angeles Trade Technical College. The meeting was arranged by the Drug Enforcement Administration and the LAPD gang detail. There were representatives from gangs all over the county, plus several law enforcement officers. The focus of the meeting was to lessen violence and threats against police officers. The gang representatives downplayed the threats against police officers, saying that lower level gang members were making the threats to make a name for themselves and get attention. The various gang representatives denied any knowledge of who sent the four billion dollar demand (summarized earlier) to the city.

Elements of 1-18th Cavalry were supporting LAPD's 77th Street Division. They were having problems in one of the projects, and had requested transportation to carry prisoners. Major James L. Sullins, the Squadron Executive Officer, described what then happened. "Command Sergeant Major White and I were out visiting the troops. We had been guarding the (77th Street) station with a group of troops and a five ton truck. Just about the time we pulled up, the cops asked for help. The police captain was excited, and needed help. We tried to get through to get permission, but had no luck, so we made a decision on our own. We figured as long as we don't guard the prisoners, it would be O.K. to help.

"We went with them, the police leading, with the CSM (Command Sergeant Major) and I following (in a Hummer). The incident was next to a (housing) project at the edge of their jurisdiction. The crowds there were getting unruly, there were about twenty arrestees, and they had been sitting for about an hour. They had no transportation, and the situation was getting worse by the minute.

"When we arrived, it was a dark street. There were about twenty of them ranging from guys in their thirties who looked like football players, down to a 13-year-old girl. There was also a guy in a wheelchair they had taken a Mac-10 (submachine gun) away from. Across from us were the low cost apartment buildings about four stories high. The balconies were full of people. The gangbangers on the street had started chanting 'gangsters unite,' and the people on the balconies were responding in unison, 'gangsters unite.' This was late at night, and the hair stood up on the back of my neck. There were a lot of shotguns there with the police, but my four riflemen in the back were the only ones with rifles. I kind of felt like we were in a 'fire sac' (a military term describing a place where the enemy has all his weapons registered or pointed, hoping you will move into his 'fire sac' and be at a great disadvantage).

"We had trouble loading them on the truck, but finally did. We took off in a hurry with six patrol cars, lights and sirens doing about 45-50 miles per hour. As we were going down the street with all those black prisoners on the back of the truck, the sight was startling and had an adverse impact on some. Women on the side of the street were screaming, and covering their eyes. It probably looked like (we had) a load of kids. It was real shattering to us to see their response. I was wondering if we were doing the right thing getting involved in law enforcement. The good will we had been building over the last several days could be destroyed, and maybe was, by the scene we presented.

"There was television at the scene, we found out later. We got accused of arresting them. That brought the division commander in a hurry!" That was the only mission involving the trucking of prisoners that was performed. The reaction of people in the street will probably never be forgotten by the few Guardsmen involved.

A drive-by shooting was reported shortly after midnight at El Centro Avenue and Barton Street in LAPD's Hollywood Area. Four victims were hit with shotgun blasts, two seriously. The suspects were not apprehended, but the vehicle was identified as belonging to a member of the Mara Saldatrucha gang.

An LAPD helicopter was assisting ground units with a search in the Hillcrest area about 2:00 a.m. A citizen phoned in saying he saw sparks and flames coming out of the back of the helicopter. Another citizen reported seeing a suspect on a roof with a rifle. When the LAPD helicopter landed at the heliport, they found the aircraft had been hit.

Lieutenant Colonel William H. Wade's 2-160th Infantry was in the process of assuming responsibility for the Baldwin Hills Crenshaw Mall from 2-185th Armor, and conducted several leader's reconnaissances throughout the area. Lieutenant Colonel Wade and the battalion operations officer, Major Daniel E. Barnett, checked on various foot patrols shortly after dark. They took separate routes through the battalion's new area of operations and intuitively felt their area was going to be a challenge.

They were finding that evenings in the area, especially on Sundays, were occasions for heavy cruising and wall-to-wall people on the sidewalks down Crenshaw. Both Hummers headed down Crenshaw to about 41st Street. They saw about 150 low riders (automobiles customized so they ride very low, and lots of loud music. There was considerable hell raising, and a lot of animosity shown the troops, including obscene gestures as well as the by-now-routine taunting.

When the Hummers got back to the mall, six rapid shots rang out. About a dozen gangbanger's cars raced north up Crenshaw, followed quickly by another dozen. Suddenly the place was empty, almost like magic. They later found that the shots had broken out the window of a video store across from the mall.

We phoned the National Guard Bureau EOC first thing Monday morning, the 11th, and told them things were extremely quiet. They were urged to assist us in getting the troops home quickly, or indiscipline could result. They were given a quick summary of how we were making the transition, and that troops were being repositioned to facilitate rapid disengagement. We got a call back in a few minutes asking for additional information on the troops being retained in federal status due to medical and legal issues.

Most of those issues were rather routine. The most significant one involved a noncommissioned officer who went public, discussing on television his frustrations with the Rules of Engagement, and most especially, the Arming Orders. The soldier had been admonished in advance not to discuss these issues, and commander had tape recorded the admonition as he was warning his soldiers. The soldier ended up in Fort Ord's stockade and was court-martialed.

We then had another key session with our Future Operations Task Force. In attendance were Commander Bayan Lewis and Lieutenant Bruce Ward of LAPD, and Mike Guerin of OES. By this time Lieutenant Colonel Dannice J. (Dan) McCann, former G3 of the 40th Division and a highly experienced operational planner, had joined the team to assist in writing the final plan. The group was introduced, the genesis of the project explained as well as the Missions Tasking Guidelines matrix. Major Jim Thigpen and Sheriff's Lieutenant Dick Odenthal then explained the intent and implementation concepts of the operations plans they were developing. By this time a relatively sophisticated time line had been graphed, showing the many actions required based on twenty four hours from the first call to soldiers deployed on the street.

A general discussion followed. There was considerable discussion about how things really happened when the riots first exploded, and how the formal mutual aid system was never properly employed. The authority given National Guard commanders to liaison and train in an inactive duty (normal weekend drill) training status was explained. Mike was assured that we wouldn't formalize execution of orders until OES issued a mission number. He was confident that Dr. Andrews would support the briefed concept for both Los Angeles and San Francisco. We also discussed coverage for other major metropolitan areas in the state. It was emphasized that if the concept had been in place previously, to include liaison officers, there would have been fewer troops called, much less had any people feel federal troops should be involved.

The Sheriff's EOC dispatched a message advising they did not expect a verdict on the Skiles case soon. The message included an analysis suggesting that the number and readiness of forces could be cut back. Unfortunately, no one seemed to be listening.

Deputy Chief Bill Booth and Captain Keith Bushey met with General Bill Stewart and I just before 1:00 p.m. on Monday. We were told that LAPD would go on tactical alert when the Skiles trial verdict came in. Deputy Chief Booth told us how much Chief Gates appreciated our services. We briefly discussed operational plans.

At the same time our Future Operations Task Force was looking out to future operational missions and response contingency plans state-wide, the division had been working on plans to phase down operations. This effort was worked under the supervision of General Stewart, the Assistant Division Commander for Maneuver, and included a four phased withdrawal plan.

Very early in the morning, police raided several homes and picked up three suspects in the Reginald Denny beatings. The suspects were all members of the notorious Eight Trey Gangster Crips. Chief Daryl Gates personally was involved in the arrest of one of the three, with a fourth suspect turning himself in. Several people called LAPD over the next several days and surrendered their videotapes of the riots to assist in apprehending criminals.

On Tuesday, May 12th, we were told that The International Committee Against Racism planned a demonstration for 4529 S. Vermont Avenue at 7:00 p.m. in the evening.

Chaplain (Captain) Bob Field of 1-185th Armor was going to add to his reputation this day. You may remember he was the chaplain who got "flashed" by a female exposing her ample bosom in broad daylight at the corner of Vernon and Vermont. Chaplain Field had to make a run to the home area in San Bernardino, and was riding in the passenger seat of a Hummer, with about five or six Guardsmen in the back. They were heading up the freeway when he noticed a red Firebird sports car traveling beside them to the right. He could see that the very attractive blonde driving the car was busy writing something. She finished writing, and then handed the note to Chaplain Field. It read, "Thanks! Let's Party!" The troops in the back were understandably eager to see what the note said, so the chaplain passed it back. The chaplain continues with the story. "She took the next exit off, and we needed to stretch our legs right then, I guess...so we did too. She had stopped, we did too. Those (who were) young bachelors in back hopped out, made a date, and partied later."

We were advised at 5:01 p.m. that the Governor planned to announce the first release of National Guard troops in five minutes, but to take no action until we saw it on television or received official notification. At 5:24 p.m. we got another phone call advising the release had been officially approved.

280

The division's withdrawal plan as originally designed and approved:

-- Phase I. This phase would send the troops from Northern California home, including the Third Brigade, 1-144th Field Artillery, 2-160 Infantry, most of the 132nd Engineers, and all of the 49th Military Police Brigade. This would reduce the 10,072 troops still on duty to 6,375, of which 4,187 would be available for street missions.

-- Phase II. This phase would release other troops with armories distant from Los Angeles, primarily from San Diego and other cities to the south and east. That included 1-185th Armor, 240th Support, and 240th Signal. The Second Brigade would be released except for their 4-160th Infantry. The troops on duty would then total 4,272, with 3,069 available for street missions.

-- Phase III. This phase included comparatively small parts of the Division Support Command and Artillery. The troops on duty would then total 3,883, with 2,742 available for street missions.

-- Phase IV. Phase IV was a little more complicated, designed for incremental phasing within. It started with what was called Task Force Weil, based on Colonel Bill Weil's First Brigade as reinforced by other elements. It could be gradually phased down until nothing was left except the 40th Military Police Company. That unit was designated to be the last out for the same reason it was the first in. They were particularly well suited for civil disturbance missions.

The written confirmation for implementation of Phase I was faxed to us at 5:27 p.m. It seemed to take forever to get anyone to authorize our release of any troops, but when it was once decided, it moved very quickly. A copy of Governor Wilson's press release was faxed an hour later.

A short time later we received a copy of a drawdown schedule from OES that detailed the projected timing of withdrawals. Phase II was scheduled for May 14th, Phase III for May 16th, and Phase IV for May 18th, but could not be implemented without express concurrence from OES acting in the name of the Governor. It was made clear that any release publicity would come from the Governor's Press Office.

A good part of the day was devoted to refining what eventually was called "Contingency Plan (CONPLAN) *Reliable Response.*" By the end of the day it had been published and distributed. It was a comprehensive document designed to provide support to Los Angeles in the event there was another civil disturbance. As all agencies collaborated in writing the plan, it could be implemented almost immediately. The plan had a military date/time group of 120800May92 (8:00 a.m. on May 12, 1992), and included nine annexes. The annexes provided information on task organizing, mission tasking guidelines, communications, responsibilities of liaison officers, aviation support, service support, maps, law enforcement organization and points of contact, and rules of engagement. Two additional annexes were to be provided later. One was a glossary of terms. The other was the Intelligence Summary that is rarely meaningful in a contingency plan, but is extremely important when updated at the last minute with the latest information available.

On Wednesday, May 13th, several convoys of troops were heading north as part of the first withdrawal of troops. Six C-130 loads of troops had departed Los Alamitos by noon, with several more sorties planned. The various Emergency Operations Centers in the Pentagon to monitor the situation were shut down.

Gang members at 7:10 p.m. were reported gathering at 107th Street and Normandie to discuss gang unity. There were about 200 estimated to be in attendance, blocking streets. About two hours later about a hundred gang members were reported in South Park. The Sheriff's Department established a command post at Imperial Highway and Normandie Avenue.

The 3-160th Infantry got the word about the gang gathering, and were told to get their Quick Reaction Force ready to roll. In the meantime, police officers went there to check out the problem, only to have rocks thrown and police sedans rocked before they withdrew. The battalion commander, Major Bill Wenger: "They wanted 120 soldiers, and told us they would send a black and white escort. At about 2100 (9:00 p.m.) they arrived. The LAPD lieutenant briefed me, we were ready to roll, and then rolled through the street 'Code 3' with five or six cars escorting us. The Guardsmen were singing a song, beating time with feet and riot batons on truck beds, singing, 'Our gang is bigger than your gang, our gang's bigger than yours...(to the tune of a nursery rhyme).'

"I think our driving through the streets of South Central (Los Angeles) tended to defuse the situation. We arrived south of 107th and Normandie. There were fifty to a hundred cars, helicopters overhead, and the media there. Lieutenant Colonel Marv Metcalf was there with about a hundred soldiers from the cav' (1-18th Cavalry). All were preparing to make a sweep and clear the area. The gangbangers heard about it, and dispersed on their own."

The order for implementation of Phase II of the Division's withdrawal plan was received at 2:45 p.m. on Thursday, May

14th, by Colonel Dick Beardsley. By this time, only 279 of 8947 available Guardsmen were actually committed to missions of any kind.

It was reported at 2:30 a.m. on Friday that gangs intended to destroy utility power sources and then attack police officers in the dark. There were several reports that if the four Denny beating suspects weren't released by the end of the week, rioting would resume. Later reports were that the rioting would begin at sundown on May 16th.

A couple of flyers were distributed calling for a general strike on Friday. The flyers included demands for the removal of all troops, the release of all arrestees, reparations to black businessmen, that Officer Powell be tried, that all four LAPD officers be charged for civil rights violations, and that the officers be turned over to the black community for trial.

The execute order for Phase III of the Division's withdrawal plan was received at 1:59 p.m., a day earlier than expected. It was very welcome nonetheless. Someone had finally figured out that having thousands of troops doing nothing was not only expensive to the Guardsmen involved (and the firms they worked for), but was also a significant drain on the State's treasury.

Intelligence for several days said this night would be "White Night," with blacks attacking whites. At least one Quick Reaction Force was called, with Company C of the 4-160th receiving a warning order that they might be needed. Very quickly old relationships began to kick in. Lieutenant Dick Odenthal used to be from this battalion. He talked direct to Captain Jeff Bygum, the company commander, giving him as much intelligence as he had.

Dick was the Battalion S-2 (Intelligence Officer) when he was a Guardsman, and Jeff was his Scout Platoon Leader. The Scout Platoon is the operational arm for the S-2, and they had developed a close working relationship. It was obvious that Dick was concerned, and he wanted Jeff to have as much information as possible before he was committed into Compton.

The troopers were loaded and told to report for a mission west of the Compton armory on Alameda Street. They ended up at the Davis Middle School on Wilmington just south of Rosecrans. The Compton Police told them there were about 300 gangbangers racing up and down the street. There were a lot of bottles thrown, windows broken, and looting going on in a situation that evidently involved two rival gangs. Captain Bygum could see two bodies in the street, though at first he didn't know if they were dead or alive. At about 3:00 a.m. a SWAT team arrived, and started moving through the area. They found one of the victims dead, and the other one still alive, so an ambulance was called. The area was cordoned off, but with obvious escape routes left open so the gangbangers would just disperse. Street sweepers got the mess cleaned up before anyone could see it during the morning rush hour.

An informant said that gangs would rally on Saturday, May 16th, to kill an LAPD officer. The Intelligence Summary also noted that the Chosen Few Motorcycle Gang reportedly stole a large amount of ammunition in the Fresno area and planned to join the gangs this date. We were also told that Fritz Patterson of OES had gotten the word from the State Department that effective 8:00 a.m. we were released from the Korean Consulate mission.

There was a large gang-sponsored picnic at the park near El Segundo Boulevard and Central from noon until 7:00 p.m. The flyers mentioned Crips, but both Bloods and Crips participated. The police did not go into the park, although they kept circling it, and had helicopters flying over. One participant said, "We were holding hands, eating together, hugging each other. That is something I will always remember. The truce did not last, but it was really something at that picnic!"

It was reported at 4:00 p.m. that gang members in the Jordan Downs housing projects were seen wearing black clothing with bulletproof vests and were heavily armed. They were planning to kill a police officer some time in the evening. Nothing came of the threat, and the gangsters wearing bulletproof vests weren't spotted outside of the projects.

Undersheriff Edmonds, General Hernandez and I met in the late afternoon to discuss strategy. It was decided to maintain a two hundred man force for a while to serve a dual purpose. The military would be seen every once in a while, raising a concern in gangbangers' minds about the presence of the military. Just as important, there would be a highly responsive force of 200 hundred soldiers available in case they were needed.

A USC sorority invited thirty five members of the 1-18th Cavalry to lunch as thanks. They had what the troops described as "a real nice sit-down lunch." For soldiers who had been generally having to eat with food balanced in their laps, this event was very much appreciated. There was a poster out in front of the sorority house reading "Welcome California National Guard. We love you." Later the soldiers brought the college students to the Coliseum to see their operational setup, vehicles and helicopters.

At 5:00 p.m. the Governor agreed to withdraw National Guard troops but decided to leave a ready response force of

1500 troops. At 5:05 p.m., it was reported there were eight people shot, three stabbed and one confirmed dead in a gang clash at the Pomona Fair Grounds. There were about two hundred gang members involved. Several hours later it was reported that about six hundred gang members were reported racing up and down Rosecrans Boulevard. A platoon of National Guardsmen was sent.

Some black soldiers were very up tight, as were Hispanics to a lesser degree, about returning to their communities after the emergency was over. They were not as tense as they were when originally committed to suppressing the riots, but they nonetheless were extremely concerned about how their neighbors would react. They knew that some neighbors considered them "traitors" to the black cause. Some units had sessions with their black soldiers to talk the problem through and help prepare them for the return home and the reaction of their neighbors.

The return home was not eased by knowing that many of their neighbors were gang members. Some of the returning Guardsmen had been gang members themselves. They certainly knew more than most about complex motivations driving members of various gangs in their neighborhoods.

Rather interestingly, Command Sergeant Major Dorsey in his counseling sessions during the riots, made it clear that if black Guardsmen were uncomfortable in the role they had been assigned, they could do something about it *after* the mission was over. In effect, he would support them getting out of their enlistment contracts. Almost a year after the riots, he was not aware of any soldiers who did that. In fact, he felt most of the Guardsmen were better soldiers, and felt better about themselves, after the riots.

Task Force Arce (pronounced Ar'see) was announced May 18th, to be effective at noon on Tuesday. Task Force Arce was designed to be a stay-behind force held in reserve after all other troops had been released. The Commander's Intent:

"My intent is to draw down forces to a force of 200 soldiers deployed forward. They will be capable of deploying on the streets within 30 minutes. A reinforcing force of 200 more soldiers will be staged at AFRC. This will be designated as TF Arce."

Lieutenant Colonel Arce selected his commanders and staff, and organized a force of 400 soldiers to be quickly ready if needed. They trained in airmobile operations, and had several training exercises involving the Lakewood Sheriff's Station. They learned to quickly arm, undergo a rapid precombat inspection, mount up and be ready for Sheriff's escorts. This force of 400 soldiers was cut in half after a short while. Task Force Arce was never called for an actual operational mission.

The balance of May was relatively quiet. A mistrial in the Skiles case was declared shortly after noon on May 19th. A city wide tactical alert was called, but the streets were quiet. Members of the Jamaican Mafia were reported on May 21st being flown from New York to Los Angeles at the request of gang members to battle the police on May 22nd.

On Saturday, May 23rd, the normal weekend escalation of activities occurred. In the afternoon, a group of 75 gang members from various gangs assembled at a local junior high school, but were dispersed by school police. At 5:30 p.m., police making arrests in the area of 88th Street and Hoover Avenue had a gang of about five hundred people try to take the arrestees away.

On Sunday evening, at 6:00 p.m., several carloads of suspects were seen going into the Imperial Courts Housing Projects. At 10:25 p.m., responding officers were met with rocks and bottles from the residents. Several gunshots were reported in the housing projects and gang members were seen running away from the scene with shotguns. Five hundred gang members were reported assembled in the Imperial Courts Housing Projects at 1:00 a.m.

All in all, it had been an unusually quiet weekend. At 8:00 a.m. on Monday, the National Guard pulled their liaison personnel out of the county EOC. Over the next several days, Task Force Arce phased out, with no response forces left by the end of the week.

Troops guarding burnt out buildings
(Photo by SSG Alan Zanger)

CHAPTER FOURTEEN

POLITICS, EGOS, AND CONTROVERSY

The riots erupted in the midst of biennial political campaigns, just six weeks before primary elections in California. At any other time, many of those not directly involved describe these activities as the "silly season." However, the riots, property and lives at risk were much too serious for people to even think in those terms at the time.

Politicians and political candidates made a great many visits into the riot-torn areas. All of them required security and sizeable escorts, but that was expected and was no real problem. There was also the rally and demonstration advertised for "Justice and Solidarity" that suddenly sprouted with the sponsor's campaign signs as soon as the crowd gathered. That again created no difficulty, but served to illustrate that motivations were sometimes suspect during those turbulent times.

It seemed obvious to many of us that politics and egos had a significant impact on various important decisions made during the riots and for several weeks afterward...although we'll never know precisely to what degree. Sometimes senior officials merely wanted to appear fully "in charge," or posture themselves to take maximum advantage of the incredible numbers of media personnel in the area. At other times, decisions were made to help justify more questionable decisions made previously.

Military officers are expected to adhere to a rigid code of integrity. An officer's word is his bond in a code that naturally evolved in a profession where lives are at stake, and where decisions must be based on the assumption of honest input and guidance. Unfortunately, others don't always feel they must adhere to such a code. As a consequence, soldiers occasionally found themselves responding to suspect guidance, driven by motivations that appeared to be more political than operational. Those decisions ranged from deployment timing and techniques, through calling for federal troops, to unconscionable delays before releasing troops to return home.

There were four particularly controversial issues surrounding the riots. They were the Rodney King verdict that triggered the riots, the slowness of the initial police response, the delays in deploying the National Guard, and the decision to call for federal troops followed by federalization of the National Guard which created problems for law enforcement officials.

1. *THE RODNEY KING VERDICT.*

The failure to convict any one of the four defendants was totally unexpected by most of the public. Expectations for findings of guilt were fueled by the media's repeated airing of a shortened version of the tape showing just the most brutal aspects of the beating. Public reactions to the jury's decisions were exacerbated by initial statements immediately afterwards from the Mayor and other political leaders expressing shock and disbelief at the verdicts. The public outcry, demonstrations, rioting, looting and burning that followed were predictable and unfortunate reactions. On the other hand, the public expectations were somewhat vindicated when two of the four

(Stacey Koon and Laurence Powell) were convicted during a federal trial that ended about a year later.

2. THE SLOW RESPONSE BY POLICE.

The slowness of response by the police has been much debated and investigated. Those delays were commented on by the media repeatedly during the riots. One wag even said that if the police had been away from Florence and Normandie any longer, police faces would have been printed on milk cartons along with missing children.

Politics tended to waft through the repetitive finger pointing that went on over police problems in responding to the riots. The fact that the Mayor and Chief of Police had not directly spoken to each other for over a year was well documented. The City Council was the other corner of the triumvirate with overall responsibility for public safety. There had been considerable acrimony in the stormy relationships between the various elements of city government for years. It was obvious even to outsiders that the machinery of city government was not smooth and well-oiled, a situation that had to detract from effective policing. The proof to corroborate empirical conclusions regarding blame was eventually supplied by a panel of experts empowered by the Los Angeles Board of Police Commissioners. After months of intensive investigation, almost no one in the city escaped criticism.

That investigation was initiated on Monday, May 11, 1992 when the Los Angeles Board of Police Commissioners appointed Judge William H. Webster to investigate LAPD preparations for civil disturbances, and police responsiveness after the riots started. Judge Webster, named Special Advisor to the Police Commission, was formerly Director of the Federal

Bureau of Investigation, and later the Central Intelligence Agency. Appointed as his Deputy Special Advisor was Hubert Williams, the President of the Police Foundation of Washington, D.C., and former Police Chief of Newark, New Jersey.

Richard J. Stone, from Webster's law firm of Milbank, Tweed, Hadley and McCoy, assumed the duties of General Counsel and Staff Director. Much of the hard work in ferreting out details during the investigation was accomplished on a *pro bono publico* basis by a large number of lawyers and paralegal assistants. There were over a hundred names of principals and staff that assisted Judge Webster listed in the final report. They participated in over four hundred interviews, typically using teams of two who conducted very thorough interrogations. In addition, Judge Webster and his associates studied police standards in other cities. They also sponsored seven town meetings to ascertain attitudes in some of the neighborhoods most heavily impacted by the riots, and conducted surveys that produced highly informative data.

On October 21, 1992, Judge Webster's "Office of the Special Advisor to the Board of Police Commissioners, City of Los Angeles" submitted its 2-volume report (hereafter called the "Webster Report"). In one of its most basic findings, the report noted that the LAPD response clearly was disorganized. Judge Webster's team felt the most important recommendations were these three:

1. Reorganize police resources away from special units and towards patrol duties.

2. The City and LAPD must do more emergency response planning and training, to include training in the use of mutual aid.

3. Make improvements to the City's Emergency Operations Center and emergency communications systems.

In addition, the following conclusions and recommendations were provided:

1. Neither the City nor LAPD prepared specific plans in enough detail to deal with the disturbance, and must share responsibility for the lack of prior planning. A Master Plan, with comprehensive inter-departmental plans, involving all City departments, is required for responses to any reasonably probable contingency. Plans must address tactics, command and control, logistics, and communications.

2. An investment is needed in modern emergency equipment for the Police Department.

3. The Police Department should adopt "problem-solving partnerships" with communities of the city.

4. Senior (Captain and above) staff officers should be placed in field commands wherever possible.

5. As many as possible of the 1600 unmarked LAPD sedans should be repainted as black and white fully-equipped patrol sedans and used in that capacity.

6. A training program is needed to enhance the ability of police officers to work with diverse communities and cultures.

The Webster Report also noted the problems with morale and *esprit de corps* as a consequence of attacks, or the perception of attacks, on LAPD. The (Warren) Christopher Commission had investigated charges of excessive force and racial intolerance in the LAPD following the Rodney King beating. This was one of the factors blamed by some for the near-paralysis of senior LAPD leadership during the crisis. The attacks clearly had an impact on police officers, who felt "damned if they did, and damned if they didn't" take strong action against minority lawbreakers.

National Guardsmen, some of whom worked for police departments of other cities, noted this ambivalent attitude of LAPD officers. Quite often they were surprised when LAPD officers failed to arrest lawbreakers, or even let lawbreakers go, during the riots. In spite of that, every soldier and marine returned from riot duty with a more thorough understanding of and appreciation for the life-threatening dangers police face every day and night in Los Angeles County. If not before, almost all of the military troops now have a much more profound regard for officers in law enforcement throughout the area.

There were many police heroes during the first hours of the riots. Publicity, however, was directed at the initial failures of the police department as the city suffered through the anguish and pain of scenes brought into every living room showing flames, looting, injuries and death. It wasn't until long after the fact that many stories about individual acts of heroism performed by police and firemen were publicized.

One of the three most important recommendations in the Webster Report mentioned the failure to properly utilize the Mutual Aid system. Mutual aid in California is a well-designed system of law enforcement officers helping neighboring law enforcement jurisdictions when situations escalate beyond local capabilities. Too little mutual aid was called too late to help control the situation while the National Guard mobilized. Experienced officers within the California Office of Emergency Services tried to implement the system early, but were unable to energize senior management.

A meeting of senior law enforcement officials to discuss mutual aid was later called by the State Office of Emergency Services on June 19, 1992 in Los Angeles. The meeting was attended by the Sheriffs from seven counties, plus senior officials from various state and local agencies. One of the more senior law enforcement participants wrote Dr. Richard Andrews, the Director of the Office of Emergency Services, a letter three days later. In the three page letter, he said "The entire meeting (of June 19th) was a graphic reminder of how fragile the line is between order and anarchy. In order to maintain that line, it was the consensus that a quick law enforcement response is essential. In this instance (the L. A. riots) that did not occur, and we all agreed to examine the process to determine what could be done to respond quickly and quell disturbances before they become contagious." He then listed, under the title "Findings," the following points:

-- "It was the overwhelming opinion that our existing Mutual Aid system and process is time-tested and proven to function well when it is utilized and followed.

-- "The Mutual Aid system was not put into place in proper fashion, nor was the request for mutual aid made in a timely manner.

-- "The Mutual Aid system was circumvented, and we must remember that even politicians need to follow time-proven practices and work within the system.

-- "National Guard troops were requested by the Mayor and committed by the Governor before a law enforcement mutual aid request occurred.

-- "The receiving agency was not ready for the assistance when it was available, nor had they planned missions for law enforcement and/or the National Guard prior to their arrival.

-- "The National Guard response should never be expected in less than 24 hours. The Sheriff's plan in Los Angeles did, in fact, allow for 24-hour response for the National Guard. The National Guard should always be 'the last in and the first out.' In this case the National Guard was there six hours faster than any plan should expect them to be (18 hours versus 24 hours after request), but they were called in before law enforcement (Mutual Aid) and were kept in the area after law enforcement was relieved."

3. *THE DELAYED RESPONSE OF THE NATIONAL GUARD*

The above conclusions from highly regarded law enforcement officials received almost no publicity. What did receive almost as much press as slowness of the police response was the perceived delay in deployment of the National Guard. This impression was fed from several sources. Television news cameramen took film of Guardsmen practicing riot control formations inside of armories rather than deploying into the streets. Interspersed with scenes of a city in flames during the worst of the riots, the question about delays was a natural one.

The next event that impacted perceptions of delays was law enforcement leadership being told in error that the National Guard was ready to go at 10:00 a.m. Thursday morning. That had an obvious impact on expectations, though none of the Guardsmen in Southern California even knew about that assertion until long after the riots. It should be remembered that they had been promised ammunition and equipment by noon, although those supplies didn't actually land until just prior to 2:00 p.m.

298

Nothing, however, had a greater impact on Guardsmen or the perception of their response, than public assertions by their Commander in Chief, Governor Pete Wilson. He started talking about the slowness of response on Thursday, and mentioned it on a daily basis into the next week. On Sunday, in his most controversial statement, he talked about "heads rolling" over the issue.

As we have seen, the City of Los Angeles and their police department were not prepared for the riots. Prior planning was inadequate and lacked specificity. What about the California National Guard? The National Guard was also caught unprepared. No professional soldier likes to be caught unprepared, but it happened in this case.

The Guard had been provided many excuses, none of them compelling. For instance, the headquarters had just been reorganized in a rather controversial decision that ended up with a significant reshuffling of senior officers. Any headquarters needs some time to settle into new assignments and responsibilities. Therefore, the timing of the reorganization turned out to be most unfortunate. To compound the problem, state agencies and law enforcement officials in Southern California had told the National Guard they wouldn't be needed. The National Guard even sent scarce riot control equipment off for others to use. Nonetheless, we in senior leadership had an obligation to make our own assessment of the likelihood of commitment in advance. As is obvious in retrospect, we made a grievous error in judgment. Again, we were caught unprepared, and shouldn't have been.

The ammunition was slow in arriving. This was due to several factors. Key was that security ammunition scattered around the state had been recalled to San Luis Obispo for inventory, reallocation for use on ranges (it was becoming old), and redistribution to fewer regional sites. While it was in San Luis Obispo, the National Guard was vulnerable. There was no excuse for this, as the regional sites could have been stocked before the security ammunition was recalled for inventory and reallocation. Sad and rather obvious lesson learned.

But was the National Guard slow? The military is famous for having a standard for almost everything, including speed of deployment. What is the standard any military force should be measured against?

The readiest ready force in the United States Army (and perhaps in the world) is the 82nd Airborne Division at Fort Bragg, North Carolina. For many years, the 82nd Airborne Division has been at the top of the Army's rapid deployment or contingency lists. The 82nd Airborne Division was and is *the* standard for the United States Army, the first to be called in an emergency worldwide.

The deployment events and timing standards for the 82nd Airborne Division are found in their Readiness Standard Operating Procedures (RSOP). This is a highly detailed, unclassified document that spells out all the actions required to quickly deploy the division. An appendix spells out all the actions required to deploy the first Division Ready Force (DRF-1) from a no-warning start. Their DRF-1 is the most ready of nine battalion-sized task forces (numbered from DRF-1 through DRF-9). Timing sequences in the document are based on "N-Hour" (N=Notification) starting with receipt and authentication of the initial order. Ten pages of detailed requirements follow, actions required to move the most ready military force in the United States Army.

The detailed requirements to properly deploy a large force of soldiers are often overlooked by the non-professional, uninitiated, or by junior soldiers for that matter. What kind of details? For the 82nd Airborne, they range from performing maintenance on vehicles to ensure they are ready to go (N+2:30), to turning in supply room keys (N+3:45), to mission briefs (N+16:00). The first aircraft of the division's most ready force is programmed for "wheels up" (departure) at N+18:00. That is eighteen hours from first notification to departure, not arrival in the commitment area, but initial departure.

The other standard is referred to as the "Garden Plot" standard. This is the title of the Department of Defense plan for response to civil disturbances. The standard is less clear in that document, but is commonly interpreted to be 24 hours for staging and 36 hours for commitment.

The actual deployment times of the federal forces were very close to standard. Ignoring whether or not they received any advance warning, comparing times after they received their official notification is instructive. The 7th Infantry Division (Light) received their notification at 4:15 a.m. on Friday. They started flying their ready brigade at 4:30 p.m. that day, with the last aircraft landing at about 5:00 a.m. Saturday. It should be noted that the Monterey Airport is some distance from Fort Ord, and the brigade force flown is considerably larger than that described for the 82nd Airborne Division. After they arrived in Southern California, their initial commitment into the riot zone was delayed for operational reasons; that is, they were initially placed in reserve, though there was no lack of readiness on the part of the soldiers.

The Marines provide a better example of actual deployment times for an active duty force. The Marines at Camp Pendleton were notified at 6:00 a.m. Friday, and convoyed to Tustin starting at 2:30 p.m. that afternoon. They had their ammunition, but not their riot control equipment, and commenced riot control training. They were deployed on Saturday, with initial elements arriving on site by about 4:00 p.m. Their total elapsed time was 34 hours, slightly faster than the accepted Garden Plot standard.

The California National Guard was notified slightly after 9:00 p.m. on Wednesday night. Guardsmen left their homes and businesses and reported to their armories to begin the almost metamorphic transition from civilian to soldier. The 40th Military Police Company had two platoons ready at 1:30 p.m. (N+16:30), was completely ready when the Sheriff's guides arrived at 2:35 p.m. (N+17:35), and was fully deployed by 3:30 p.m. (N+18:30). That particular unit, incidentally, wasn't notified until 11:10 p.m. Wednesday night, so some might feel two hours should be subtracted from their deployment time.

The second company had an even more impressive odyssey time-wise. This 670th Military Police Company, split in two locations hundreds of miles to the north, was notified at 3:15 a.m. Thursday. By noon they were airborne, and were committed on the streets by 4:00 p.m. (N+13) Thursday afternoon. Those first two companies were quickly followed by a full battalion, with a second battalion committed before N+24.

Perhaps a couple of points should be made. One is of great importance to the senior commanders. That is, the National Guard started committing troops *before* any joint military-law enforcement command and control arrangements were agreed to and in place. That was clearly a risk, but a risk they were willing to take based on confidence in both the Guardsmen and their leadership at all involved levels, as well as confidence in the law enforcement officers to whom they reported. Those extremely important joint command and control decisions were being agreed to in Sheriff Block's conference room at the same time the 40th Military Police Company was entering the riot zone.

The second point regards the logistical challenges that had to be met before Guardsmen were sent into hazardous situations. The problem with ammunition was only the most publicized. There weren't adequate numbers of face shields, flak vests, riot batons, and lock plates (for weapons) on hand in the state. Logisticians had to gather this equipment from depots and the National Guard of neighboring states before troops could be properly equipped and committed. As a mechanized division that normally travels in tracked vehicles, transportation also had to be arranged. Rules of Engagement to match the L.A. riot situation had to be written, approved, disseminated to 43 different armories, reproduced, read and signed by every Guardsman.

On Thursday, June 4th, the Governor appointed retired Active Army Lieutenant General William H. Harrison to look into the National Guard's delays. His report to the Governor was dated October 2, 1992. General Harrison didn't have much if any help in the way of staff, so his effort should not be compared to the Webster Report. General Harrison's report has many minor errors, but none of them impact on his conclusions and recommendations which faulted National Guard planning, and determined that the response was slow.

General Harrison's report doesn't address acceptable standards for mobilizing the National Guard and committing them in support of law enforcement, nor compare the timing with Active Army standards or the actual deployment of the federal troops. He did however, mention the same 24 hour expectation for National Guard troops that was also discussed in the letter to OES. His conclusion that the National Guard was slow is his own opinion, but an important opinion. It should be emphasized that nothing written here is meant to derogate General Harrison's efforts. He is an outstanding senior officer of unquestioned professionalism and integrity. We simply disagree on this issue. To summarize the various time lines:

-- 24 hours is the time shown in the Sheriff's plan for commitment of the National Guard and agreed to in various planning sessions.

-- 18 hours is the "wheels up" standard for departure of the first unit of the 82nd Airborne Division.

-- 24 hours is the staging time standard derived from the Department of Defense's Garden Plot plan.

-- 24 hours was the staging time actually taken by federal troops when called.

-- 36 hours is the commitment time standard derived from the Garden Plot plan.

-- 34 hours was the actual time taken by federal troops for commitment.

-- 18.5 hours was the time taken by the first National Guard unit on the street (actually less than 16.5 hours after that unit was first notified).

-- 19 hours was the time taken by the second National Guard unit on the street (actually less than 13 hours after that unit was first notified).

-- 24 hours was the time taken to commit two additional National Guard battalions on the street.

The above summarizes facts that have been carefully checked. Readers can draw their own conclusions, from facts which are particularly compelling when considering that citizen-soldiers are being compared to full time active duty soldiers and marines.

4. *THE CALL FOR FEDERAL TROOPS AND FEDERAL-IZATION OF THE GUARD.*

The fourth controversial issue concerns the call for federal troops and federalization of the National Guard. The federal troops were requested by the Mayor and the Governor, in spite of the fact there were more than enough National Guard troops.

After the military force was federalized, many changes were made. The deployment schemes were changed, requiring no stationing of any force anywhere smaller than a platoon, with a commissioned officer in charge. Rules of Engagement and Arming Orders were changed. However, the change that had the greatest impact on law enforcement was the refusal to perform most law enforcement functions. As stated in the Webster Report, "(The Joint Task Force)...required each request for assistance to be subjected to a nebulous test to determine whether the requested assignment constituted a law enforcement or a military function. As a result, after the federalization on May 1 (the date was actually May 2nd), not only were the federal troops rendered largely unavailable for most assignments requested by the LAPD, but the National Guard, under federal command, was made subject to the same restrictions, and therefore had to refuse many post-federalization requests for help."

This issue was also addressed in the June 22nd letter to the Director of OES following the June 19th state wide meeting of law enforcement officials in Los Angeles. That letter stated "The calling in of federal troops appears to have been a mistake. This resulted in the National Guard becoming federalized, which severely limited their flexibility and the missions they were able to undertake."

There was some evidence of claiming credit where little or no credit is due. One glaring example is the Army's After Action Report about the Los Angeles riots submitted to the Department of the Army by the Army's Forces Command. Forces Command was the headquarters that the Joint Task Force reported to. In their After Action Report, Forces Command said "Disturbances in St. Croix *and Los Angeles* (emphasis added) required federal forces to restore order." This was stated even though the riots were over before the National Guard was federalized on May 2nd, and before any federal troops were committed to the streets.

In 1992, senior officials in Washington were aggressively discussing the increased necessity for use of the military services in domestic roles. Part of the debate was fed by biased and inaccurate reports ignoring the fact that National Guard men and women were the ones who helped law enforcement restore order to the streets. Inaccuracies of that kind were not being encouraged by the three federal general officers sent to Los Angeles. They knew better and were too honorable to support such inaccuracies.

The frustrations experienced by law enforcement officials in Los Angeles with federal troops undoubtedly ended up ultimately working to the advantage of the National Guard. Local law enforcement officials had not asked for federal troops, but acquiesced to the request initiated by the Mayor and the Governor. After the frustrations of the Los Angeles riots, it is clear that knowledgeable law enforcement officials next time will actively fight to retain their National Guardsmen in *state* status.

The call up of federal troops also had an adverse impact on the morale of National Guard troops in a couple of ways. First was the lack of confidence in them manifested by the Governor, their Commander in Chief, especially after the battle to regain control of the streets had already been won. Perhaps more frustrating was being pulled off the streets so federal troops could be employed, only to then spend many long days and nights sitting around armories and staging areas away from their families and jobs or school, with nothing to do.

Politics and personality conflicts waft through the preceding discussion of the four most controversial issues surrounding the riots. It would be merely interesting, if life and death issues weren't ultimately involved.

Some of the contention contributed to a schism that had been growing between the Governor and his National Guard for months if not years. He hadn't visited the National Guard headquarters in Sacramento, nor visited any troops in the field. He was the first California Governor in years without a Military Liaison Officer to maintain liaison and close ties between the two offices. His own Adjutant General, Major General Robert C. Thrasher, did not have direct access to the Governor. In short, there was not a close working relationship between the Governor's office and the National Guard, and they didn't know each other. This worked to their mutual disadvantage when tensions rose in April of 1992.

Guardsmen were shocked when their Commander in Chief went public to criticize them as they deployed into the streets. This just isn't done. No commander criticizes his soldiers. Loyalty works both ways, and is especially important in a profession where those in command must ask subordinates to put their lives at risk. Many knew that the Governor was a former Marine, and found some statements attributed to him rather hard to believe. Others concluded that his three years service as a lieutenant was simply too short and at too junior a level to learn all of the basic precepts of military leadership.

A Ph.D. and noted researcher in Northern California made the natural assumption that the Governor had been misquoted by the press. On May 11, 1992 he wrote the Governor, recounting the sacrifices made by the National Guard men and women during floods, earthquakes, and drug interdiction missions in California. His final paragraph notes:

"An early expression of your unflinching support for the California National Guard would go a long way toward dispelling misconceptions and biased statements which have been published in the general press. As Commander in Chief of the California National Guard, you ought to give that recognition to the deserving and dedicated men and women serving in our Guard."

However, in most cases the Governor had been accurately quoted in the press. As previously noted, the Governor on the first Sunday of the riots said, "Someone's head may very well roll" when discussing his anger over delays in implementing his order to deploy National Guard troops.

The comment regarding someone's head rolling quickly spread among the ranks of National Guardsmen. General Covault, as the federal Joint Task Force commander, felt the

308

impact of those unfortunate comments almost immediately. He went out to visit the troops he had just assumed responsibility for, and became extremely concerned with the fact that some Guardsmen had lost what he termed "battle focus." By that he meant that soldiers on the street were manifesting more concern about the Governor publicly criticizing their senior leaders, rather than focussing on the threat from gangbangers in the street.

The press focussed on Major General Thrasher as the target of the Governor's frustration. General Thrasher had announced his intention to retire even prior to the riots. Nonetheless, his name surfaced on a recurring basis as the scapegoat for criticism. The speculation became somewhat subdued when the Governor asked General Thrasher to remain for three months beyond his intended retirement date, and publicly applauded Thrasher's career with the Guard.

General Thrasher finally retired on August 1, 1992. The largest newspaper in Sacramento announced that with a headline reading "Guard chief criticized over riot role retires." The column went on to quote personnel from the Governor's office saying General Thrasher was not forced out. Unfortunately, the speculation was fueled again when the Harrison report was released. The Governor's office published one of their shorter press releases on December 1, 1992, stating:

"Governor Pete Wilson and retired Army Lt. Gen. William H. Harrison will release the report on the performance of the California National Guard during the Los Angeles riots at a press conference scheduled for 2:30 p.m., Wednesday, December 2, in Room 1190 of the State Capitol."

Obviously omitted from the press release, the Governor chose to announce the replacement for General Thrasher,

Major General Tandy Bozeman, at the same press conference. The net result, whether intended or not, was to again tie General Thrasher to adverse comments, such as those in the Harrison report.

From the start there appeared to be a carefully orchestrated effort to control releases to the press. The California National Guard's Public Affairs Officer, Colonel Roger L. Goodrich, spent his first three days in Southern California trying to set the record straight. He was then muzzled, and told that all statements relating to National Guard response times were to be cleared in advance with the Governor's office. As Roger would be the first to admit, candor sometimes got the best of him. One of his many quotable quotes occurred when he talked about the Governor's request to bring in federal troops. He said "We need them like a hole in the head, we have more than enough troops!"

One of Colonel Goodrich's two assistants was working the issue of ammunition delays. He discussed the issue with the Governor's Deputy Communications Director on the first Thursday night, and they agreed on the details and how they would be explained. The Assistant Public Affairs Officer then granted an interview with the local NBC affiliate regarding the ammunition delays. The short interview played that night and during the morning news.

The Governor's representative then phoned the newsman involved, and demanded a retraction because she felt the interview made the Governor look bad. The newsman refused, but did offer her an opportunity to address the issue on camera. She dropped the issue. She then phoned the National Guard's Assistant Public Affairs Officer, and told him that "Under no circumstances are you to embarrass the Governor!" He responded "You are thinking about the political aspects. I'm concerned about the lives of troops."

That day it became increasingly apparent to the Guard's Public Affairs Office that the press statements out of the Governor's Office differed from what had been previously agreed. More important, those statements differed from what they saw as the facts. When the Governor's Deputy Communications Director was apprised of the problem, she invited the National Guard to provide their own draft of a press release. Several proposals were sent over by the Military Department during the next few days. Not surprisingly, none of them were accepted or released.

As time went by, it became increasingly obvious that various state officials had adopted a siege mentality. Many of those officials were contacted for interviews to ensure the accuracy of this book. Some accepted appointments, then quickly cancelled when they got the word that it would be "inappropriate" to grant an interview. During a meeting with the Governor's staff just prior to the press conference in late November regarding release of the Harrison Report, the subject of this book came up. As one example of the paranoia, a senior official of OES quickly assured the Governor's staff of his fealty, advising them that he had refused to return my call. One might surmise that some people had things to hide! As is obvious to the reader, enough others provided information to assure accuracy of this accounting.

One of the more curious episodes occurred shortly after the riots. On the second day of National Guard commitments to the streets of Los Angeles, a directive came down requiring every unit to provide specific details about the timing of their deployment. The requirement included time of notification,

311

how long it took to assemble, when troops were ready to deploy, when they received mission orders, who they reported to, when they were deployed in the streets, and other administrative details. This requirement came down during the height of the rioting with a demand that the information be immediately furnished in company-level detail. Commanders were understandably perturbed when they received such administrative demands while they were trying to bring riots under control. However, being good soldiers, they did what they were told.

At the same time, the California National Guard's Inspector General, Active Army Colonel Barry Penzel, was directed to investigate the delays. He led a team of investigators who quickly ferreted out details at the same time the riots were being brought under control.

What made the episode particularly curious? After the staff in Sacramento had organized all the information from commands in the field and combined it with the Inspector General's findings, the Governor's office refused to accept it. The best guess is that by refusing to even accept the report, they tried to retain credibility.

As is often the case with something as important and newsworthy as the L. A. riots, the press coverage was both good and bad. Time Magazine inaccurately quoted Governor Wilson and others during the conference call that occurred just after 2:00 p.m. Thursday, April 30th. In the column headed "Grapevine" for the issue of June 15th, the conversation was related:

(Governor Wilson talking) "If you give each man one bullet, and a larger quantity to unit commanders, can you, No. 1, ensure that Guard's safety, and No. 2, accomplish your

312

mission?" Guard commanders said they could. Wilson exploded, "then divide up the f---ing ammunition and get out there!"

The column ended up saying, "Meanwhile, the talk in some law-enforcement (sic) circles is that if any major urban unrest occurs, Wilson may just skip the frustration and ask for the Marines."

The conversation involving the Governor did not occur as related. Many of us were involved in that phone conversation, including the Sheriff of Los Angeles County, Sherman Block. Sheriff Block is not only the chief law enforcement officer for one of the most populous regions in the country and regional coordinator for the mutual aid system, he enjoys a national reputation. He chose to respond to Time Magazine, and was quoted in their letters to the editors on July 6th:

"As Sheriff of Los Angeles County, I take strong exception to the tone of the brief item (Grapevine, June 15) discussing the investigation launched by California Governor Pete Wilson into why the National Guard took 17 hours to respond to the Los Angeles riots. I have worked closely with the California National Guard for a number of years and have found it extraordinarily competent in every way. My respect for the Guard was further enhanced by its superior performance during the riots.

"I resent the suggestion that 'the talk in some law-enforcement circles is that if any major urban unrest occurs, Wilson may just skip the frustration and ask for the Marines.' That certainly isn't the talk in the Los Angeles County Sheriff's Department. Thanks to the support of the California Guard, local law enforcement was able to restore order to the streets, and the Guard maintained that order in its usual professional manner. You should not unfairly impugn 26,000 of the finest men and women of the state--the citizen soldiers of the California National Guard."

Rather interestingly, the only sentences in Sheriff Block's letter that Time Magazine chose not to print read: "The decision to ask for Marine and active Army support was not made by this department. By the time the request was made, additional support was unneeded."

Another column written by the syndicated columnist Harry Summers, a highly decorated retired Army Colonel, was much appreciated by the troops. In a column headed "Fire discipline all the way to L.A.," Summers wrote a thought-provoking article about the importance of fire discipline over the centuries. The two latest examples he cited were the extraordinary discipline demonstrated by the 1st Armored Division in the Persian Gulf, and that demonstrated by the California National Guard in Los Angeles. They were two entirely different circumstances, but if anything, fire discipline is vastly more important when the targets are United States citizens rather than enemy soldiers.

Considerable risks were taken by National Guard men and women when they went into the streets of South Central Los Angeles. Many of these troops felt they were treated unfairly by the press. However, the press was no more than following the lead of the Governor.

The Governor and his staff got very little sleep for the first three nights. Even his own security detail complained privately that they weren't getting enough sleep to perform properly. The problems with what appeared to be bad judgment could be as simple as the insidious effects of cumulative sleep loss. That is something military officers are trained to carefully guard

314

against. Soldiers are taught that sleep is fuel to fight with, a resource like everything else. It must be managed. That may be a lesson the Governor and his staff learned the hard way.

It may have been a simple case of the Governor being given poor advice and counsel. Every person in senior office, whether civilian or military, is forced to rely on the honest, intelligent, carefully reasoned advice of subordinates. Perhaps the advice he received was less than the quality he deserved.

The controversies continue to bubble, but probably none will be remembered with such pain as the various trials surrounding the prelude to and consequences of the riots. Those trials served as constant reminders of the suffering endured by so many during the riots.

The federal retrial of the four police officers accused of excessive force involving Rodney King ended April 17, 1993. Officers Theodore Briseno and Timothy Wind won acquittal. Sergeant Stacey Koon and Officer Laurence Powell were sentenced to thirty months in federal prison. They remained free pending appeals until October 12, 1993, at which time they were incarcerated in the Federal Prison Camp at Dublin.

There had been literally dozens of people assaulted at the corner of Florence and Normandie on April 29, 1992. The most notorious trials that resulted involved those accused of beating truck driver Reginald Denny. By early December 1993, verdicts had been reached. Damian Williams was sentenced to ten years for felony mayhem. Henry Watson was sentenced to three years probation, and Antoine Miller to slightly over two years probation plus a hundred hours of community service.

Controversy for years to come is expected to swirl about the leniency or severity of sentences administered for those particular trials.

CHAPTER FIFTEEN

HINDSIGHT AND PROSPECTS

South Central Los Angeles was ripe for an explosion. All the ingredients were there. The area was in a state of decay, with too little major investment and renewal. There were too few jobs, and most of those available paid very little. Family units were often broken. There was little sense of community as older more established families moved out of the area and others moved in. Most public schools found they were not meeting needs, with young people dropping out daily. Many of those young people found the identity and structure they wanted in neighborhood gangs. Paint peeled, weeds grew, and graffiti appeared everywhere as more and more people stopped trying to keep their small part of the neighborhood attractive. In short, there was an aura of hopelessness and despair everywhere.

Complicating this unhealthy milieu was the fact that relationships between the police and those policed had deteriorated from mere estrangement to active contempt. Mutual respect had all but disappeared. The Rodney King incident and the subsequent failure to convict the four police officers involved was seen, if not worse, at least as corroboration of deep-seated suspicions.

The riots that erupted the afternoon and evening of April 29, 1992 were anticipated by many of those in authority. Some pundits felt that rioting should have been anticipated by even more officials in spite of reassurances by some church and community leaders just two days before the verdicts that they could control their people. Extraordinarily complex situations are always much clearer in hindsight. The truth is, while some could and did predict there would be rioting, absolutely no one predicted the shape, substance and extent of those riots.

There were many mistakes made during the riots. The lack of responsiveness, by far the most publicized issue, was covered in detail in the previous chapter. Another point should be made, however, about ammunition delays. There was much talk, press, and even an investigation into the delays in getting ammunition to the Guardsmen. Nobody was more frustrated over those delays than military commanders on the scene. Nonetheless, the delays proved to be a blessing in disguise. Military commanders would have faced a moral dilemma if the ammunition had been on hand. Command and control arrangements weren't even decided until half an hour *after* the first troops were sent out. There were a great many other things to organize before troops were committed. If we had ammunition on hand during the early stages, we would have undoubtedly been ordered to immediately send the troops out, long before the police had their act together, and certainly before we did. At that time one or more of us responsible for the lives of those Guardsmen would have had a decision to make, and it likely would have resulted in at least one resignation. Thankfully, we weren't faced with that tough decision.

Far too many soldiers were called, approaching 15,000 at one point. That was a political, not a military decision. We went from hundreds to literally thousands of soldiers sitting around armories and staging areas with nothing to do. Even worse, they were kept way too long, as the "last in, first out" rule for the military was ignored. Morale suffered as they were kept from family, schools and their normal civilian jobs, almost always at greatly reduced pay. Soldiers will always remember that political leaders kept them on duty for an unconscionably long time, much longer than any previous riot in California, or any other state for that matter.

Sometimes the loyalty of the soldiers, regardless of their color or background, was surprising. This became increasingly obvious as fewer soldiers were committed to the streets, and more and more sat around the armories. Their commanders were challenged to keep them motivated. Unfortunately, quite a few lost jobs and had broken marriages and relationships as a result of the duty, and especially because they were away from home so long after the riots were over. After the rioting ended in the streets, that tension was replaced by other concerns. One was the frustration of differing rumors on when they would finally be allowed to return home. For some soldiers, especially younger ones, there also turned out to be justifiable concerns about their student status in school, or their jobs.

There were a lot of pay problems and delayed payments. This unfortunately is often typical when Guardsmen are mobilized without warning for unusual duty, and was exacerbated when they are changed from state to federal, and back to state pay systems. As a result, some soldiers lost credit card privileges and had other credit problems due to delayed payments. Many of these were minority soldiers, who sometimes had a tough time getting credit approved to begin with.

At least one soldier had his house burgled during the riots. Several of the troops were gone when new children were born. Other troops missed their child's first steps. When discussing these things, there was a surprising lack of bitterness. It was almost, "Oh well, it goes with the territory."

A related issue was the call for federal troops and the federalization of the National Guard. The call should never have been made. The riots were over by the time the federal troops were on the scene. There was the fact that even though federalized, circumstances kept National Guardsmen and their families from taking advantage of military perquisites that normally offset pay differentials. Circumstances precluded they or their families using the military medical, commissary, post exchange and other benefits of service in the armed forces.

The Joint Task Force Commander, Major General Covault, was unfairly accused of failing to accept missions because he did not understand that *posse comitatus* did not apply to the 1992 riots. In responding to accusations in the Webster Report, he said: "They (the Webster Commission) never looked beyond the legal issue. The JTF-LA Commander and his staff understood from the outset that the *Posse Comitatus* Act had no effect, and the Act in no way limited the decision-making process within the JTF headquarters. Accordingly, the JTF-LA Commander was free (subject to limitations that could have been set by the Attorney General) to use his force in any capacity, including typical law enforcement functions."

General Covault's orders from his Commander in Chief were very straightforward. The Presidential Executive Order of May 1st directed the military to, "restore law and order in and about the City and County of Los Angeles, and other districts of California." The mission had been accomplished before he arrived. General Covault said, "It was not the military's mission to solve Los Angeles' crime problem, nor were we trained to do so." That almost says it all. He was briefed daily on the sniping and drive-by attacks on his soldiers and marines. Like any good commander, he was concerned about the safety of his

320

troops, troops he increasingly saw as vulnerable targets for gangbangers. He had a tough time getting permission to get his troops off the streets and released.

The other controversial issue involving the Joint Task Force, at least among the troops on the street, was the requirement to keep their magazines out of their weapons in accordance with Arming Order One. General Covault's response regarding this issue: "Soldier's armed status needed to be consistent with the threat. Arming Orders were changed as the situation became less hostile. Having a set of Arming Orders is one of the most effective command and control measures available in a civil unrest environment."

General Covault did what he felt best following federalization. He received very little operational guidance from higher headquarters, which is what any good commander would prefer. In his words, they "chose to defer to the 'commander on the ground' (Covault)." It is always easy to snipe in hindsight. In spite of the fact that the riots were over when he arrived, he nonetheless ended up with the ultimate responsibility for the lives of thousands of troops exposed to daily gunfire. Many commanders would have taken a different tack on mission acceptance and Rules of Engagement. However, he accomplished his mission, and returned all troops unhurt. I doubt anyone could have done it better.

Some of the military lessons learned during the Los Angeles riots may be of interest to the general reader. Most have been mentioned during the course of the narrative, but bear repeating:

-- *Arming Orders.* Arming Orders are designed to provide a shorthand to describe specific degrees of weapons readiness depending on the situation. Bayonets should generally be prescribed only when aggressive crowd control is anticipated. Not permitting soldiers to put magazines in their weapons puts them at a decided disadvantage. Gangbangers recognize when magazines are not in place, and soldiers are adversely impacted psychologically when they are not trusted to have their magazines in place. Such restrictions should normally be used only when working with extremely green troops, or when the threat is almost nil. Neither was the case in South Central Los Angeles.

-- *Communications.* Radio communications using most military radios are severely restricted in built-up areas. Alternative means, such as cellular phones, or adequate radio equipment, are needed.

-- *Rifle lock plates.* Lock plates are installed on rifles in civil disturbance situations to preclude accidentally switching from semi-automatic to automatic fire. If this federal requirement continues, units should install the lock plates and keep them installed. The lock plate is designed to easily snap off if automatic fire is needed, but that need is doubtful short of combat.

-- *Training.* Some have suggested that special riot control training is needed. The Harrison Report implies that, but when he briefed his report, he made it clear that traditional riot control training is archaic. Normal combat training is what is needed for the "urban warfare" or what the military calls "Low Intensity Conflict" as was encountered in Los Angeles. The soldiers who were committed in the streets of Los Angeles had the proper training, as was obvious by the results. The only additional training that may have been desirable for some soldiers is what is called "MOUT" training, short for Military Operations in Urban Terrain. Such training is usually of lower

322

priority for mechanized troops such as the 40th Infantry Division, as compared to the "light fighters" of the 7th Infantry Division (Light) who joined them later in Los Angeles. Rules of Engagement, Arming Orders and other training are situationally dependent, and differ with each emergency.

-- *Intelligence.* Military intelligence is predictive, versus the event-oriented intelligence normally used by the police. Military commanders are used to detailed intelligence estimates prepared by officers who receive extensive training in this very special field. Decent intelligence estimates were not developed until the riots were over, because police intelligence was alien to the military, and it took a while to learn the new "enemy." Most of the intelligence efforts then ended up being directed towards educating soldiers on their primary "enemy," the gang-banger.

-- *Deployment Scheme.* There were differences of opinion on whether it was better to deploy nothing smaller than a platoon with a commissioned officer in charge, or much smaller deployments down to the fire team level, with noncommissioned officers (sergeants) in charge. Platoon level deployments were supported by active duty officers, while smaller deployments were favored by the National Guard, in spite of the risks admittedly involved. The National Guard took the streets back from the gangs. They did it by literally blanketing the affected area with Guardsmen. In effect, they became the "beat cops," walking two by two, replacing those who stopped walking beats many years ago in Los Angeles. They had a decidedly calming effect in the neighborhoods.

The gangs are what make the streets especially dangerous. It was interesting to see comparisons drawn between the gangs and the troops. There were repeated comments by police officers to gang members likening the troops to a "bigger gang." They evidently felt it was an example the gangbangers could relate to. Sometimes the troops did it themselves, like the troops singing "My gang's bigger than your gang, my gang's bigger than yours..." when driving off to confront gangbangers.

Simplified comparisons between soldiers and gangbangers are tenuous at best. Gangs are organized, usually have some form of uniform (although perhaps not much of a uniform), and tend to be young. Both have discipline, but there is no way military discipline should be compared to the discipline found in gangs. In fact, the differences between the gangs and disciplined troop units are rather profound.

Many gang members, the same age as many of our soldiers, tended to be extremely frustrated. They were generally bitter about the "establishment," especially law enforcement. Most are undereducated, if not illiterate. But here one has to be careful about stereotypical generalizations. There are educated gang members in almost every gang, and a lot of very smart ones, even if undereducated.

If the gang problem is being solved, we don't see it. Truces between gangs make news occasionally. Truces, however, have rarely endured. It is not surprising when one considers that one of the reasons (though just one reason) youngsters join gangs is to belong. Not just belong, but belong to something unique. They belong to a unique gang, from their area, often with specific apparel, always with specific signs and tags, and sometimes with unique tattoos.

Unfortunately, the gang provides too many young people in South Central Los Angeles with their only real sense of belonging and protection that mainstream Americans usually find in their family. The gang too often also is the only source of satisfaction, or provides the only sense of accomplishment, in a world that is full of frustrations.

There are programs being worked to make inroads into the gang problem. They are generally small, local, and under-funded. Programs to provide opportunities for undereducated, underemployed gang members to work their way into the mainstream are almost always too little, and too late. The military at one time provided a route out of the ghetto or barrio. That generally changed over a decade ago when the entrance requirements, whether active or reserve, were made significantly more stringent. A high school diploma is only one requirement now, as all applicants for enlistment must take tough written examinations. What's more, with the military shrinking now, recruiters can afford to be even more selective. In the meantime, the number of gang members in Los Angeles County passed 100,000 some time ago, and continues to climb.

The best solution would be a booming economy, with industry scrambling to employ entry level workers. Unfortun-ately, the riots hit an area already severely depressed, with one out of three people otherwise eligible unemployed. What's more, there have not been enough improvements since then. Peter Ueberroth's Rebuild Los Angeles organization had a rocky start. The campaign promises of politicians during and immediately after the riots appear to have been just that...campaign promises. What little has been done has come almost entirely from the private sector. Peter Ueberroth later resigned from the effort, and talk of lowered goals followed a short time later. It is extremely doubtful that Rebuild Los Angeles results will match the original expectations of many Angelenos.

The number of weapons in the hands of gang members also continues to climb. Thousands of weapons were looted during the riots. Soldiers and marines on the streets saw those weapons every night, and sometimes during the day. The number of weapons recovered in the year following the riots was almost inconsequential.

Probably the most important story to come out of the 1992 riots involves the indiscriminate use of weapons by gangbangers while the disciplined soldiers and marines held their fire. The fire discipline of those young troops borders on the incredible. There were countless provocative incidents where troopers held their fire even though sorely tempted to respond with lethal force. Incidents the first several nights often occurred where there was no electricity or lighting. Troops were understandably tired and nervous. Their extraordinary restraint served as affirmation of the training methods and commitment of leaders at all levels. Most telling, that restraint showed the discipline, maturity and good judgment exercised by literally thousands of individual soldiers and small unit (squad and fire team) leaders.

The table on the opposite page is a summary of assaults against troops detailed in Appendix 4. The troops withheld fire except when responding to the incidents on May 3rd and 5th when they were assaulted by automobiles. The increased assaults on Tuesday, May 5th appear to have been the result of planned escalation of violence involving several gangs.

As repeatedly mentioned, there is gunfire every night in some parts of Los Angeles. It was felt important that the chart opposite only show where soldiers were specifically targeted. Soldiers described the sound of bullets whizzing by their heads, or bullets hitting walls or pavement "sounding like hail." No one can tell those troops they weren't targeted.

326

ASSAULTS ON MILITARY FORCES

1992 Date	Shootings Directed At			Assaults On	
	ARNG	USMC	USA	ARNG	USMC
30 April	24*				
1 May	10			2 R&B**	
2 May	4			2 R&B, 1 Auto	
3 May	4	3		1 Auto	1 R&B, 1 Auto
4 May	3	1			
5 May	11			1 Auto	
6 May	2		1	1 Thrown object	
7 May	1				
8 May	1				
9 May	1				
10 May	2				
11 May	1				
12 May	1				

* The Los Angeles Sheriff's log shows "Two dozen reports of shots fired at Guardsmen." Details were not recorded the first night, so this figure should be viewed with some scepticism.

** R&B = Rocks and Bottles. Auto = Assault using an auto. Thrown Object was a large object thrown down on top of a military vehicle from a freeway overpass.

There were 325,000 rounds of M-16 ammunition issued to Guardsmen, plus pistol ammunition, and over a thousand canisters of tear gas. Tear gas, subject to the vagaries of the wind, almost always impacts upon the innocent as well as the guilty. During the Berkeley riots gas was used in large quantities, and once drifted across a hospital. National Guard commanders in Los Angeles were very much aware of the problems in using gas, and none was used in 1992.

It is a modern miracle that with hundreds of thousands of rounds issued to almost 15,000 National Guardsmen, Army Soldiers and Marines, no innocent people were hurt. The National Guard fired a total of twenty-two bullets in self defense, killing one and injuring another. Both were individuals with a history of problems with the law. The marines fired considerably more rounds, but injured no one.

There were other successes to offset the problems. The performance of the troops exceeded all expectations. The Webster Report includes an interesting Community Attitude Survey conducted by more than 300 people over a three day period about three months after the riots. There were fifty three questions asked of over 2000 households. One question asked them which were the "*most* effective public safety agencies in handling the LA riots?" The number one answer was the National Guard, closely followed by the LA Fire Department, with all others receiving less than a third as much support. Even more telling was the question regarding what stopped the riots. Eighty percent felt it was the presence of the National Guard. Even the Harrison Report complimented the performance of soldiers and junior leaders. Most complimentary of all were law enforcement officials, and their opinion is perhaps the most important of all. That is because law enforcement officials have a comprehensive awareness of how very dangerous those streets really are, and the risks the troops were exposed to.

There were many efforts to compare the Los Angeles riots of 1992 with the Watts riots of 1965. These two respectively are now the first and third largest riots in U.S. history (Detroit's 1967 riots were the second largest). The military after action report following the Watts riots described the situation leading up to the unrest. The report noted that the riots occurred in a badly overcrowded area with one story, single family homes. Unemployment was widespread, with the great majority of those having employment working at menial tasks for inadequate pay. The area had too many broken homes, too many school dropouts, and too much illiteracy. Sound familiar? It should, because little changed in that regard when comparing the 1965 and 1992 riots. However, most honest comparisons by knowledgeable observers are notable for the many differences in the two riots, in spite of the fact their flash points were only four miles apart:

-- *Geography*. The Watts riots occurred in a comparatively compact area of 60 square blocks. That sounds like, and is, a lot of city. But it pales in comparison to the 1992 riots, which quickly exploded over literally hundreds of square miles in this huge county. In addition, the rioting was extremely contagious, immediately spreading to other cities in California, plus additional cities across the United States and Canada. This undoubtedly resulted from the shortened version of the videotape given widespread national and international television coverage.

-- *Timing*. All large inner-city riots have occurred almost entirely during the hours of darkness. What little formal advance planning that occurred prior to the 1992 riots was based on that expectation. One example was the late roll call time specified for LAPD's Metro Squad. Unfortunately, in the 1992 riots, there was a great deal of daytime riotous activity on

329

both Wednesday and Thursday, and to a much lesser degree, on Friday.

-- *Duration.* The Watts riots required five days to control. The 1992 riots were effectively under control in about 36 hours.

-- *Racial aspects.* The Watts riots were marked by clearly racial lines. The population of the affected area was 55% black, and the dissension ended up with blacks versus whites. This was not the case in 1992, where men, women and children of all colors were involved. Over 50% of the arrestees were Hispanic, with a great many of them being illegal immigrants.

-- *Gangs.* There were gangs in South Central Los Angeles in 1965, but they were much tamer in those days. Now the gangs are much, much more numerous and pervasive, considerably more violent, and more heavily armed.

- *Fire Discipline.* The Watts riots had accurately been described as occurring in a "free fire" zone, with comparatively few constraints imposed on the use of weapons by law enforcement officers and the National Guard. None of the military after action reports following those riots address the amount of ammunition fired by soldiers. No one wanted to talk about the vast quantities of ammunition expended, with literally thousands of pistol, rifle and machine gun rounds fired by Guardsmen. It was entirely different during the 1992 riots, where every bullet fired by a Guardsman or Marine was strictly accounted for in an atmosphere of carefully observed fire discipline.

-- *Injuries to Innocent People.* We will never know how many innocent people were injured or killed during the Watts riots. All that is known for certain is that too many of those killed and injured were innocent victims of misunderstandings and stray bullets. The 1992 riots were an entirely different story. The military involved in the Los Angeles riots know where every bullet went, and know that no innocent people were injured or killed.

No narrative would be complete without again mentioning the heartwarming attitude of Angelenos to the troops deployed into their streets. That is an enduring memory almost always recalled by the soldiers. They will never forget the "thumbs up," waves, horn blowing, smiles, and words of welcome when they first hit the streets. They remember the hugs and kisses from a surprising number of folks, and the incredible amount of food and drink that was offered. They cherish the notes from children that flowed from the schools. They recall the parents and children who wanted photos taken with the troops.

The troops will always remember the businesses that refused to take their money, and those businesses that donated everything from food and drink to office supplies and newspapers. Furniture was donated to add to the comfort of troops. Dealers loaned television sets, VCRs, and videotapes. Truckloads of bottled water were donated by companies. A full truckload of yogurt with granola was delivered to the troops. They loved it. These few examples illustrate what was happening all over the county.

The attitude of millions of Angelenos more than made up for the comparatively few that gave the troops problems. When soldiers and marines were asked some months later to relate their most memorable recollection of the riots, they almost always commented on the incredible support of the people before mentioning the dangers they faced.

331

In the meantime, the environment that proved so ripe for riots in 1992 is still susceptible to unrest. Response agencies, at all levels, are very much aware of that fact, and much has been done to prepare for such an eventuality.

The Los Angeles Police Department admittedly was not ready for the riots. A very good police department, some say a great police department, many LAPD officers were deeply disappointed in, and embarrassed by, their initial response. Dedicated LAPD leaders like Bayan Lewis, Keith Bushey, Paul Mock, Ross Moen, Neal Fine and literally hundreds of others that worked closely with the military are obviously committed to precluding any recurrence of the delayed response of 1992. Plans are being revised.

During the riots, participants had problems with such simple factors as common terms. Platoons are very different formations to a policeman, highway patrolman or military officer. The order "cover me" was shown to have an entirely different meaning to police and soldiers than to marines. Exercises were therefore planned and conducted in 1993 that surfaced many, though not all such differences, so accommodations could be worked out prior to having to make diverse systems work together during crises.

It will not be easy. The new Chief of Police for Los Angeles, Willie L. Williams, has his hands full. His department when he assumed control was losing officers faster than they were being replaced by the Police Academy. His department is also concerned because organized crime seems to be migrating to the West Coast as the result of recent crackdowns in the East. Nonetheless, Chief Williams appears undaunted, and has already made significant progress in ensuring his department is ready for future civil disturbances. Unfortunately, that task may turn out to be Chief William's easiest. Much, much more difficult will be healing the rifts that have grown between the populace and their police.

The rifts (virtual chasms in some cases) exist in many neighboring police jurisdictions as well as in Los Angeles. During the riots, soldiers saw a lot of the enmity that exists between police officers and some of the people. It appeared to be less of a problem with the Los Angeles Sheriff's Department. Regardless, the police can't do it all themselves. Community, school and church leaders must be willing to help lead people in meeting the police half way. It will take compromise on both sides to break down what have become seemingly impermeable barriers. Calloused attitudes on both sides have developed over a period of many years, and won't change overnight. Changes must be made, however, and both sides will be much happier and better off as a result of the huge effort that must be invested to ensure success.

State officials have recommited themselves to the Mutual Aid system. It works and should have been immediately implemented for the 1992 riots, and undoubtedly it will be for any future civil disturbances. The value of the system was reemphasized when the Mutual Aid Review Task Force met in June of 1992. They noted that the Fire Mutual Aid System worked very well. Unfortunately, too little of the Law Enforcement Mutual Aid System was requested, and requests from LAPD that did come were too late to have a truly effective impact.

The Governor's Emergency Council was convened on a periodic basis prior to the Wilson Administration. Both times it was convened prior to the 1992 riots were during emergencies. The Emergency Council will undoubtedly be reinstituted on a periodic basis for planning sessions as it was in the past.

Improvements have also been made in the Military Department's response capability. Immediately following the riots, the Military Department's Task Force for Emergency Preparedness examined and recommended necessary changes in the California National Guard's emergency planning, training, operations, and logistical systems.

Some of the key recommendations developed by the task force centered on a command group to accompany the Adjutant General during any future large scale emergencies, plus a complete reorganization of the Military Department's Emergency Operations Center. Those recommendations have since been implemented.

The task force's charter was simplified because much had already been accomplished in the several weeks between the end of the riots and the last troops finally being released. Major commands of the California National Guard already had contingency plans written and approved, equipment pre-positioned, and ammunition in place.

In addition, an exercise was conducted in February of 1993, testing the Military Department's new Crisis Action Center and contingency plans. The exercise involved various entities the Military Department will work with during an emergency, including OES, as well as representatives of the military field commands. Later in the month, National Guard units were mobilized in an exercise to test plans with law enforcement officers in Los Angeles.

There is always a temptation for senior officers to want to take credit for the successes of their troops. However, there is an important maxim that applies to the military when remembering the lessons of 1992, or looking to the future. That is, the influence of generals is comparatively limited once the fight begins. Generals sometimes can pick the time and place to do battle. They are expected to synchronize combined arms to maximize the synergistic effects of all the weaponry and other resources at their disposal. Generals commit the reserve, and fight for additional resources when they are required.

However, in discussing the real impact of generals once the battle is joined, General Sherman hit the mark in a comment he made to the War Department during the Civil War. He is said to have told them he had good sergeants, lieutenants, and captains, and that those are far more important than good generals. So they are, and such was certainly the case in Los Angeles. The troops were widely scattered over the streets of Los Angeles County, too widely scattered for rigid command and control by senior officers. Circumstances forced them to "power down" to more junior soldiers. Senior officers dispatched their troops and then prayed, because there often was not much more they could do.

The Lord responded. It was a near miracle that no troops were hurt by gangbangers. This is particularly clear when one recollects the number of times military men and women were assaulted. Troops described the "whrrr" of bullets going right by their heads, the "ping" of bullets striking metal close by, the "whack" of bullets hitting wood or concrete, the sharp "swish" of bullets ripping through nearby leaves. It is difficult to avoid developing an almost missionary zeal when one looks back at the dozens of accounts, and thinks, "My God, so many came very close to getting hit!"

At the same time that miracle, or near miracle, is contemplated, one must consider the other half of the big story. The troops were constantly hassled, taunted, and harassed by gangbangers. They had guns waved at them every day, in addition

335

to being targets of gunfire, rocks and bottles. It is remarkable, if not incredible, that they exercised such restraint and fire discipline. For just as important as the fact that no soldier was hit, is the fact that unlike previous riots, no innocent people were injured by the troops.

What is being done to preclude another riot? Millions of us Angelenos, past and present, continue to drive every day on the elevated freeways through Los Angeles trying to ignore the serious problems on the streets below. Much as we'd like to think otherwise, very little progress has been made in solving basic economic and social ills there.

There is considerable focus on policing, although it appears that focus does not include enough resourcing. However, law enforcement can't do it alone. The insidious cancer that infects South Central Los Angeles won't be cured until economic and social ills there are properly addressed, and the general quality of life greatly improved.

No one should take a great deal of comfort if riots don't explode again, or if they are quickly squelched if they do erupt. More problematic is the possibility of further escalation of the endemic lawlessness that already exists every day and night in parts of Los Angeles. An average of over four people are killed every day in the county. Los Angeles' pride won't be fully restored until more of the area is safe for its citizens. Mothers must be comfortable letting their children play in the front yard, or the corner park. People must be able to walk to the market without fearing for their safety.

Los Angeles has a new mayor and a new chief of police. Everyone is hoping things get better. If they don't, more rioting may occur. If those riots prove beyond the capability of law enforcement to quickly control, authorities should not count on another near miracle like 1992. Nevertheless, if help is needed, California is fortunate to have many thousands of law enforcement officers and Guardsmen who are now veterans, "blooded" with experience forged in the fires and furies of the 1992 L.A. riots.

APPENDIX ONE

TROOP LIST

CALIFORNIA NATIONAL GUARD (10,456 total *)

Headquarters, State Area Command
  Headquarters, Los Alamitos Armed Forces
    Reserve Center
  143rd Evacuation Hospital
  170th Criminal Investigation Detachment

Headquarters, 40th Infantry Division (Mechanized)(-)
  40th Infantry Detachment (Rear Command Post)
  132nd Engineer Battalion
  240th Signal Battalion
  1-18th Cavalry Squadron (-)
  40th Military Police Company
  140th Chemical Company
  Companies D, E. F 140th Aviation Regiment
  160th Infantry Detachment (Long Range Surveillance)
  Platoon, 2668th Trans Co (attached)

Headquarters: 1st, 2nd, and 3rd Brigades
  2-159th Infantry Battalion
  2-160th Infantry Battalion

*At highest level.

40th Infantry Division (Mechanized) (Continued)
   3-160th Infantry Battalion
   4-160th Infantry Battalion
   1-184th Infantry Battalion
   1-149th Armor Battalion
   1-185th Armor Battalion
   2-185th Armor Battalion
   3-185th Armor Battalion

Headquarters, Division Artillery
   Battery F, 144th Field Artillery
   1-144th Field Artillery Battalion
   2-144th Field Artillery Battalion
   3-144th Field Artillery Battalion

Headquarters, Support Command, 40th ID (M)
   40th Support Battalion
   240th Support Battalion
   540th Main Support Battalion

Headquarters, 49th Military Police Brigade
   143rd Military Police Battalion
   185th Military Police Battalion

Headquarters, California Air National Guard
   146th Airlift Wing (C-130 Transport plus Security Police)
   129th Rescue Group (Security Police)
   163rd Reconnaissance Group (Aerial Photos and Security
      Police)
   144th Fighter Interceptor Wing (Security Police)

U. S. ARMY (2,023 total*)

Headquarters, 7th Infantry Division (Light) (-)
7th Military Police Company
Aviation Elements, 7th ID (L)

Headquarters, 2nd Brigade, 7th ID (L)
5-21 Infantry Battalion
2-27 Infantry Battalion
3-17 Infantry Battalion

Headquarters, Support Command, 7th ID (L)
7th Forward Support Battalion

U. S. MARINE CORPS (1,508 Marines total*)

Special Purpose Marine Air-Ground Task Force (BGen
Marvin T. Hopgood, Jr.)
3rd Battalion, 1st Marines
1st Light Armored Infantry Battalion
Combat Service Support Detachment 11
1st Combat Engineer Battalion (elements)
7th Engineer Battalion (elements)
Military Police Company
Marine Air Group 16 (elements)

*At highest level

APPENDIX TWO

RULES OF ENGAGEMENT
(29 April - 1 May 1992)

I understand that I may be deployed to perform law enforcement support missions including crowd control, traffic control, perimeter security, protection of public safety employees such as firefighters, area security or roving patrols. I understand the following rules on the use of deadly and non-deadly force:

NON-DEADLY FORCE

1. Non-deadly force involves the use of physical contact, restraint, baton, M16A1/2 with bayonet or chemicals such as tear gas or MACE.

2. Non-deadly force will always be the minimum necessary to protect yourself, a team member, or a law enforcement officer or citizen from serious bodily injury.

3. Non-deadly force should only be used at the discretion of a superior officer or noncommissioned officer, a law enforcement officer, or in emergency situations.

USE OF DEADLY FORCE

1. Deadly force refers to the use of any type of physical force in a manner that could reasonably be expected to result in death whether or not death is the intent.

2. The use of deadly force is authorized only where all three of the following circumstances are present:

  a. All other means have been exhausted or are not readily available.

341

b. The risk of death or serious bodily harm to innocent persons is not significantly increased by its use.

c. The purpose of its use is one or more of the following:

(1) Self-defense to avoid death or serious bodily harm (threat of harm is not restricted to firearms, but may include assault with bricks, pipes or other heavy missiles, incendiary and explosive devices, or any other material which could cause death or serious bodily harm).

(2) Prevention of a crime which involves a substantial risk of death or serious bodily harm.

(3) Defense of others where there is substantial risk of death or serious bodily harm.

(4) Detention or prevention of the escape of persons against whom the use of deadly force is authorized in subparagraphs (1), (2) and (3) above.

CIVIL DISTURBANCE TRAINING

I acknowledge that I have received basic civil disturbance training prior to my actual deployment in support of law enforcement.

I HAVE READ AND UNDERSTAND THE ABOVE USE OF DEADLY FORCE.

_____
Signed/date

342

ARMING ORDERS

Arming Order	Rifle	Bayonet	Pistol	Baton	Magazine/Chamber	Control*
AO-1	Sling	Scabbard	Holstered	Belt	In pouch/Empty	OIC/NCO
AO-2	Port	Scabbard	Holstered	Belt	In pouch/Empty	OIC/NCO
AO-3	Sling	Fixed	Holstered	Hand	In pouch/Empty	OIC/NCO
AO-4	Port	Fixed	Holstered	Hand	In pouch/Empty	OIC/NCO
AO-5	Port	Fixed	Holstered	Hand	In weapon/Empty	OIC/NCO
AO-6	Port	Fixed	In Hand	Belt	In weapon/locked	OIC

* OIC = Officer in charge, NCO = Noncommissioned officer in charge

Author's note: In high threat areas, soldiers were normally at a modified AO-5, *without* bayonets fixed. This is much safer, and Arming Orders have since been modified to reflect this.

APPENDIX THREE

GANGS IN LOS ANGELES COUNTY

This list is based on information from the Los Angeles City Police Department, the Los Angeles County Sheriff's Department, the Western States Information Network, and gang members. It should not be considered current or all-inclusive. Gang sets are constantly changing. They routinely shrink, expand, change names or affiliation, organize new sets, and sometimes completely disappear. A few of these gangs are from outside the county, but have created problems within the county.

Blood Sets

Athens Park Boys
Bishop Sets
  Elm Street Bishops
  Block Bishops
  92 Bishops
Pueblo Bishops
Bounty Hunter
Bloodstone Villains
Bee Bop Watts
Black P-Stone
Blood Fives
Belhaven Bloods
Brim Sets
  62 Brims
  Aliso Village Brims

Brim Sets (Cont'd)
  59 Brims
  Rollin' 60's Brims
Carson Cabbage Patch
Crenshaw Mafia Gang
Denver Lane Sets
  Denver Lane
  Pasadena Denver Lanes
  Pasadena Devil Lanes
89 Family Blood
Harvard Park
Hacienda Village
Home Shopping Club Bloods
Inglewood Family Blood
Jungle Bloods

Bloods (Continued)

Lot Boys (Bounty Hunters)
Mid City Gangsters
Miller Gangsters
Outlaws
Piru Sets
  Block Piru
  Campanella Park Piru
  Cedar Block Piru
  Centerview Piru
  Cross Atlantic Piru
  Compton Piru
  Circle City Piru
  Fruit Town Piru
  Holly Hood Piru
  Leuder Park Piru
  Lime Hood Piru
  Mob Piru

Piru Sets (Cont'd)
  Nutty Block Piru
  151 Piru
  Pain Piru
  Paicoma Piru
  Pomona Islands Piru
  Rollin' 30's Piru
  Tree Top Piru
  Westside Piru
Swan Sets
  77 Swans
  79 Swans
  80 Swans
  83 Swans
  84 Swans
  Main Street Swans

Crip Sets

Acacia Crips
Altadena Block Crips
Anzac-Grape Street Watts
Avalon Gangster Crip Sets
  A-Line
  53 Street
  88 Street
  116 Street
Back Street Crips
Beach Town Mafia Crips
Bible Crips
Boulevard Crips
Broadway Crips
52 Broadway Gangster Crips
Carver (Park) Crips

Compton Crips
Compton Westside Crips
Corner Pocket Crips
Dodge City Crips
Durlock (Doorah) Crips
East Coast Crips Sets
  1st East Coast
  43 East Coast
  59 East Coast
  62 East Coast
  66 East Coast
  68 East Coast
  69 East Coast
  76 East Coast
  89 East Coast

Crip Sets (Continued)

East Coast Crips Sets (Cont'd)
94 East Coast
97 East Coast
102 East Coast
118 East Coast
190 East Coast
Eight Tray (or Trey) Gangsters
Eighty Seven Gangster Crips
Eighty Three Main Street Crips
Fifty Six (56) Syndicate Crips
Fifty Three (53) Gangster Crips
Forty Three Gangster Crips
Fronthood Crips
Front Street Crips
Fudge Town Crips
Geer Street Crips (Geer Gang)
Grandee Crips
Grape Street Watts Crips
Harbor City Crips
Harlem 30's Crips
Hat Gang Crips
Hoover Street Crips
43 Hoover
52 Hoover
54 Hoover
59 Hoover
74 Hoover
83 Hoover
92 Hoover
94 Hoover
107 Hoover
112 Hoover
Imperial Village Crips
Insane Crips
Kitchen Crips

Lantana Block Crips
Long Beach Boulevard Mafia
Main Street Crips
Marvin Gangster Crips
Menlo Gangster Crips
Mona Park Crips
Myrtle Street Crips
Neighborhood Crips Sets
Lynwood N-Hood
108 N-Hood
111 N-Hood
113 N-Hood
NBC (N-Hood Block Crips)
Ninety Eight Main St. Crips
Ninety Gangster Crips
(Westside Crips)
Nut Hood Watts Crips
107 Underground Crips
113 Block Crips
117 Street Watts Crips
Original Valley Crips
Ozone
Palm & Oaks Crips
Palmdale Gangster Crips
Palmer Block Crips
Park Village Crips
Payback Crips
P. J. Watts Crips
Playboy Gangster Crips
Pocket Hood
Pope Street Crips
Raymond Crip Sets
Raymond Avenue Crips
Inglewood Raymond
Pasadena Raymond

Crip Sets (Continued)

Rollin' 20's
Rollin' 30's
Rollin' 40's
Rollin' 60's
Santana Block Crips
Schoolyard Crips
Seventy First Street Hustlers
Shack Boys (76 East Coast)
Shotgun Crips
Sintown Crips

Spooktown Crips
Three Fifty Seven (357)
   Pomona Crips
Triagnew Park Crips
Venice Shoreline Crips
Watergate Crips
West Boulevard Crips
West Covina Gangster Crips
Westside Crips

Hispanic Gangs*

Adidas Boys
Al Capones (Capones)
Alley Boys
Al Capones (Capones)
Alley Boys
Alley Cats
Alpine Street
Arta
Avenues (Aves)
Azusa
Bad Boys Organization
Baja Trece (13)
Ballard Street
Barrio Loco
Barrio Los Padrinos
Barrio Mojados
Barrio Paramount

Barrio Pobre
Barrio Small Town
Barrio Van Nuys
Barrio Viejo Virgil
Barrio West
Bassett
Beer Wolvez
Big Top Locos (Diamonds)
Black Diamonds
Bloomington
Blythe Street
Boyz From The Hood
Brick City Boys
Bricktown
Bryant Street
Bunker Hill
Burbank Trece (13)

* The letters "B" and "V" are used interchangeably in converting Spanish to English. Therefore, both Barrio and Varrio are correct and interchangeable.

Burlington Locos
Camarillo
Canal Boys
Canoga Park Alabamas
Car Wash Locos
Carnales (Los Carnales)
Carson 13
Central City Criminals
Chicali Trece (13)
Chino Center
City Terrace
Clantone (C-14)
Clarence Street Locos
Clover (E/S Clover)
Columbus Street Gangsters
Compton Flats (Midget Dukes)
Compton Trece (13)
Compton Varrio
Compton Varrio 70 (CV70)
Coronado Street Boys
Crazy Boys
Crazy Riders
Cuarto Flats
Culver City Boys
Cycle World Boys
Cypress Park (CP's)
Dead End
Diamonds
Dogtown
East L. A. Trece (13)
Eastlake Boys
Eastside Los (ESL)
Eastside Punks
Eastside Torrance (EST)
Eastside Trece (13)

Eastside 7th Street Locos
Echo Park
El Monte Flores
El Segundo
El Sereno (ESR)
Evergreen
Fickett Street
Fives
Florencia (F-13)
Friends
Frogtown
Gardena Trece (13)
Ghetto Boys
Glassell Park Loco
Guardia Loco
Hang Out Boys
Happy Valley
Harbor City
Harpys
Hart Street
Hazard
Highland Park
Hollywood Rebels
Home Boys
Homies Trece (13)
Humphrey Boys
Inglewood Trece (13)
Intruders
Jokers
Juarez Mara Villa
Kinto Kisle
Krazy Katz
L. A. Warriors
La Hood
La Loma

Hispanic Gangs (Continued)

La Mirada (San Bernardino)
La Mirada Hustlers
La Mirada Locos
La Pee Wees
La Primas
La Rana
La Via
Laguna Park Vikings
Langdon Street
Largo Varrio (Compton)
Latin Lords
Latins (Miscellaneous)
Lennox Trece (13)
Lil Eastside
Lil Valley
Lincoln Heights Boys
Little Criminals
Little Locos
Little Winos
Locas
Loco Park
Locos (La Puente)
Locos 13
Logan Heights (San Diego)
Lopez Mara Villa
Los Carnales
Mara Salva Trucha (or Mara Saldatrucha)
Mara Villa
Menezabal
Metro
Michaeltorena Locos
Midget Dukes (Compton Flats)
Midnight Criminal Force
Midnight Locos Carnales
Moon Lite Katz (MLK)
Northside Redondo

Nela Boys (N/E L.A.)
New Relations
Night Crawlers
North Hollywood Boys
North Hollywood Locos
Ochentas
Opal Street
Orkas
Orphans
Otay (San Diego)
Paca Flats
Paca Trece (13)
Pacas (Latin Time Pacas)
Pacoima Brown Stone Locos
Paramount Varrio
Park Dillon
Party Locos
Perris Mara Villa
Pico Nueva
Pierce Boys
Playboys (Latin Playboys)
Pomona Hazard
Project Boys
Ramon
Rancho San Pedro (RSP)
Rascals
Rebel 13
Rebels
Reseda Boys
Reseda Westside
Ricardo Street Locos
Rockwood
Southside L.A.
Southside Trece (13)
Salva Trucha (Salvadoran)
San Fer

Santa Fe
Santa Monica
Santa Nita
Santa Paula Criminals
Sepas
Shaking Cats
Sol Trece (13)
Sotel
Soto Street
South Los
Spring Valley (San Diego)
State Street Boys
Street Boys
Street Saints
Street Villains
Temple Street
The Magician Club (TMC)
The Mob Crew
The Wanderers
Tiajuana Locos
Tiny Boys
Tokers
Toonerville
Tortilla Flats
Trece (13) Loco
Valerio Street
Valley Clantone
Van Nuys Boys
Varrio Carson
Varrio Keystone
Varrio La Loma
Varrio Latin Kings
Varrio Nueva Estrada (VNE)
Varrio Salitre Rifa (VSR)
Vaughn Street Boyz

Venice Trece (13)
Ventura Avenue
Vicky's Town
Vineland Boys
V54 Varrio Norwalk
Watts Colonial (Weigand)
   (Watts)
Westside Criminals
Westside Locos
Westside Playboys
Westside Trece (13)
Westside Verdugo (Rialto)
Westside Vista
White Fence
Whittier Locos
Whittmore Street
Wild Bunch
Wilmas (Miscellaneous)
Wilmas Eastside
Wilmas Westside
1st St. Flats E/S - Primara
   Flats
1st St. Flats W/S - Primara
   Flats
16th Street (San Diego)
18th Street (Miscellaneous)
18th Street Eastside
18th Street Northside
18th Street Southside
18th Street Westside
21st Street
22nd Street
23rd Street
28th Street
29th Street

Hispanic Gangs (Continued)

32nd Street
3rds (Thirds)
36th Street

38th Street
4th St. Flats (Quarto Flats)

Asian Gangs

Asian Sisterhood
Dirty Punks Gang
Innocent Bitch Killers
Innocent But Killers
Lady Rascal Gangsters
Nip Family
Ruthless Girls
Santa Ana Boys

Silver Middle Girls
Southside Scissors
United Bamboo (Chu Lien
  Bien)
Viet Ching
Wah Ching
Wally Girls
Yakuza

Other Gangs

Fourth Reich Skinheads
Samoan Warriors

Tongan Crips
White Aryan Resistance

APPENDIX FOUR

ASSAULTS ON THE MILITARY

Date/Time

30 Apr   On this date, the Los Angeles Sheriff Department log
              shows "Two dozen reports of shots fired at Guardsmen."
              Details were not recorded the first night of the military
              commitments to the streets.

Date/Time	Location	Incident	Target(s)
1 May 0243	Under New Century Freeway	Sniper shots from overpass	3-160th Inf CAL ARNG
0800	Crenshaw Plaza Shopping Center	Sniper from rooftop shot betw. troops	2-185th Armor CAL ARNG
Noon	110 Freeway So. of I-10 Freeway	2 sniper shots at convoy from roof	1-185th Armor CAL ARNG
1815	Northrup Avn in Hawthorne	Shots fired near gate	3-160th Inf CAL ARNG
1930	Redondo & Washington	Automatic Weapons	3-185th Armor CAL ARNG
1945	157th St. & Crenshaw	Shots from motel. 2 males arrested.	3-160th Inf CAL ARNG
1950	L.A. Swap	Sniper fire	240th Sig Bn CAL ARNG
1953	Florence & Firestone	Rocks & Bottles thrown	4-160th Inf CAL ARNG

Date/Time	Location	Incident	Target(s)
2135	Under New Century Fwy	Automatic fire from overpass	2-144th Arty CAL ARNG
2155	Near Firestone Sheriff's Station	Rocks & Bottles thrown	4-160th Inf CAL ARNG
2330	NW corner of 65th & Menlo	Sniper shots	4-160th Inf CAL ARNG
2400	Olympic & Western	9mm fired at troops on roof. Slugs found in a.m.	4-160th Inf CAL ARNG
2 May 0001	156th St. & Crenshaw	2 rounds from sniper.	4-160th Inf CAL ARNG
0120	Fwy exit at Spring St.	Sniper shots at Hummer	Mil Police CAL ARNG
0130	Pacific Coast Hwy & Cedar (L. B.)	20-30 auto. rounds fired by sniper	270th MP CAL ARNG
0719	2200 Redondo (Long Beach)	Veh tried to run down soldier. Driver arrested.	40th DISCOM CAL ARNG
2100	Firestone area	Rocks & bottles thrown by gangs	4-160th Inf CAL ARNG
2300	Jefferson & Kingston	Bottles thrown by 3 gangbangers	40th DIVARTY CAL ARNG
2358	Hall of Justice & Jail	Drive-by shooting from 101 Fwy	649th MP CAL ARNG

353

Date/Time	Location	Incident	Target(s)
3 May 0015	Sixth & Western	Sniper shots	3-185th Armor CAL ARNG
0700	Anaheim Blvd. & Orange (L. B.)	Sniper shots	1st LAI USMC
1228	Compton Blvd. (Compton)	Drive-by shooting from Monte Carlo	3-1 Marines USMC
1755	71st & Compton (Compton)	Several sniper shots	3-1 Marines USMC
1900	Long Beach	Drive-by shooting from blue truck	1st LAI USMC
1940	Pico & New Hampshire	Datsun tried to run down soldiers. (Driver killed)	40th Spt Bn CAL ARNG
2040	Santa Fe & Walnut	Veh. tried to run down Marines. (Driver arrested)	3-1 Marines USMC
2055	90 Fwy & Fox Hills Mill (Culver City)	Drive-by shots from Fwy	3-144th Arty CAL ARNG
2144	42nd & Central	Sniper shots	(Unconfirmed) CAL ARNG
2147	101 Fwy north of Hall of Justice	Drive-by shots from freeway	3-160th Inf CAL ARNG
2220	21st & Pacific (Long Beach)	Bottles thrown Two arrested	1st LAI USMC

354

Date/Time	Location	Incident	Target(s)
3 May 2304	26th & Vermont	Sniper shots	3-185th Armor CAL ARNG
4 May 2247	Adams & Orchard	Several sniper rounds	49th MP Bde CAL ARNG
2308	Vermont & Slauson	Drive-by shooting	132nd Engr CAL ARNG
2310	Fox Hills Mall (Culver City)	2 sniper rounds fired	2-159th Inf CAL ARNG
2315	Carson Mall (Carson)	Several shots fired. Suspect arrested.	3-1 Marines USMC
5 May 0008	Martin Luther King & Hoover	3 shots fired	3rd Bde, 40th CAL ARNG
0110	Slauson & Vermont	Drive-by shots from Gold Nova	132nd Engr CAL ARNG
0330	Fox Hills Mall (Culver City)	Drive-by 8-10 shots (hit Hummer)	2-159th Inf CAL ARNG
0400	La Brea & Juniper (Inglewood)	Drive-by shooting	3-160th Inf CAL ARNG
0558	59th & Vermont (See also 0110 entry)	4 Juveniles shoot at soldiers. All arrested.	132nd Engr CAL ARNG
0815	Manchester & St. Andrews	Drive-by shots. 5 juveniles arrested	3rd Bde, 40th CAL ARNG

355

Date/Time	Location	Incident	Target(s)
5 May 0830	Compton & Pine (Compton)	2 shots fired by sniper	4-160th Inf CAL ARNG
0845	Compton Armory, Alameda Street	2 shots fired by sniper	540th Spt Bn CAL ARNG
2155	Santa Monica Blvd & St. Andrews Place	Assault by veh, driver wounded and arrested	1-184th Inf CAL ARNG
2210	Fremont High School	Drive-by shooting	2-160th Inf CAL ARNG
	Fremont High (Separate Incident)	Sniper fires several rounds	2-160th Inf CAL ARNG
2240	Santa Monica Blvd & Tamarina	2 shots fired by sniper	1-149th Armor CAL ARNG
6 May 0400	Jefferson & Hauser Boulevards	Sniper fired 5-7 rounds	3-185th Armor CAL ARNG
1830	Weatherby's Gun Store	Drive-by 1 round fired	3-17th Inf US Army
2030	710 Freeway & Del Amo	Mil Veh hit & badly damaged by thrown object	540th Spt Bn CAL ARNG
2310	5500 block of Wilshire Blvd	Shots fired by sniper on roof	3-185th Armor CAL ARNG
7 May 2251	Northbound on Stadium Way	Drive-by, 2 small caliber rounds hit Hummer	670th MP CAL ARNG

356

Date/Time	Location	Incident	Target(s)
8 May 2300	Sports Arena Parking Lot	Drive-by from MLK at troops or helicopter	1-18th CAV CAL ARNG
9 May 0130	Ramada Inn (Compton)	4-5 sniper rounds fired from N.E.	4-160th Inf CAL ARNG
10 May 0230	Compton Town Center (Shopping Mall)	3 sniper rounds fired at troops on roof from south	4-160th Inf CAL ARNG
11 May 2100	Vermont & Coliseum Dr	Shots fired, believed 9mm.	1-185th Armor CAL ARNG
12 May 1533	Coliseum Parking Lot	Shots fired at helicopter as it took off	1-18th CAV CAL ARNG

357

SOURCES

	Input*
Adams, MAJ Gary PM 40th ID	T
Aguilar, SGT Henry M. Svc Btry 2-144th FA	P
Aguilar, 1LT Lawrence 2-159th Inf	T
Alberts, LTC Warren L. OTAG	T
Aleman, CPL Juan D. HSC 1st LAI USMC	P
Allen, SPC Kevin B. Btry B 3-144th FA	P
Allen, CDR Ramon Compton PD	T
Anderson, SSG Phillip R. HHB 2-144th FA	P
Andrews, SPC David P. Co D 3-160th Inf	P, T
Andrews, Marilyn (Guardsman's Wife)	P
Antonetti, LTC Lou OTAG/2-159th Inf	P
Appel, MAJ David K. OTAG	P, R
Arce, LTC Charles M. HHC 1st Bde, 40th ID	P
Ardilla, SFC David A Co C 3-185th Armor	T
Armstrong, CPT Troy 2-159th Inf	O, T
Arruda, CPT William T. Co B 132nd Engr	T
Ayala, SSG Gary 40th MP Co	T
Aylward, 1LT Rory J. 1-185th Armor	T
Bannon, 1SG R. Dennis Co B 3-185th Armor	T
Barker, 1SG Richard A. 4-160th Inf	T
Barnett, MAJ Dan HHC 2-160th Inf	P
Barrow, SGM Fred 40th Finance Co	P, R

* B= Briefing, Panel etc.
  O = Photos, Tapes etc.
  P = Personal Interview
  R = Report or Written Input
  T = Telephone Interview

Bay, 1SG Bruce E. 2-159th Inf	T
Beardsley, COL Richard OTAG	P
Beechum, 1LT Gary 4-160th	T
Belt, 1SG Richard A. Btry A 2-144th FA	P
Bentley, 2LT William K. HSC 1st LAI USMC	P
Bernatz, LTC John C. HHC 40th Inf Div	R, T
Berumen, Det. Joe LAPD (CRASH Detail)	P
Betts, SGT Everett E. 3-160th Inf	T
Bitetto, SGT Jim LASD PJP Honor Rancho	T
Black, SFC Dan 40th MP Co	O, T
Black, 1SG Pat 40th MP Co	T
Bogges, SFC Toby Co E 2-160th Inf	O, P
Bolton, SPC Christopher 270th MP Co	T
Bona, SSG Arnel B. 270th MP Co	T
Boslaugh, SFC Robert E. 649th MP Co	T
Branch, SSG Perry T. Btry B 3-144th FA	P
Brandt, BG Robert J. HHC 40th ID	P
Brayton, SGT Matt W. Co A 3-160th Inf	P
Brennan, BG Daniel OTAG	R
Brown, SPC Christopher M. Btry B 3-144th FA	P
Brown, 1SG Jim 4-160th Inf	O, T
Burns, SPC Tyson M. Co D 3-160th Inf	P
Bushey, Commander Keith D. LAPD	R, T
Buss, LCpl Jeremy J. HSC 1st LAI USMC	P
Butler, SPC Dion L. Btry B 3-144th FA	P
Bygum, CPT Jeff 4-160th Inf	T
Caceres, PFC Christopher T. HHB 3-144th FA	P
Calleia, Anton L.A. Mayor's Office	T
Carrillo, Det. Jose M. LAPD CRASH Detail	P
Carroll, SFC Brian 160th Long Range Surveillance Det	R, T
Casper, SSG Richard W. Cc C 1-185th Armor	T
Clark, SGT Jay D. 2-160th Inf	P
Covault, MG Marvin 7th Inf Div US Army	R
Cornelius, MSG Milo HHT 1-18th CAV	T
Culver, SFC Charles D. 2-159th Inf	T
Currier, CPT Donald J. 270th MP Co	T
Davis, SSG Mark K. 649th MP Co	T

359

Delaney, CSM Robert W. HHC 4-160th Inf	T
DePoian, Phil L.A. Mayor's Office	T
Dillon, CPL David Co. D 3-160th Inf	P
Dodd, CPT Mark HHC 1-184th Inf	T
Donahue, Dan NGB Washington DC	P
Dorsey, CSM Charles J. HHC 2nd Bde, 40th ID	T
Dotter, SPC John Troop B 1-18th Cav	T
Downey, SGT Donald T. Co B 1st LAI USMC	P
Dunn, CPL James E. HHB 3-144th FA	P
Durante, LTC Kirk L. 3-17th Inf US Army	T
Eckman, CPT Dwayne P. Co B 1-185th Armor	T
Elder, SPC Robert E. Co D 3-160th Inf	P
Elick, SGT Mike 2-160th Inf	P
Erdenberger, SPC Steven E. 1-185th Armor	T
Espinosa, SSG Jaime C. HHB 3-144th FA	P
Farrell, MSG John R. PAO Cp Pendleton USMC	P
Fenstermacher, 1SG Doug 4-160th Inf	T
Field, Robert W. Chaplain (CPT) HHC 1-185th Armor	T
Fields, BG Jerry 49th MP Bde	R, T
Fine, CSM Neal L HHC 1st Bde, 40th ID (& LAPD)	T
Finn, SGT Gregory G. Co C 2-185th Armor	T
Florer, SFC George M. Svc Btry 3-144th FA	P
Flores, SSG Alfred A. Btry B 2-144th FA	P
Flores, SGT Ramon Co B 3-160th Inf	T
Flores, LT Joe Compton PD	T
Flynn, LTC Ron HHC 2nd Bde 40th ID	T
Formosa, SFC Leonard W. 2-185th Armor	T
Fox, MSG Donald E. 4-160th Inf	T
Galang, 2LT Edward F. Co D 1-185th Armor	T
Gay, SGT Carvel Co D 3-160th Inf	P, T
George, PSG Paul 270th MP Co	P
Gilbert, SSG Dan P. HHB 2-144th FA	P
Givens, 1LT Jack E. Cc C 132nd Engr	R, T
Gladney, SPC Kenneth M. B 132nd Engr Bn	T
Glass, LTC Randy D. 2-27th Inf Bn US Army	T
Goldberg, CPT Seth M. Co D 1-185th Armor	T
Gong, LTC John HHC 240th FSB	O, R

Gonzales, SGT Edward Co D 3-160th Inf — P
Goodrich, COL Roger L. Jr OTAG — P/R/T
Gormley, SGT Jesse B. 4-160th Inf — T
Gosney, CPT Bonnie C. 140th Chemical Co — R
Grafton, SFC Raymond D. HHC 3-160th Inf — P
Granado, 2LT Gilbert R. HHC 1-149th Armor — T
Gravett, COL Peter J. HHC 40th ID — R, P
Green, CPL Thomas M. Jr. HSC 1st LAI USMC — P
Gregson, COL W. C. "Chip" USMC — R, T
Guerrero, SSG William F. HHB 3-144th FA — P
Gurney, SPC Chet 4-160th Inf — T
Haglund, SSG Wayne R. Btry B 3-144th FA — P
Harbo, SSG Richard A. HHC 3-160th Inf — P
Harrel, MAJ Linda C. HHC 40th ID — P, R
Harrel, MAJ John S. HHC 1-185th Armor — T, R
Haskins, CPT Larry 4-160th Inf — T
Hathaway, SGT Jim 4-160th Inf — T
Hecht, 1LT Brian Co C 2-159th Inf — T
Henderson, CPT Scott 2-160th Inf — P, R
Hernandez, MG Daniel J. HHC 40th ID — P
Herrera, CPT Art L.A. Sheriff Dept — R
Hooper, SFC Allen L. Co B 1-185th Armor — T
Hopgood, BG M. T. (Ted) 1MEF USMC — T
Hoskot, COL N. R. Jr. (Nick) USMC Pendleton — P
Humphreys, LTC Bill HHC 40th ID — T
Ironfield, SSG Milton H. HHB 2-144th FA — P
Irwin, CPT Bruce H. Co B 2-159th Inf — R
Isbister, SSG John D. Co A 1-185th Armor — T
Jiminez, SPC Emilio B. Co C 1-185th Armor — T
Jones, SFC Malcolm S. HHB 3-144th FA — P
Keating, CPT James A. Co C 3-160th Inf — P
Kessler, SSG Stephen D. Co D 3-160th Inf — P
Klein, LTC Robert HHC 240th Signal Bn — T
Koontz, MAJ James A. HHC 1-184th Inf — R
Kramer, CPL Herman H. HSC 1st LAI USMC — P
Kramer, MAJ Jeff HHB 40th Divarty — P, R
Lee, CPT Edward 670th MP Co — T

361

Lee, In H. Korean Businessowner | P
Levi, 1LT Erskine Troop B 1-18th Cav | T
Lewis, Deputy Chief Bayan L.A.P.D. | B/R/T
Lindquist, LTC Edwin B. "Skip" HHC 40th ID | R
Lloyd, SPC Ernest W. Co D 3-160th Inf | P
Lochner, CPT Keith D. HHC 1-185th Armor | T
Lucero, SGT Armando C. Svc Btry 2-144th FA | P
Lum, 2LT Frank E. 649th MP Co | T
Lyon, PFC Clint J. HHB 3-144th FA | P
Martinelli, SSG Edward C. Btry B 3-144th FA | P
Matey, SGT Robert A. 2-185th Armor | T
Mathewson, LTC Joseph R. HHC 4-160th Inf | P
May, SPC Turhan L. Btry B 3-144th FA | P
McClary, SGT Dennis M. 3-185th Armor | T
McCloskey, CPL Timothy G. HSC 1st LAI USMC | P
McGill, SGT David Co D 4-160th Inf | T
McGreevy, SSG Thomas D. HHB 3-144th FA | P
Mendizabal, PFC Otto R. Co B 1-l85th Armor | T
Metcalf, LTC Marvin G. HHT 1-18th CAV | P
Metcalf, COL Richard HHC 2nd Brigade. 40th ID | P
Minetti, LTC Jerry HHB 40th Div Artillery | P, T
Miranda, SGT Tom L. HHB 3-144th FA | P
Montee, SFC Richard E. 3-185 Armor | T
Moore, SPC Derry X. Btry B 3-144th FA | P
Morishita, PFC Christopher K. Co D 3/160th Inf | P
Mueller, Robert S. III US Dept of Justice | T
Mularz, CPL Russ 40th MP Company | T
Muller, SFC Martin A. HHB 3-144th FA | P
Muzzall, SGT Adrian S.C. HSC 1st LAI USMC | P
Myron, Chief Paul L.A. Sheriff Dept | T
Nunez, PFC Richard M. Co B 132nd Engr | T
Ober, SFC Jim HHC 40th ID | O
O'Connell, Terry Gov Affairs Consultant | P
Odenthal, LT Dick L.A. Sheriff Dept | R
Ogalue, Captain Barry Private Security Svc | P, R
Oliver, SFC Thomas K. Co B 132nd Engr | T
Olvera, SGT Louie Jr. Co C 1-185th Armor | T

Ouimet, CPT Mark T. OTAG   P
Pelton, 1LT Steven J. 270th MP Co   T
Petry, SFC Tom 2-159th Inf   T
Poole, MAJ Barbara J. HHC 40th ID   T
Ponce, PFC Gonzalo Co D 3-160th Inf   P
Portante, COL Guido J. Jr. OTAG   P
Prendergast, SSG John Troop B 1-18th Cav   T
Pulgencio, CPT Bruce HHT 1-18th Cav   T
Quattlebaum, PFC Algernon J. Btry B 3-144th FA   P
Rabe, 2LT Richard A. Co B 132nd Engr   T
Ramos, SSG Salvador Troop B 1-18th Cav   T
Randall, PFC Bruce J. HHB 3-144th FA   P
Ray, SGT Dawn 2-160th Inf   P
Reaza, SGT Alfred Troop B 1-18th Cav   T
Reichert, CAPT Daniel J. HSC 1st LAI USMC   P
Reynolds, COL Curwood OTAG   P
Reynolds, 1SG Robert A. Co A 1-185th Armor   T
Roberts, SGT Wesly S. 649th MP Co   T
Robertson, GySgt Jerry W. HSC 1st LAI USMC   P
Rocha, SFC Angel 4-160th Inf   T
Rogers, MAJ Lee HHC 3-160th Inf   T
Romero, SGT Miguel A. Btry A 2-144th FA   P
Rosso, 1LT Andrew H. Co A 3-160th Inf   P
Schnaubelt, MAJ Chris HHC 2nd Bde-40th ID   T
Schrieken, WO1 Steven HHC 40th Inf Div   P
Scott, LTC Terry HHC 2-185th Armor   P
Sexton, Chaplain (CPT) M. Steve HHC 2-185th Armor   T
Skidmore, CPT Alan J. Troop B 1-18th Cav   T
Skinner, SSG George T. Co B 1st LAI USMC   P
Slaughter, CPT Douglas A. Compton PD & 3-160th Inf   T
Smiley, 1LT Jeff 4-160th Inf   O, T
Smith, MAJ Cherie D. OTAG   T
Snodderly, 1SG Vernon 2-160th Inf   T
Stanton, MSG Ken 40th Divarty   P
Stewart. SSG Solomon Jr. Co D 3-160th Inf   P
Stockman, SGT Michael J. Btry B 3/144th FA   P
Sullins, MAJ (Now WO1) Jim HHT 1-18th Cav   T

Sullivan, MAJ Dennis F. 40th Div Artillery   T
Swann, CPT Tim J. 4-160th Inf   T
Taylor, SFC Dana L. 2-185th Armor   T
Telles, SFC Ralph E. 2-185th Armor   T
Thompson, SSG Robert S. HHC 3-185th Armor   T
Thrasher, MG Robert C. OTAG   P, R
Throckmorton, LTC Rick HHB 40th Div Artillery   P, R
Tooley, SGT David P. Co C 3-185th Armor   T
Tran, CPL Liem H. Btry B 3-144th FA   P
Traylor, SPC B. Scott HHB 3-144th FA   P
Trippel, 1LT Dieter 40th MP Co   T
Troncoso, SGT Richard Troop B 1-18th   T
Tweten, SGT Keith E.   Co B 132nd Engr   T
Vamorano, SGT Rene 40th MP Co   O, T
Van Horn, LT Errol LASD PJP Honor Rancho   T
Vaughn, 1LT Steven C. 2-160th Inf   T
Vogel, SSG Norman E. Svc Btry 2-144th FA   P
Wade, LTC William H. II HHC 2-160th Inf   P
Welch, MSG Greg 146th ANG Security Flt ANG   T
Wenger, LTC William V. HHC 3-160th Inf   T/R/P
West, CPT John HHB 2-144th FA   R
Willet, SGT Michael D. 2-160th Inf   P
Wilson, SGT Chris F Btry 144th FA   T
Wood, 1SG John B. Btry B 2-144th FA   P
Wynhamer, SFC Robert Btry C 2-144th FA   P
Ybarra, SSG Jerry Btry C 2/144th FA   P
Young, CPT Gary W. 1-184th Inf   R, T
Zezotarski, CPT Stan OTAG PAO   P
Zmarzlak, 2LT Robert L. HHC 1-185th Armor   T
Zysk, COL Edmund C. OTAG   P

Plus state officials, local citizens, Salvadoran immigrants, gang members, and law enforcement officers who preferred to remain anonymous. Military personnel not otherwise identified were from the California National Guard.

BIBLIOGRAPHY

After Action Reports (Various Military Commands and Law Enforcement Agencies). 1992.

The City in Crisis (2 Volumes) A Report by the Special Advisor (William H. Webster) to the Board of Police Commissioners on the Civil Disorder in Los Angeles, 1992.

Civil Disturbance Handbook. Sacramento: California National Guard, 1993.

Crips & Bloods, An Informational Guide for the Investigator. The Western States Information Network, (by Phil Steed, Criminal Intelligence Analyst). 1988.

Daily Staff Journals/Duty Officer's Logs (EOC).
1. L.A. Police Department, 29 April-26 May 1992.
2. L.A. Sheriff's Department, 29 April-3 May 1992.
3. Military Department, 29 April-1 May 1992.

Emergency Operations Center Standard Operating Procedures. Sacramento: California National Guard, 1991

Emergency Procedures Manual. Sacramento: California National Guard, 1992

Fire Statistics for the Period 29 April-2 May 1992 (City of Los Angeles). Letter dated 27 May 1992 from David J. Driscoll, County Fire Warden, Forestry and Fire Warden Department, County of San Bernardino.

Future Mobilization & Deployment of the California National Guard in Civil Disturbance Operations. Sacramento: Task Force for Emergency Preparedness: 1992.

365

Harrison, Lieutenant General William H. (U.S. Army, Retired) *Assessment of the Performance of the California National Guard During the Civil Disturbances in Los Angeles, April & May 1992, Report to the Honorable Pete Wilson, Governor, State of California,* 1992.

"L.A. Style" A Street Gang Manual of the Los Angeles County Sheriff's Department. Prepared by Members of "Operation *Safe Streets (OSS)"* Street Gang Detail, 1992.

Military Deployment (City Under Fire - April 29-May 4, 1992). Los Angeles: LAPD Tactical Planning Section, 1992.

Military Support to Civil Disorders. Sacramento: California National Guard, 1993.

Operations Other Than War, Vol. III, Civil Disturbance (L. A. Riots), Newsletter No. 93-7. Fort Leavenworth, KS: Center for Army Lessons Learned (CALL), 1993. Note: While this document has many good items of information, there are so many errors that the reader must be very careful what information is quoted.

Operation Reliable Response (Contingency Plans).
1. Greater Los Angeles Area, Los Alamitos: Headquarters, 40th Infantry Division, 1992.
2. Greater Bay Area. Alameda: 49th Military Police Brigade, 1992
3. Greater Sacramento Area: Fairfield: Troop Command, 1992.

Operation Safe Streets. Los Angeles County: L.A. County Sheriff's Department (A tutorial on gangs). 1992.

Readiness Standard Operating Procedures. Fort Bragg, N.C.: The 82nd Airborne Division, Chapters 1, 2, 4, and Appendix 2 (Battalion TF Alert Sequence Task List) to Annex F (DRF 1 Assumption and N-Hour Procedures) to Chapter 4. As of 1992 (Unclassified)

Report Concerning the California National Guard's Part in Suppressing the L. A. Riots of August, 1965. Sacramento: California National Guard, 1965.

INDEX